East Anglia

An Anthology

East Anglia

An Anthology

Edited by Miles Jebb

BARRIE & JENKINS
LONDON

in association with The National Trust

British Library Cataloguing in Publication Data
Jebb, Miles
    East Anglia: an anthology.
    1. East Anglia
    I. Title II. National Trust
    942.6085'8

    ISBN 0–7126–2029–X

Typeset by Deltatype Ltd, Ellesmere Port, Cheshire
Printed and bound in Great Britain by
Mackays of Chatham PLC, Chatham, Kent

Contents

Acknowledgements

The author and publisher gratefully acknowledge the following, who have kindly given permission for the use of copyright material:

Publication of the extract from Queen Victoria's Journal has been granted by gracious permission of Her Majesty the Queen.

Alastair Press for an extract from 'Our Villages' by Ronald Blythe, in *Suffolk for Ever*, ed. Celia Jennings, © the Suffolk Preservation Society; and an extract from *Love on a Branch Line* by John Hadfield.

The Edward Ardizzone Estate for an extract from *The Young Ardizzone*, © 1970 Edward Ardizzone.

Barrie & Jenkins Ltd for extracts from 'Cambridgeshire' and 'The Coast, Norfolk' by Frances Cornford in *Collected Poems*, published by the Cresset Press.

Marjorie Bell for an extract from *A Street in Suffolk* by Adrian Bell.

A. & C. Black Ltd for an extract from *Norfolk and Suffolk* by W. G. Clarke.

Blackie & Son Ltd for an extract from *Suffolk Scene* by Julian Tennyson.

The Bodley Head Ltd on behalf of the Estate of L. P. Hartley for an extract from *The Shrimp and the Anemone*.

Jack Burton for an extract from *The City of Churches*.

The Executors of the Estate of C. C. Bush (Michael Home) for an extract from *Autumn Fields* and an extract from *Spring Sowing*.

Jonathan Cape Ltd on behalf of the Estate of Percy Lubbock for extracts from *Earlham*; and on behalf of the Estate of Arthur Ransome for extracts from *The Big Six*, *Coot Club* and *We Didn't Mean to Go to Sea*.

Century Hutchinson Ltd for an extract from *Corduroy* by Adrian Bell; and for an extract from *A Suffolk Childhood* by Simon Dewes.

Chatto & Windus Ltd and W. H. Freeman for an extract from *Joseph and his Brethren*; on behalf of the Estate of Shane Leslie for extracts from *The Cantab*; and on behalf of the Executors of the Estate of R. H. Mottram for an extract from *The Boroughmonger*.

William Collins Sons & Co. Ltd for an extract from *A Canvas to Cover* by Edward Seago.

Constable & Co. Ltd for an extract from *Looming Lights* by George Goldsmith Carter.

Cornell University Press for an extract from *Saints' Lives and Chronicles in Early England* by Charles W. Jones, copyright © 1947 by Cornell University.

The Estate of O. G. S. Crawford and Antiquity Publications Ltd for an extract from *Antiquity*, March 1940.

Curtis Brown Ltd, London on behalf of Professor Eric Robinson for an extract from *The Shepherd's Calendar* by John Clare, ed. Eric Robinson and Geoffrey Summerfield (Oxford University Press, 1964) and an extract from 'The Mores' by John Clare, in *Selected Poems and Prose of John Clare*, ed. Eric Robinson and Geoffrey Summerfield (Oxford University Press, 1967), both works copyright Eric Robinson.

David & Charles Publishers plc for an extract from *Forgotten Railways*, Vol. 7, by R. S. Joby.

J. M. Dent & Sons Ltd for an extract from 'Philip Sparrow' in the *Complete Poems* of John Skelton, ed. Philip Henderson.

Henry Engleheart for an extract from 'Pin Mill' by Francis Engleheart in *A Selection of Poetry*.

Eyre & Spottiswoode Ltd for an extract from *Happy Countryman* by C. Henry Warren and an extract from *Anglo-Saxon Chronicle*, ed. Dorothy Whitelock.

Faber & Faber Ltd for an extract from *Ask the Fellows who Cut the Hay* by George Ewart Evans; and an extract from *Britten* by Imogen Holst.

Jane Hales for an extract from *The East Wind*.

Michael Hamburger and Carcanet Press Ltd for an extract from 'In Suffolk' in *Collected Poems* (1985).

Sir Thomas Hare, Bt, for Sarah Hare's will.

W. Heffer & Sons Ltd for an extract from *The Skaters of the Fens* by Alan Bloom; and an extract from *In Breckland Wilds*, by W. G. Clarke.

David Higham Associates Ltd on behalf of Robert Baldick for an extract from the *Memoirs* of François René de Chateaubriand, published by Hamish Hamilton Ltd; on behalf of Ronald Blythe for an extract from *Akenfield*, published by Allen Lane Ltd; and on behalf of the Estate of Dorothy L. Sayers for extracts from *The Nine Tailors*, published by Gollancz Ltd.

Longman Group UK Ltd for an extract from *Here We Are Together* by Robert S. Arbib.

Macmillan, London and Basingstoke for an extract from *A Victorian Boyhood* by L. E. Jones.

Methuen & Co. Ltd for extracts from *Medieval People* by Eileen Power.

Jane Moore for an extract from *The Common Stream* by Rowland Parker.

The Sir Alfred Munnings Art Museum for extracts from *An Artist's Life* by Sir Alfred Munnings, published by Museum Press.

John Murray (Publishers) Ltd for an extract from 'East Anglian Bathe' by John Betjeman in *Collected Poems*; and for an extract from *Another Part of the Wood* by Kenneth Clark.

Penguin Books Ltd for an extract from 'The Reeve's Tale' in *The Canterbury Tales* by Geoffrey Chaucer, translated by Nevill Coghill (Penguin Classics, 1951), copyright © Nevill Coghill, 1951, 1958, 1960, 1975, 1977.

The Peters Fraser & Dunlop Group Ltd on behalf of the Estate of Edmund Blunden for an extract from 'Winter: East Anglia' in *Poems*, published by Cobden-Sanderson; and on behalf of the Estate of Hilaire Belloc for an extract from *The Hills and the Sea*, published by Methuen & Co. Ltd.

Laurence Pollinger Ltd on behalf of the Estate of John Cowper Powys for an extract from his *Autobiography*, published by John Lane.

The Harry Price Library, University of London, for an extract from *The Most Haunted House in England* by Harry Price, published by Longman Green.

Ken Rice for an extract from *Blue and White Crusade*.

The Royal Literary Fund for extracts from *Norfolk Assembly* by R. W. Ketton-Cremer.

Norman Scarfe and the Suffolk Records Society for extracts from *A Frenchman's Year in Suffolk*, translated and edited by Norman Scarfe.

Martin Secker & Warburg Ltd for an extract from *Anglo-Saxon Attitudes* by Angus Wilson.

Dr Barbara Shorvon for extracts from *A Countryside Chronicle* by S. L. Bensusan, published by William Heinemann Ltd.

George Target for an extract from 'Welcome to Norwich a Fine City' in *Writers of East Anglia*, edited by Angus Wilson.

Unwin Hyman Ltd for an extract from *History is on our side* by Joseph Needham.

Sir Laurens van der Post for an extract from 'Edward Seago: the Land and the Painter' in *Writers of East Anglia*, edited by Angus Wilson.

A. P. Watt Ltd on behalf of Rosemary Beresford, J. C. Beresford, B. W. Beresford and Ruth Longman for extracts from *The Diary of a Country Parson* by James Woodforde, ed. John Beresford; and on behalf of the Estate of Jane White for an extract from *Norfolk Child*.

Mrs M. Wentworth Day for extracts from *Harvest Adventure* by James Wentworth Day and from his piece in *The East Anglian Magazine*, November 1970.

Every effort has been made to contact the copyright holders of the material quoted; but if any has been inadvertently overlooked the necessary correction will be made in any future edition of this book.

The author's best thanks go to Linden Lawson at Barrie & Jenkins and to Philip Hood for the text illustrations.

Introduction

East Anglia's gentle landscape, with its jigsaw of lanes and hedges, fields and copses, has an understated and deeply affecting charm. Though the primeval fenlands are gone for ever, the extensive broads and isolated marshes hold a fascination for many, particularly ornithologists. The long, low coastline of sedimentary cliffs, of rolling shingles and muddy estuaries, has in large measure escaped the ribbon developments of the South Coast; and the region is blessed by the absence of the sort of decayed industrialization that we see in the North West or in South Wales. By a stroke of good fortune, the period of East Anglia's greatest relative prosperity was in the fifteenth century, well before the Industrial Revolution. What is more, much of the wealth of that time was channelled into the parish churches, whose incomparable display has always been recognized as the great glory of this corner of England. And all around these inspiring focal points there is scattered the rich and varied architecture of ancient timber-framed buildings, red-brick houses, country mansions and old village and town centres.

Originally, East Anglia was the kingdom of the East Angles, which comprised Norfolk and Suffolk only. Later it came to mean the whole of the hump on the map, with variable penetrations inland. My definition of East Anglia has been the National Trust's administrative region, which is Norfolk, Suffolk, Essex and Cambridgeshire (including the former Huntingdonshire); but I've included only the *northern* part of Essex, because the remainder is so bound up with London and the Thames Estuary.

I have also taken 'East Anglia' to imply not merely a topographical entity but a historical and social setting as well, inhabited by 'East Anglians'. The instances of their kindnesses and their cruelties, of their foresight and their follies, suggest a broad spectrum of the human condition which I should not care to attempt to summarize. But I suppose it is true to say that the traditional characteristics of East Anglians have been powerfully shaped by their environment, and that, as Jack Burton has put it,

The land and people one same nature share;
Not overpowering, but warm and fair.

An anthology is like a sketch or cartoon, rather than a detailed picture. It can be no more than a personal selection from a broad field of other men's flowers, many of them doomed to blush unseen. In picking my way through East Anglia, and making my flower arrangements, my main aim has been to select passages which can be read with pleasure and interest. I have done my best to prevent the extracts from overrunning their essential point, but I have refrained from including short snippets. I have rigorously avoided cuts within the quotes, which always leave an unanswered question in the mind of the reader. And I've been fairly restrictive in quoting more than once from any given author, so as to give a wide range and curb my own preferences. For simplicity, each passage shows merely the name of the author and the year when the text was first printed (or, in certain instances, assumed to have been written), but all other details are given in the list of sources.

Any book dealing with the essence of an English region must mainly be concerned with the past, if only because local distinctiveness was then so much more pronounced than now. When it comes to compiling a regional anthology, the past is even more significant, for the reason that modern descriptions, particularly of the natural scene, seldom stand comparison with the wealth of descriptions in the past. There can be little doubt that this is connected to the progressive development of photography; today there is less incentive to interpret visual scenes by means of the written word. Certainly East Anglia has for two centuries been renowned for its school of landscape painters (from Constable and Cotman to Munnings and Seago), whose testimony surpasses words. But before photography their pictures were only seen by few, and it was mainly through literature that images were evoked in the mind. Some of the descriptions in this collection (for instance, those of the coast) convey what we still see today; many are of scenes that have vanished or been radically transformed. Either way, what is clear is the passionate admiration felt by so many of their authors for the East Anglian countryside.

Many are the organizations involved with conservation in East Anglia, but none bears so large a responsibility as the National Trust. Its properties range from stately homes to mills and cottages, and it is responsible for 23,000 acres of countryside and thirty-six miles of coastline. But the Trust cannot just rest on its laurels; it needs to be able to acquire more land under threat of development. So it has launched an appeal for support for its East Anglia Coast and Countryside Fund. I hope that this anthology may induce some readers to give practical help towards the East Anglia evoked for us by so many writers – the East Anglia of all those curious little corners and surprises, the East Anglia we love, the East Anglia of the East Anglians.   Miles Jebb

Ancient Countryside

East Anglia, a bright and breezy land.

No part of England is more interesting than East Anglia, as regards both its natural features and its historic associations. It lies between the estuaries of the Ouse and the Orwell, and contains the brightest and breeziest of all English counties. Though it has a lower rainfall than the rest of the United Kingdom, it is amply watered by magnificent lakes, broads, and navigable rivers. Emerald and white, azure and gold are the prevailing colours of its coast-line, washed by the North Sea's foam and broken by sand-dunes, chalk, and red and yellow sand cliffs. Nowhere has Nature been more lavish of colour than in this picturesque region, within the shadow of whose old grey churches, crowning its wooded uplands or nestling in its valleys, sleep generations of men who played their parts in some of the most eventful scenes in the national drama. Hither in the sixth century came the tribes that gave to England her name. Here centuries later settled the great migration of Flemings who laid the foundations of England's textile industries; and here, too, at the most memorable and stormiest period in the Island story, was formed that famous Eastern Counties' Association which fostered the Puritan revolution and raised for Cromwell the flower of that army of stalwarts 'whose backs no enemy ever saw'.

Picturesque East Anglia lies towards the sea. The country westward widens out into the great plateau of the Fens; but even these lonely fenlands have a beauty of their own. The wayfarer there breathes the air of boundless freedom. His outlook is on far horizons. He has the open sky above him, with cloud-scenery, sunrise, and sunset of surpassing splendour. Here, too, at night, especially during the long winter nights, above the purity of untrodden snows, the heavens are aglow more brilliantly than elsewhere with the light of rolling systems moving on in their eternal silences.

A. E. Fletcher, 1904

Norfolk, the inner fastness of East Anglia.

> Eastward, beyond the open Fenland skies,   2
> Beyond the furthest point the eye can see,
> The country of the ancient North-folk lies,
> Swept by the wind, and guarded by the sea;
> The people there are watchful and reserved:
> But true their hearts – once honour be deserved!
>
> This haunt of harrier, bittern, swallow-tail
> A loveliness possesses all its own;
> If some seek splendour on a grander scale,
> Others see beauty where good crops are grown;
> The land and people one same nature share:
> Not overpowering, but warm and fair.
>
> When morning breaks in shades of grey and gold,
> Church towers of flint appear on every side:
> Mark out the holy, sacred sites of old,
> And claim the landscape for the Christ who died;
> Each tower reflects the clear East Anglian light:
> Each stands secure and silent through the night.

Jack Burton, 1987

Essex, a land of plenty.

This shire is moste fatt, frutefull, and full of profitable thinges, exceding   3
(as farr as I can finde) anie other shire, for the generall comodeties, and
the plentie. Thowgh Suffolke be more highlie comended of some
wherwith I am not yet acquaynted: But this shire seemeth to me to
deserue the title of the englishe Goshen, the fattest of the Lande:
comparable to Palestina, that flowed with milke and hunnye.

John Norden, 1594

The ancient countryside – of twisting roads, hedges and paths, of hamlets and isolated farms – lies largely on the rich loamy soil, as here delineated in Suffolk by Arthur Young, the leading agricultural theorist, who latterly lived at Bradfield.

A strong loam, on a clay-marl bottom, predominates through the   4
greatest part of the country, as may be seen by the map annexed;

extending from the south-western extremity of Wratting Park, to North Cove, near Beccles. Its northern boundary stretches from Dalham, by Barrow, Little Saxham, near Bury, Rougham, Pakenham, Ixworth, Honington, Knattishall, and then in a line, near the river which parts Norfolk and Suffolk, to Beccles and North Cove; but every where leaving a slope and vale of rich friable loam adjoining the river, of various breadths. It then turns southward by Wrentham, Wangford, Blithford, Holton, Bramfield, Yoxford, Saxmunham, Campsey, Ash, Woodbridge, Culpho, Bramford, Hadleigh; and following the high lands on the west side of the Bret, to the Stour, is bounded by the latter river, with every where a very rich tract of slope and vale from thence to its source. Such is the strong land district of Suffolk taken in the mass; but it is not to be supposed that it takes in so large an extent without any variation: a rule, to which I know few exceptions, is, that wherever there are rivers in it, the slopes hanging to the vales through which they run, and the bottoms themselves, are of a superior quality, and in general composed of rich friable loams; and this holds even with many very inconsiderable streams which fall into the larger rivers. The chief part of this district would in common conversation be called clay, but improperly. I have analized many of these strong loams, and found them abounding with more sand than their texture would seem to imply; so that were they situated upon a gravel, sand, or chalk, they would be called *sandy loams*; but being on a retentive clay-marl bottom, are properly, from their wetness, to be termed *strong* or *clayey loam*.

Arthur Young, 1794

The ancient countryside extended also over the clays of Essex, here described in typically hard-hitting style by William Cobbett, another doughty inquisitor into agricultural practices. (The 'Wen' is his pejorative term for London.)

From the *Wen* to Norwich, from which I am now distant seven miles, there is nothing in Essex, Suffolk, or this county, that can be called a *hill*. Essex, when you get beyond the immediate influence of the gorgings and disgorgings of the Wen; that is to say, beyond the demand for crude vegetables, and repayment in manure, is by no means a fertile county. There appears generally to be a bottom of *clay*; not *soft chalk*, which they persist in calling clay in Norfolk. I wish I had one of these Norfolk men, in a coppice in Hampshire or Sussex, and I would shew him what *clay* is. Clay is what pots, and pans, and jugs, and tiles, are made of; and not soft, whitish stuff, that crumbles to pieces in the sun, instead of baking, as hard as a stone, and which, in dry weather, is to be broken to pieces, by nothing short of a sledge-hammer. The narrow ridges, on which the wheat is sown; the water furrows; the water standing in the dips of the pastures; the rusty iron-like colour of the water, coming out of some of the banks; the deep ditches; the rusty look of the pastures; all show, that here is a bottom of clay. Yet there is gravel too; for the oaks do not grow well. It was not till I got nearly to Sudbury that I saw much change for the better. Here the bottom of chalk, the soft dirty-looking chalk, that the

Norfolk people call clay, begins to be the bottom, and this, with very little exception (as far as I have been) is the bottom of all the lands, of these two fine counties of Suffolk and Norfolk.

William Cobbett, 1821

This area was among the first to become extensively enclosed, an agricultural and scenic transformation involving the construction of hedges and ditches, to the great benefit of farmers. Thomas Tusser, who had retired to the country to farm in Suffolk and then Essex, was naturally much in favour of enclosures.

Where all things in common do rest,   6
    Corn field with the pasture and mead;
Though common ye do for the best,
    Yet what doth it stand ye in stead:
There common as commoners use,
For otherwise shalt thou not chuse.

What layer much better than there,
    Or cheaper (thereon to do well?)
What drudgery more any where,
    Less good thereof where can ye tell?
What gotten by summer is seen,
In winter is eaten up clean.

Example by Leicestershire,
    What soil can be better than that?
For any thing heart can desire,
    And yet doth it want, ye see what.
Mast, covert, close pasture, and wood,
And other things needfull as good.

All these doth enclosure bring,
    Experience teacheth no less:
I speak not, to boast of the thing,
    But only a truth to express.
Example, if doubt ye do make,
By Suffolk and Essex go take.

More plenty of mutton and beef,
    Corn, butter, and cheese of the best,
More wealth any where, to be brief,
    More people, more handsome and prest,
Where find ye? (go search any coast,)
Than there, where enclosure is most.

More work for the labouring man,
    As well in the town as the field;

Or thereof (devise if ye can)
   More profit, what countries do yield?
More seldom, where see ye the poor,
   Go begging from door unto door?

In Norfolk, behold the despair
   Of tillage, too much to be born,
By drovers, from fair to fair,
   And others destroying the corn.
By custom and covetous pates,
By gaps, and by opening of gates.

Thomas Tusser, sixteenth century

Robert Reyce, of Preston, near Lavenham, saw another advantage in the enclosures: one relating to national defence rather than economics. It is pleasant to think of the invaders becoming bogged down in the hedges and ditches, but fortunately the theory was never properly put to the test.

I must confesse as all other earthly benefitts are accompanied with some   7
incommodities, for it is objected it lyeth open and is ready for forreigne
invasion, there bee so many havens, harbours, creekes, and other places
of ready discent, that the enemy is soon entered, and this is more
confirmed by the frequent proofe of the silly Dunkirkes who before the
peace concluded between Spaine and England, robbed our shores, came
into our havens, and carried away our loden vessels, rifling often times
whole townes: Butt that which is common to all other sea bordering
shires (as what shore is free from their insulting, audacious, and their
furtive preying) ought nott here to bee reckned as a perticuler incommo-
ditie, neither may those furtive assaults, with a more momentary returne
bee reputed as a warlike invasion, which whensoever it shall bee
effected, by that time the invaders meet with our deep myrie soyle, our
narrow and fowle lanes, our manifold inclosures, severed with so many
deep ditches, hedges, and store of wood, bushes and trees, seing the
impassablenesse of this Country, with any martiall forces, albeit there
were noe other meanes of resistance, they will have just cause to repent
their rashnesse.

   Robert Reyce, 1618

The best way to observe the countryside is to travel on foot, though to do so requires effort.

One summer morning I started out of Chelmsford by the northern road   8
with a long day's tramp before me. The first halt was made at Broomfield,
a little village surrounding a green, on whose gravelly soil the broom
plant probably grew of old. The church has abundance of Roman brick
worked into its walls, and a round tower of Norman age. From hence the

road ran along the valley of the Chelmer. Presently I came upon a delightful park, with the river flowing through it, and deer and cattle browsing in the shade of the trees. This beautiful place, known as Langleys, is said to have been staked upon a throw of the dice, and lost, by Sir Richard Everard, the last of the old Essex family of Everards, in 1705. It stands in the parish of Great Waltham. The single street of the village, with ancient houses and small shops, winds round the spacious green churchyard. Here I found a litter of planks and ladders with workmen busy at repairing the church. What was intended I did not know; certainly little mischief could be done to the massive Norman tower, the finest feature of the building, and as to the fate of the Perpendicular and still more modern detail I must own myself indifferent. It was now high noon. Throwing myself down on a grassy bank under the shade of a spreading oak just outside the village, the murmur of the Chelmer was in my ears, and the old water-mill built over the river-bed showed its irregular gables over the willows. The hum of insects in the drowsy heat lulled me as I lay stretched on the grass, and a rare temptation assailed me unawares. Why should I not rest here all day if I chose? Why toil any more along the hot and dusty road? Why slavishly worship an Itinerary of my own devising? Then the spirit of obstinacy asserted itself; the hatred of being beaten brought me to my feet again, and set me once more upon the blinding road. Presently the road began to rise, the trees grew fewer, and on the stony ground beyond the hedge I heard the peculiar shuffling sound that marks the presence of a flock of sheep.

Reginald Beckett, 1907

Long-distance walking also requires a sense of direction. In 1863 an American, Elihu Burritt, walked all the way to John o'Groats to obtain first-hand evidence of the state of British agriculture. He began his walk at Tiptree, because of the model farming there, and spent the first night at Great Bardfield.

Immediately after breakfast the following morning, my kind host accompanied me for a mile on my walk, and put me on a footpath across the fields, by which I might save a considerable distance on the way to Saffron Walden, where I proposed to spend the sabbath. After giving me minute directions as to the course I was to follow, he bade me good-bye, and I proceeded on at a brisk pace through fields of wheat and clover, greatly enjoying the scenery, the air, and exercise. Soon I came to a large field quite recently ploughed up *clean*, footpath and all. Seeing a gate at each of the opposite corners, I made my way across the furrows to the one at the left, as it seemed to be more in the direction indicated by my host. There the path was again broad and well-trodden, and I followed it through many fields of grain yellowing to the harvest, until it opened into the main road. This bore a little more to the left than I expected, but, as I had never travelled it before, I believed it was all right. Thetford [Thaxted] was half way to Saffron Walden, and there I had intended to stop an hour or two for dinner and rest, then push on to the end of the day's walk as speedily as possible. At about noon, I came suddenly down upon the town, which seemed remarkably similar to the one I had left, in size, situation, and general features. The parish church, also, bore a strong resemblance to the one I had noticed the previous evening. These old Essex towns are 'as much alike as two peas', and you must make a note of it, as Captain Cuttle says, was the thought first suggested by the coincidence. I went into a cosy, clean-faced inn on the main street, and addressed myself with much satisfaction to a short season of rest and refreshment, exchanging hot and dusty boots for slippers, and going through other preliminaries to a comfortable time of it. Rang the bell for dinner, but before ordering it, asked the waiting-maid, with a complacent idea that I had improved my walking pace, and made more than half the way:

'How far is it to Saffron Walden?'

'Twelve miles, Sir.'

'Twelve miles, indeed! Why, it is only twelve miles from Great Bardfield!'

'Well, this is Great Bardfield, Sir.'

Elihu Burritt, 1864

On a warm summer evening a walk yields even more delights, as was found by the poet George Crabbe and his family. Crabbe was at the time living in a house in what is now the park of Glemham House.

The summer evenings especially, at this place, dwell on my memory like a delightful dream. When we had finished our lessons, if we did not adjourn with my father to the garden to work in our own plats, we generally took a family walk through the green lanes around Glemham; where, at every turn, stands a cottage or a farm, and not collected into a street, as in some parts of the kingdom, leaving the land naked and forlorn. Along these we wandered sometimes till the moon had risen, – my mother leading a favourite little niece who lived with us, my father reading some novel aloud, while my brother and I caught moths or other insects to add to his collection. Since I have mentioned novels, I may say that even from the most trite of these fictions, he could sometimes catch a train of ideas that was turned to an excellent use; so that he seldom passed a day without reading part of some such work, and was never very select in the choice of them. To us they were all, in those days, interesting, for they suggested some pleasing imaginings, the idea of some pretty little innocent-looking village heroine, perhaps, whom we had seen at church, or in a ramble; and while he read Mrs Inchbald's deeply pathetic story, called 'Nature and Art', one evening, I believe some such association almost broke our hearts. When it was too dark to see, he would take a battledore and join us in the pursuit of the moths, or carry his little favourite if she were tired, and so we proceeded homeward, while on the right and left, before and behind, the nightingales (I never heard so many as among those woods) were pouring out their melody, sometimes three or four at once. And now we

10

fill the margin of our hats with glow-worms to place upon the lawn before our windows, and reach the house only in time for supper.

George Crabbe (the younger), 1834

The country from Ipswich to Norwich as seen by a compulsive traveller as she rode through it on her 'Great Journey to Newcastle and to Cornwall' of 1698. Despite attempts at standardization, the computation of a mile still varied. In some places the Old British Mile of 2428 yards was still used.

Thence I went to Woodbridge 7 mile, mostly lanes enclosed countrys; this is a little Market town but has a great meeting for the Dessenters; thence to Wickham 5 mile more – but these are all very Long miles.

Thence to Saxmunday [Saxmundham] 8 miles more, this is a pretty bigg market town, the wayes are pretty deep, mostly lanes very little commons; I pass'd by severall Gentlemens seates – one Mr Dormers which stands in a fine parke the entrance from the Road thro' rows of trees discovered the front and building very finely to view, being built with stone and brick and many sashes lookes like a new house, with the open iron barr gates between pillars of stone the breadth of the house; so to Bathfort [Blyford] 8 miles where is the remaines of the walls of an Abby and there is still a very fine Church, all carv'd in stone hollow work one tire [tier] above another to the tower that ascends not very high but finely carv'd also; hence I descended into lower grounds banck'd on each side with a brick wall but low, and so a walk on it for foote people and severall arches here and there to draine off the water, so that those bancks are to secure the Road from the marshy fenny water that oft a great extent on both sides is subject to; thence I passed by some woods and little villages of a few scattered houses, and generally the people here are able to give so bad a direction that passengers are at a loss what aime to take, they know scarce 3 mile from their home, and meete them where you will, enquire how farre to such a place, they mind not where they are then but tell you so farre which is the distance from their own houses to that place; I saw at a distance as I descended some of their hills a large place that look'd nobly and stood very high like a large town; they told me it was called either Stowle [Southwold] or Nole I cannot tell which.

I rode in sight of St Georges Channell in the way from Colchester and Ipswitch and so to Norwich, sometymes it was in view then lost againe; to Beckle [Beccles] is 8 mile more which in all was 36 miles from Ipswitch – but exceeding long miles – they do own they are 41 measured miles; this is a little market town but its the third biggest town in the County of Suffolke, Ipswich, Berry [Bury St Edmunds] and this; here was a good big Meeteing place at least 400 hearers and they have a very good Minister one Mr Killinghall, he is but a young man but seemed very serious, I was there the Lords day; Sir Robert Rich is a great supporter of them and contributed to the building the Meeteing place, which is very neate, he has a good house [Roos Hall] at the end of the town with fine gardens; there are no good buildings the town being old timber and plaister-work except his and one or two more, there is a pretty bigg Market Cross and a great market kept, there is a handsome stone built Church and a very good publick Minister whose name is Armstrong he preaches very well; they say notwithstanding the town is a sad Jacobitish town; this chooses no parliament men.

At the towns end one passes over the River Waveny [Waveney] on a wooden bridg railed with timber and so you enter into Norfolk, its a low flatt ground all here about so that the least raines they are overflowed by the River and lye under water, as they did when I was there, so that the roade lay under water which is very unsafe for strangers to pass, by reason of the holes and quick sands and loose bottom; the ordinary people both in Suffolk and Norfolk knitt much and spin, some with the rock and fusoe as the French does, others at their wheeles out in the streete and lanes as one passes; its from this town to Norwitch 12 miles.

Celia Fiennes, 1698

Alfred Munnings was the son of a farmer at Mendham. It was from physical experiences such as this that his depictions of the East Anglian countryside, as well as of horses, derive their immediacy.

Once I remember I had been despatched in haste to catch a waggoner   12
who had started at six in the morning with his load and had forgotten his delivery bills or tickets. All went well until I was nearing the village of Metfield, when Jack, the black pony I was riding, suddenly made something an excuse to take me home. We fought until he reared and backed into a ditch and I lost the reins, for he walked all over me! As you can't hurt a boy of ten, I crawled out and followed the brute, weeping. I was ashamed of myself, and all mud from head to foot. Then, suddenly, through an open gate leading into a ploughed field, I saw that rascally pony with dangling rein trotting across to a ploughing team. The ploughman stopped his horses and hid himself behind them, and as my pony came up to smell his horses he quietly stepped out and took the reins. That incident is plainly engraved on my mind. The cold, raw day; the heavy clay of the furrows; my pony – a smart, clipped-out black, a mouse colour we know so well – his ears pricked, smelling the patient team; the wise, kind farm-hand in his weather-stained corduroys, sack on shoulders, coming out and taking charge, waiting for me to come up.

The clay on my boots weighed me down so that I was breathless and all but weeping again as I approached. The ploughman helped me to clean off those heavy masses of clinging clay, lifted me once more into the saddle and sent me off. I often wonder who that kind son of the soil was. As a horseman, his wages then would be eleven shillings a week.

My next fear as I got to the gate was whether Jack would try to take me home; but I was ready for him with my stick and fear of what my father would say if I didn't get those bills to the waggoner ahead, and I had the brute going full split before he had time to think. When I caught the waggoner some miles ahead he looked me up and down. I was covered in mud, and hated him to know I'd been off.

Alfred Munnings, 1950

Travelling by coach was easier than walking or riding. The scene set here is for the passage of Mr Pickwick and Sam Weller from Eatonswill (Sudbury) to Bury.

There is no month in the whole year, in which nature wears a more   13
beautiful appearance than in the month of August. Spring has many beauties, and May is a fresh and blooming month, but the charms of this time of year are enhanced by their contrast with the winter season. August has no such advantage. It comes when we remember nothing but clear skies, green fields, and sweet-smelling flowers – when the recollection of snow, and ice, and bleak winds, has faded from our minds as completely as they have disappeared from the earth, – and yet what a pleasant time it is! Orchards and corn-fields ring with the hum of labour; trees bend beneath the thick clusters of rich fruit which bow their branches to the ground; and the corn, piled in graceful sheaves, or waving in every light breath that sweeps above it, as if it wooed the sickle, tinges the landscape with a golden hue. A mellow softness appears to hang over the whole earth; the influence of the season seems to extend itself to the very waggon, whose slow motion across the well-reaped field, is perceptible only to the eye, but strikes with no harsh sound upon the ear.

As the coach rolls swiftly past the fields and orchards which skirt the road, groups of women and children, piling the fruit in sieves, or gathering the scattered ears of corn, pause for an instant from their labour, and shading the sun-burnt face with a still browner hand, gaze upon the passengers with curious eyes, while some stout urchin, too small to work, but too mischievous to be left at home, scrambles over the side of the basket in which he has been deposited for security, and kicks and screams with delight. The reaper stops in his work, and stands with folded arms, looking at the vehicle as it whirls past; and the rough cart-horses bestow a sleepy glance upon the smart coach team, which says, as plainly as a horse's glance can, 'It's all very fine to look at, but slow going, over a heavy field, is better than warm work like that, upon a dusty road, after all.' You cast a look behind you, as you turn a corner of the road. The women and children have resumed their labour: the reaper once more stoops to his work: the cart-horses have moved on: and all are again in motion.

Charles Dickens, 1837

The son of the local doctor at Hadleigh sits up beside the carriage-driver on the Mothers' Meeting outing in 1919.

The harness jingled and the clip-clop of the hooves echoed on the   14 gravelled roads and, behind us, the mothers kept up an incessant chatter and Jack Robinson said, 'Would you like to hold the reins?'

That, indeed, was a proud moment when I took the reins and drove my first pair of carriage horses with that precious cargo behind. Truth to tell, there was not much driving to do, for the road was pretty straight and there was little traffic on it, but it was a great thing for me to be driving the leading carriage of such a cavalcade.

And Jack Robinson, it appeared, had every confidence in me, for now he was turning round and chatting to the ladies behind him and – it appeared – making sure that Mrs Carter had – as was her custom – fallen asleep; for, when he faced his front again, he took out his little clay pipe and loaded it and, shielding the match, lit up and, crossing his arms on his knees, was all satisfaction.

When we reached the overhead rail bridge at Manningtree, Jack Robinson told me to pull up and draw into the Station Hotel yard, for here the horses had their first rest and, as there is a very steep hill (it has been graduated since then), all the mothers, except the very old ones, were expected to walk up to and join us at the top; so now all, except old Mrs Betts and Mrs Goody in our brake, climbed down and Jack watered his horses and wiped them down and presently the other carriages joined us and, from my perch on the box, I watched the procession of mothers as they all puffed and panted up the hill.

We joined them again at the top, where they re-embarked and so we drove on to Clacton, with the sun now shining and the horses sweating slightly and the lovely exhilarating smell of horse in our nostrils.

I remember it was the time of the hay harvest and the meadows were merry with the reapers and the heavy smell of new mown hay and the bees sucking the last sweetness out of the clover, and the roads, that were soon to be all tarred, for the last time showing a surface of granite and gravel that was kind to the feet of horses. But this now was Essex and even such a little way over the border, there was a difference which I found – and still find – quite indefinable, but is there for ever, as though when you cross the Stour you leave, for good and all, the land of the Angles and come into the softer land of the Saxons.

That, I think, can be the only reason.

Simon Dewes, 1959

Twenty-nine species of birds are enumerated in the breathless doggerel of John Skelton. Skelton, a Court poet and tutor to Prince Henry (later Henry VIII), was rector of Diss. The birds are holding a service in memory of a sparrow killed by a cat. The owner of the sparrow was Jane Scroupe, a schoolgirl in a convent at Norwich.

Lauda, anima mea, Dominum!
To weep with me look that ye come
All manner of birdès in your kind;
See none be left behind.

To mourning lookė that ye fall
With dolorous songės funerall,
Some to sing, and some to say,
Some to weep, and some to pray,
Every birdė in his lay.
The goldfinch, the wagtail;
The jangling jay to rail,
The fleckéd pie to chatter
Of this dolorous matter;
And robin redbreast,
He shall be the priest
The requiem mass to sing,
Softly warbeling,
With help of the reed sparrow,
And the chatteringė swallow,
This hearsė for to hallow;
The lark with his long toe;
The spink, and the martinet alsó;
The shoveller with his broad beak;
The dotterel, that foolish peke,
And also the mad coot,
With baldė face to toot;
The fieldfare and the snite;
The crow and the kite;
The raven, called Rolfė,
His plain-song to sol-fa;
The partridge, the quail;
The plover with us to wail;
The woodhack, that singeth 'chur'
Hoarsely, as he had the mur;
The lusty chanting nightingale;
The popinjay to tell her tale,
That toteth oft in a glass,
Shall read the Gospel at mass;
The mavis with her whistle
Shall read there the Epistle.
But with a large and a long
To keepė just plain-song,
Our chanters shall be the cuckoo,
The culver, the stockdoo.
With 'peewit' the lapwing,
The Versicles shall sing.

John Skelton, 1506

*A smaller selection of birds, as seen and heard in Dedham Vale, listed in elegant
pentameters by a Suffolk pastoral poet.*

The purple dove, that mourns his murdered fair;   16
The crook-beak'd hawk, that wastes the peopled air;

The woodcock, haunter of the banks below;
The raven sable-winged; the owlet slow;
The pecker green with scarlet-rolling eye;
The crow obstreperous; the chattering pye;
The speckled thrush, that charms the woody hall;
The blackbird sweetly loud; the creeper small;
The checquered jay, that screams along the groves;
The sooty daw, that thro' the steeple roves;
The finch, whose breast with gold and saffron shine;
The linnet sweet; the redbreast half divine;
The spink, low chirping in the hawthorn glade;
The wren, that twitters in the bramble's shade;
And last, yet sweetest of the chanting train,
That fill the groves with nature's melting strain,
The latent nightingale exerts her throat;
Amaz'd the traveller hears the changeful note:
Behold him mute, and softly fixed to hear;
The bold, melodious thrills enchant his ear!

William Hurn, 1777

But the countryside is not merely a dreamlike elysium; it is also the setting for the annual birth and death in nature, as in these lines by an adopted East Anglian.

Here weather is all, all's weather.   17
A spring has gone by, cold,
A calendar summer, cold,
An autumn drawn out, late,
With apples firm on the bough
In December, and brambles dropping
Berries as red, unripened,

Ungathered, too, by faltering senses,
A mind that waited, waited
For a season to be fulfilled
While the moments fell away,
The weathers turned, too fast,

And seeing once more was postponed
For a year, reserved for the formal recurrence
That, yearly, fails to occur,
When a long lifetime's years
Could prove not long enough
For seeing only, for learning to see
Mere bud, flower, fruit
In its own time, its weathers;
See it wilt, in its own time, droop,
See it ripped, wrenched, swallowed.

Michael Hamburger, 1980

Nature comprises rot as well as growth. William Broome, who lived at Stuston, describes both of these in what is intended as an allegory of the vices of gossip and the virtues of probity.

On a fair Mead a Dunghill lay,   18
That rotting smoakt, and stunk away;
To an excessive Bigness grown,
By Night-men's Labours on him thrown.
Ten thousand Nettles from him sprung;
Who ever came but near, was stung.
Nor ever fail'd He, to produce
The baneful Hemlock's deadly Juice:
Such as of old at Athens grew,
When Patriots thought it Phocion's Due;
And for the Man its Poison prest,
Whose Merit shone above the rest.
Nor far from hence, strong-rooted stood
A sturdy Oak; it self a Wood!
With friendly Height, o'ertopt the Grove,
And Look'd the Fav'rite Tree of Jove.
Beneath his hospitable Shade,
The Shepherds all, at Leisure, plaid;
They fear'd no Storms of Hail, or Rain;
His Boughs protected all the Plain:
Gave Verdure to the Grass around,
And beautify'd the neighb'ring Ground.

William Broome, eighteenth century

Pollarded trees in hedges also disfigured the enclosed countryside, though they served a useful purpose.

Almost every bank of every field is studded with *pollards*, that is to say,   19
trees that have been *beheaded*, at from six to twelve feet from the ground,
than which nothing in nature can be more ugly. They send out shoots
from the head, which are lopped off once in ten or a dozen years for fuel,
or other purposes. To add to the deformity, the ivy is suffered to grow on
them, which, at the same time, checks the growth of the shoots. These
pollards become hollow very soon, and, as timber, are fit for nothing but
gate-posts, even before they are hollow. Upon a farm of a hundred acres
these pollards, by root and shade, spoil at least six acres of the ground,
besides being most destructive to the fences. Why not plant six acres of
the ground with timber and underwood? Half an acre a year would most
amply supply the farm with poles and brush, and with every thing
wanted in the way of fuel; and why not plant hedges to be unbroken by
these pollards? I have scarcely seen a single farm of a hundred acres
without pollards, sufficient to find the farm-house in fuel, without any
assistance from coals, for several years.

However, the great number of farm-houses in Suffolk, the

neatness of those houses, the moderation in point of extent which you generally see, and the great store of the food in the turnips, and the admirable management of the whole, form a pretty good compensation for the want of beauties. The land is generally as clean as a garden ought to be; and, though it varies a good deal as to lightness and stiffness, they make it all bear prodigious quantities of Swedish turnips; and on them pigs, sheep, and cattle, all equally thrive. I did not observe a single poor miserable animal in the whole county.

William Cobbett, 1830

And enclosures themselves destroyed ancient pastures. John Clare worked as a hedge-setter and day labourer around his native Helpston. Appropriately, he scorned to enclose his verse with punctuation.

Now this sweet vision of my boyish hours   20
Free as spring clouds and wild as summer flowers
Is faded all – a hope that blossomed free
And hath been once no more shall ever be
Inclosure came and trampled on the grave
Of labours rights and left the poor a slave
And memorys pride ere want to wealth did bow
Is both the shadow and the substance now
The sheep and cows were free to range as then
Where change might prompt nor felt the bonds of men
Cows went and came with evening morn and night
To the wild pasture as their common right
And sheep unfolded with the rising sun
Heard the swains shout and felt their freedom won
Tracked the red fallow field and heath and plain
Then met the brook and drank and roamed again
The brook that dribbled on as clear as glass
Beneath the roots they hid among the grass
Where the glad shepherd traced their tracks along
Free as the lark and happy as her song
But now alls fled and flats of many a dye
That seemed to lengthen with the following eye
Moors loosing from the sight far smooth and blea
Where swept the plover in its pleasure free
Are vanished now with commons wild and gay
As poets visions of lifes early day
Mulberry bushes where the boy would run
To fill his hands with fruit are grubbed and done
And hedgerow briars – flower lovers overjoyed
Came and got flower pots – these are all destroyed
And sky bound mores in mangled garbs are left
Like mighty giants of their limbs bereft
Fence now meets fence in owners little bounds
Of field and meadow large as garden grounds

In little parcels little minds to please
With men and flocks imprisoned ill at ease

John Clare, 1824

Even aspects of beauty can be artificial if detached from reality.

The pre-war countryside was ecologically glorious and economically 21
stagnant. Towering hedges were full of the descendants of the oaks
which had provided the timber for the houses. Immense elms stood
everywhere – coffin wood. The pastures in the river valleys during June
rose to the cows' flanks. Cottages were mostly patched, rarely restored,
and their gardens unsophisticated and often very beautiful. It was a
waiting scene, waiting for a finished Suffolk to depart, waiting for the
war, waiting for the post-war transformation. Pastiches of this lost East
Anglia are now part of the grist of the tourist industry. It was a world
which was still producing its own architectural patterns and colours via
local brick and lime kilns, long-strawed wheat and bodging. Many of the
larger houses were covered in creeper, ivy, wistaria or Virginia creeper,
the latter brought to England by those most celebrated of all Suffolk
gardeners, the Tradescants from Walberswick. The house in which
Gainsborough's nephew Dupont lived in Sudbury was locked in a
wistaria cage.

   Ronald Blythe, 1989

*The intimate and pastoral landscape of East Anglia has for over two centuries
been interpreted by the great artists of the region. Here is the art of Thomas
Gainsborough, a native of Sudbury, as expressed by another master of the art, a
native of Dedham, a few miles downstream on the Stour.*

The landscape of Gainsborough is soothing, tender and affecting. The 22
stillness of noon, the depths of twilight, and the dews and pearls of the
morning, are all to be found on the canvases of this most benevolent and
kind-hearted man. On looking at them, we find tears in our eyes, and
know not what brings them. The lonely haunts of the solitary shepherd –
the return of the rustic with his bill and bundle of wood – the darksome
lane or dell – the sweet little cottage girl at the spring with her pitcher –
were the things he delighted to paint, and which he painted with
exquisite refinement, yet not a refinement beyond nature.

   John Constable, 1836

Constable himself was deeply in love with the scenery of Dedham Vale.

The beauty of the surrounding scenery, the gentle declivities, the 23
luxuriant meadow flats sprinkled with flocks and herds, and well

cultivated uplands, the woods and rivers, the numerous scattered villages and churches, with farms and picturesque cottages, all impart to this particular spot an amenity and elegance hardly anywhere else to be found; and which has always caused it to be admired by all persons of taste, who have been lovers of Painting, and who can feel a pleasure in its pursuit when united with the contemplation of Nature.

Perhaps the Author in his over-weaning affection for these scenes may estimate them too highly, and may have dwelt too exclusively upon them; but interwoven as they are with his thoughts, it would have been difficult to have avoided doing so; besides, every recollection associated with the Vale of Dedham must always be dear to him, and he delights to retrace those scenes, 'where once his careless childhood strayed', among which the happy years of the morning of his life were passed, and where by a fortunate chance of events he early met those, by whose valuable and encouraging friendship he was invited to pursue his first youthful wish, and to realize his cherished hopes, and that ultimately led to fix him in that pursuit to which he felt his mind directed: and where is the student of Landscape, who in the ardour of youth, would not willingly forego the vainer pleasures of society, and seek his reward in the delights resulting from the love and study of Nature, and in his successful attempts to imitate her in the features of the scenery with which he is surrounded; so that in whatever spot he may be placed, he shall be impressed with the beauty and majesty of Nature under all her appearances, and, thus, be led to adore the hand that has, with such lavish beneficence, scattered the principles of enjoyment and happiness throughout every department of the Creation.

John Constable, 1833

The representational skill in his pictures was startling in his own time.

We found that the scenery of eight or ten of our late friend's most important subjects might be enclosed by a circle of a few hundred yards at Flatford, very near Bergholt; within this space are the lock, which forms the subject of several pictures – Willy Lott's house – the little raised wooden bridge and the picturesque cottage near it, seen in the picture engraved for Messrs Finden's work, and introduced into others – and the meadow in which the picture of 'Boat-building' was entirely painted. So startling was the resemblance of some of these scenes to the pictures of them, which we knew so well, that we could hardly believe we were for the first time standing on the ground from which they were painted. Of others, we found that Constable had rather combined and varied the materials, than given exact views. In the larger compositions, such as 'The White Horse' and 'The Hay Wain', both from this neighbourhood, he has increased the width of the river to great advantage; and wherever there was an opportunity, he was fond of introducing the tower of Dedham Church, which is seen from many points near Flatford.

C. R. Leslie, 1845

Ever since, visitors to Dedham have been able to see the sights he saw.

The man who could faithfully depict the beauties of the Vale of Dedham   25
had little cause to regret that his range was limited or to long for a wider
one. Words cannot convey the charm of this lovely vale. Its beauty is too
subtle to be grasped in detail, too various to be described in general terms.
Just now as I lean against a field gate beside the Flatford road, it is full of
lights and shades and overhung by slowly drifting clouds. Where the
shadows lurk the outlines of the trees and homesteads are hardly
definable; even the borders of the fields and pastures are scarcely
perceptible; but where the sunlight falls every waterside willow and
poplar, every cottage and hedgerow, and farmstead stands out clear and
beautiful, each a picture in itself. Subject to the clouds' drift, the swathes
of light and shade steal in quick succession through the vale, and
presently the tall square tower of Dedham Church – so conspicuous a
feature of Constable's picture of the vale – reveals itself amid a grove of
trees. Around the church lies the village which gives its name to the vale,
and beyond it and the slow-flowing river are the Essex cornfields. Go into
the National Gallery and look at Constable's 'Cornfield', and you will see
one of these Essex fields. In the foreground of the picture is a winding
lane, beyond which the yellow corn is bathed in sunlight. Through an
open gateway you see the corn-stalks bowing before the wind. Beyond
the field is Dedham Church, which the artist could seldom keep out of his
pictures of his homeland. Beside the lane is a brook into which the
brambles dip their bending briars, arching from banks where wave the
white umbels of wild parsleys. Along the rough wagon track a dog drives
a flock of sheep, while their young shepherd lies down to drink of the
waters of the brook.

     William Dutt, 1901

An explanation of the causes of East Anglian artistic vision.

But most relevant of all to Edward Seago's work is the fact that the   26
enlargement of European vision which culminated in Impressionism
owed a great deal to East Anglia, particularly to the county of Norfolk and
more particularly to its capital, the city of Norwich where Edward Seago
himself was born. I myself do not know precisely why the three counties
of East Anglia should have been cast for this particular role. There are,
after all, other parts of Great Britain as unspoilt, and more obviously
dramatic visually, which appear better equipped as candidates for such a
function. All I am certain of is that it was no accident, and that the cause
had a great deal to do with those things in the East Anglian scene which
make my senses, nourished on the immensities of Africa, feel more at
home there than anywhere else in Great Britain.

     There is a kind of communion between man and his surroundings,
a kind of partnership between the human being and nature, an
exposition of harmony and rhythm of natural forces that I find nowhere

else in the British Isles. There is confirmation for me of this interpretation in another dimension of the feeling arts. There is, for instance, the music of England's greatest twentieth-century composer, the late Benjamin Britten, who too was born and lived in East Anglia. He brought into his own music the same elemental idiom of nature that the East Anglian painter, at his best, introduced into European art.

Laurens van der Post, 1977

Rivers and Broads

The eastward-flowing rivers of Suffolk and Norfolk are here portrayed as playful goddesses, about to sport with father Neptune at Lothingland, which is transformed romantically to 'Lovingland'.

When those Suffolcean floods, that sided not with Stoure,
Their streames but of themselves into the ocean powre,
As Or, through all the coast a flood of wondrous fame,
Whose honored fall begets a haven of her name.
And Blyth a daintie brooke, their speedy course doe cast,
For Neptune with the rest, to Loving-land to hast:
When Waveney in her way, on this septentriall side,
That these two easterne shires doth equally divide,
From Laphamford leads on, her streame into the east,
By Bungey, then along by Beckles, when possest
Of Loving-land, 'bout which her limber armes she throwes,
With Neptune taking hands, betwixt them who inclose,
And her an iland make, fam'd for her scite so farre.
But leave her Muse awhile, and let us on with Yar,
Which Gariena some, some Hier, some Yar doe name;
Who rising from her spring not farre from Walsingham,
Through the Norfolcean fields seemes wantonly to play,
To Norwich comes at length, towards Yarmouth on her way . . .

Michael Drayton, 1622

Of these rivers, the smallest is the Blyth.

This is the valley of the Blyth. The stream ripples and glances over its 28 brown bed warmed with sunbeams; by its bank the green flags wave and rustle, and, all about, the meadows shine in pure gold of buttercups. The hawthorn hedges are a mass of gleaming blossom, which scents the breeze. There above rises the heath, yellow-mantled with gorse, and beyond, if I walk for an hour or two, I shall come out upon the sandy cliffs of Suffolk, and look over the northern sea.

George Gissing, 1903

The Waveney serves as a gentle border between two sympathetic tracts of land, one Norfolk and the other Suffolk.

Listen to me –   29
There is a little river, fed by rills
That winds among the hills,
And turns and suns itself unceasingly,
And wanders through the cornfields wooingly,
For it has nothing else to do, but play
Along its cheery way:
Not like great rivers that in locks are bound,
On whom hard man doth heavy burdens lay,
And fret their waters into foam and spray.
This river's life is one long holiday
                    All the year round.
Listen and long –
It hears the bells of many churches chime,
It has a pleasant time:
The trees that bow to it their branches strong,
Hide many birds that make its spring one song,
And orchard boughs let fall their flowery wealth,
To float away by stealth,
And land in tiny coves a mile below,
Or round and round the stems of rushes veer
Like snowy foam, but truly none is here,
So calmly gurgle on the waters clear
                    With endless flow.

Jean Ingelow, nineteenth century

Meanwhile the Ouse flows out to the north, after gathering its tributaries; similarly, the long ninth line gathers the previous eight lines in this classic Spenserian stanza.

Next these the plenteous Ouse came far from land,   30
By many a city and by many a towne,
And many rivers taking under hand
Into his waters as he passeth downe,
The Cle, the Were, the Guant, the Sture, the Rowne.

Thence doth by Huntingdon and Cambridge flit,
My mother Cambridge, whom as with a Crowne
He doth adorne, and is adorn'd of it
With many a gentle Muse and many a learned wit.

Edmund Spenser, c.1591

The Cam, a father-figure to Cambridge, mourns a dead undergraduate (the 'sanguine flower' is the hyacinth, associated with death in Greek legend). Milton was at Christ's College.

Next Camus, reverend Sire, went footing slow,   31
His Mantle hairy, and his Bonnet sedge,
Inwrought with figures dim, and on the edge
Like to that sanguine flower inscrib'd with woe.
Ah; Who hath reft (quoth he) my dearest pledge?

John Milton, 1638

The rivers were all put to good use for mills.

Every village along the Stour seems to have had its water-mill. I do not   32
know what the Doomsday count was, but even today they are
numerous, though mostly disused. They must represent an enormous
traffic in former times, both by road and river. Waggons took the road
before dawn and came rumbling through the countryside loaded with
grain to be milled; and great barges, horse-pulled, nosed their way down
the river to Ipswich, loaded with flour to be distributed all over the
country. To-day the water-mills are little more than relics of their former
selves. Mostly the mill-houses have been bought and done up as private
residences, and very peaceful and desirable they look, with the mill-pool
shining close by and the white, weather-boarded mill itself towering over
all. Naturally we sought out these old mills; lolled over the mill-pool and
watched the purple-backed swallows dipping beneath the bridge for
gnats; dreamed ourselves back (never a difficult thing to do where mills
are concerned) to the time when the building throbbed and shook as the
roaring water drove the massive gear. Always the most stirring sight was
the water-wheel, its great iron bulk wafering away with rust, its pit lined
with ferns and water-weeds.

C. Henry Warren, 1967

The variety of river fish, as recorded by Thomas Browne, who commanded great respect as Norwich's most learned man in scientific matters.

Many river fishes also and animals. Salmon no common fish in our   33
rivers, though many are taken in the Owse. In the Bure or north river, in

the Waveney or south river, in the Norwich river butt seldome, and in the winter butt 4 yeares ago 15 were taken at Trowes mill in Xtmas, whose mouths were stuck with small wormes or horsleaches no bigger than fine threds, some of these I kept in water 3 moneths; if a few drops of blood were putt to the water they would in a litle time looke red. They sensibly grewe bigger then I first found them, and were killed by an hard froast freezing the water. Most of our Salmons have a recurved peece of flesh in the end of the lower jawe, wch when they shutt there mouths deeply enters the upper, as Scaliger hath noted in some.

The Rivers, lakes, & broads abound in the *Lucius*, or pikes of very large size, where also is found the *Brama*, or Breme, large & well tasted; the *Tinca*, or Tench; the *Rubecula*, Roach, as also Rowds and Dare or Dace; *perca* or pearch, great & small, whereof such [as] are taken in Braden on this side Yarmouth in the mixed water make a dish very dayntie, & I thinck are scarce to bee bettered in England; butt the Blea[k], the chubbe, the barbell, to bee found in divers other Rivers in England, I have not observed in these. As also fewer mennowes then in many other rivers.

The *Trutta*, or trout, the *Gammarus*, or crawfish, butt scarce in our rivers, butt frequently taken in the Bure or north river & in the severall branches thereof, & very remarkable large crawfishes to bee found in the river wch runnes by Castleaker & Nerford.

Thomas Browne, c.1680

The birds in among the reeds.

But by the time the sedge warblers are back in the reed beds, and the dykes are full of amorous frogs, there is much to tempt one to take a cruise on the rivers or a ramble along the river walls. Every marsh and swampy rond is then bright with golden clusters of marsh marigolds; on the sun-warmed sides of the walls yellow coltsfoot has pushed its way up through the clods, and purple patches of dead nettle attract the early roving bees. On the boggy lands green rushes are gradually hiding the withered growths of rush and sedge; the silken sallow catkins are sending out their yellow anthers, and the ruddy bog myrtle fills the air with its sweet, strong scent. Sunward the river is agleam with flashing ripples; elsewhere the water is as blue as the sky. As you cross the rush marshes, redshanks and peewits rise from their nesting grounds, crying plaintively; now and again a snipe is flushed, and uttering that strange bleating note which has gained it the name of 'summer-lamb', betakes itself to erratic flight. In almost every dyke where there is dead sedge or gladden, moor-hens are beginning to make their nests, and the loud challenge of the pugnacious cocks is heard along the riversides; while from the shores of the larger Broads comes the harsh 'cark' of the coot. The reed beds are full of sedge warblers, playing the mocking-bird to sparrow, thrush, and finch; occasionally a louder, quicker 'chucking' tells of the presence of a reed warbler. By the time the reed warblers – which arrive later than the sedge warblers – are heard, you may listen for the

34

strange insect-like 'reeling' of the shy little grasshopper warblers, which lurk among the scrub of sweet gale and sallow and in the lush marsh grass. On the floating rafts of broken reeds and sedges, with which the wind and tide have covered the surface of some of the creeks, those dignified and graceful little dyke-rangers, the yellow wagtails, are strutting, carefully searching for crawling insects or darting their beaks at those upon the wing. In the marsh farm gardens tits and finches are busy among the fruit-buds, and the goldfinch, which is not so rare in Norfolk as in some counties where the bird-catchers are more in evidence, is often heard singing among the apple trees.

William Dutt, 1923

The riverine scenery in summer, as seen by an artist: white sails and white swans.

With the first fresh winds of summer the river yachts leave their winter moorings – their white sails appear all over the marshes like butterflies in sunshine. All the summer long there is scarcely a day when those scattered flecks of white are absent from the landscape. I love to watch them as they lean from the wind, set ablaze with sunlight; and then deprived of their whiteness by a passing shadow, and left in grey dimness until a sudden gleam will light them up again.
    There is plenty to watch on those windy days down by the river bank. I have often found a sheltered spot by the edge of the water and settled down to await events, and seldom have I had to wait long before something happens in the world of man or beast. Any place will do, for there is not a yard of that soggy ground which does not teem with life in some form or another. I never seek out something to watch; things just catch the eye, one after another, and the afternoon becomes a pageant of interesting episodes. Sometimes the piece is opened by a daddy-longlegs, flying like a jelly-fish swims, with its legs dangling beneath, being carried aimlessly along by the wind. Or it may be a dragon fly, in that wonderfully controlled flight, darting here and there, now hovering for a moment, and then peeling off to explore some other part of the bank. When I have kept very quiet I have seen water voles creep along the muddy brink, and even nose around the ground about my feet. Then they have sensed the presence of man; for a brief moment they have sat motionless, before plunging with a plop into the water.
    During this time there may have been other things to watch overhead – a marsh harrier, or a kestrel hanging on the wind, or, perhaps, a heron in slow and stately flight, and shiny-winged rooks jeering it on its way.
    At any moment a pair of swans may appear round a bend in the river. They seem to work their own particular beat, and there is one place I know which appears to be a frontier line. One pair of swans work downstream to that point, and another pair swim upstream so far but no further. I was there the other day and saw two of those proud parents with a line of eight cygnets astern. We fed them with pieces of bread, and

35

they trod water at a frantic rate to stand tip-tail, with their long necks extended, to take the morsel from my hand. A lump rippled down each long neck as the bread passed on its journey.

Edward Seago, 1947

White snow and silver water here provide a bright background for grief. Ralph Knevet was chaplain to the powerful Pastons of Oxnead, on the river Bure, and wrote this moving elegy on the death of Katherine Paston ('Calista'), wife of Sir William Paston.

When Hills and Valleys, wrap't in sheets of snow,   36
Did penance for their summer luxury,
And Winter old unto the world did show,
The skeletons of trees, muffling the sky
With vapours cold, and strewing frequently
The earth with watery confects, there I stood
On that fair tract, where Bure creeps lazily
To pay his tribute to a greater flood,
Cleapt Yar, none of the meanest of blue Neptune's brood.

There I beheld the snowy swans retreat,
Unto the silver creeks, with motion sad:
Each face of things expressed a ruin great,
But two-faced Janus all in sable clad,
Those joyous sports, and merriments forbad,
Which whilom he was wont to tolerate:
The gods themselves (it seems) a feeling had,
Of our disasters, when Calista's fate,
Our sorrows, and her endless joys did propagate.

Ralph Knevet, 1637

Winter saw the wildfowlers active on the rivers and broads, those man-made expanses of water derived from peat-diggings.

What are the marsh-men doing during this Arctic weather? Well, these   37
are really hard times with them, as all labour has to be stopped, and they can only snare and shoot wildfowl. This they accomplish by fitting a flat-bottomed punt with runners of iron, or hard wood, and filling it with fodder, or marsh hay, to lie upon and keep themselves warm; then, in the fore-part, they erect a screen of rushes, furze, or twigs, with an aperture to see through, and an arrangement of crossed sticks, upon which to rest their fowling-pieces. Their guns are old-fashioned muzzle-loaders, with enormously long barrels, and look as dangerous to the sportsmen as to the birds. Let us watch a 'gunner', and see how he sets about his work. See, here he comes out of his boat-hut, from the chimney of which curls the thin, blue, peat smoke, indicating a cosy

warmth in his little home. He is warmly wrapped up – an old white cap is pulled down over his ears; a white comforter is folded round his throat; and over his clothes is drawn a long, white smock, reaching below his knees. This is his uniform. In his mouth is the inevitable stumpy, clay pipe (a 'nose-warmer'), about 2 in. long, and as black outside as in. Over his shoulder is a rope, attached to the bow of his punt, which he now commences to drag after him over the ice, after first carefully depositing his trusty firelock on the crossed stand before mentioned.

Presently he comes to a likely place, and, leaving his boat, creeps quietly along to a reed bed, and peeps at some objects two or three hundred yards off. Having satisfied himself as to the identity of these dark objects, he comes back to his punt, and enters it, kneeling in the stern, with his face to the bow; then, from under the fodder bed, he draws out two stout sticks, shod with iron, and, taking one in each hand, thrusts their points into the ice and quietly propels himself along.

As he approaches the reed rond, by a circuitous route, he keeps himself all the time well hidden behind the screen in the bow of his craft. When within 50 yards of his unsuspicious victims, he lays down his propellers, and rests his gun in such a position that it points a couple of feet over the backs of the ducks, so as to just catch them as they rise on the wing. He then gives a tremendous war-whoop, and at the same time pulls the trigger of his gun. Then comes an exciting scene, as he chases the wounded birds, and wrings their necks, some of them having been only slightly hit, and give a long chase before being captured – or escaping. He then returns to the battle-field, collects the dead, throws them into the boat, reloads his gun, and pipe, and, taking his boat in tow, looks out for a fresh shot.

Ernest Suffling, 1895

By a time-honoured cycle of labour, the broadsmen scraped a living locally round the year. Richard Lubbock, rector of Eccles, was Norfolk's leading naturalist. His classic work specifies several species which have since become extinct in the county.

When I first visited the broads, I found here and there an occupant, squatted down, as the Americans would call it, on the verge of a pool, who relied almost entirely on shooting and fishing for the support of himself and family, and lived in a truly primitive manner. I particularly remember one hero of this description. 'Our broad', as he always called the extensive pool by which his cottage stood, was his microcosm – his world; the islands in it were his gardens of the Hesperides, – its opposite extremity his *ultima Thule*. Wherever his thoughts wandered, they could not get beyond the circle of his beloved lake; indeed, I never knew them aberrant but once, when he informed me, with a doubting air, that he had sent his wife and his two eldest children to a fair at a country village two miles off, that their ideas might expand by travel: as he sagely observed, they had never been away from 'our broad'. I went into his house at the dinner hour, and found the whole party going to fall to most thankfully upon a roasted Herring Gull, killed of course on 'our broad'. His life presented no vicissitudes but an alternation of marsh employment. In winter, after his day's reed-cutting, he might be regularly found posted at nightfall, waiting for the flight of fowl, or paddling after them on the open water. With the first warm days of February, he launched his fleet of trimmers, pike finding a ready sale at his own door to those who bought them to sell again in the Norwich market. As soon as the pike had spawned, and were out of season, the eels began to occupy his attention, and lapwings' eggs to be diligently sought for. In the end of April, the island in his watery domain was frequently visited for the sake of shooting the ruffs which resorted thither, on their first arrival. As the days grew longer and hotter, he might be found searching, in some smaller pools near his house, for the shoals of tench as they commenced spawning. Yet a little longer, and he began marsh mowing, – his gun always laid ready upon his coat, in case flappers should be met with. By the middle of August, teal came to a wet corner near his cottage, snipes began to arrive, and he was often called upon to exercise his vocal powers on the curlews that passed to and fro. By the end of September, good snipe shooting was generally to be met with in his neighbourhood; and his accurate knowledge of the marshes, his unassuming good humour, and zeal in providing sport for those who employed him made him very much sought after as a sporting guide, by snipe shots and fishermen; and his knowledge of the habits of different birds enabled him to give useful information to those who collected them.

Richard Lubbock, 1849

The broadsman's carefree attitude towards birds and eggs was bound to become outdated, and Arthur Ransome was always very much concerned about the threats to wildlife. He moved from the Lake District to East Anglia in 1934.

'You ain't never seen pods lifted?' he said. 'Seventy year to-morrow I see 'em first.'

    'Seventy years,' said Tom.

    'My birthday to-morrow,' said the old man.

    'To-day or to-morrow?' said Tom.

    'You're right. Gone midnight. Seventy year to-day.'

    'Many happy returns,' said Tom.

    'Many of 'em,' said Joe, Bill and Pete.

    The old man chuckled. 'Live to ninety we do,' he said. 'Another twelve year anyways. On my birthday seventy year gone my old uncle let me sit along of him by the eel sett same as you're sitting along of me. Above Potter was his old setts. . . . Drink up. There's plenty more.' He filled up the teapot from the kettle. 'You know Potter, you do? But there been changes since then. There weren't no houses at Potter then, saving the wind pumps. And there weren't no yachts, hardly. Reed-boats and such, and the wherries loading by the bridge. And there were plenty of netting then, and liggering for pike, and plenty of fowl. . . .'

39

'Did anybody look after the birds?' said Tom, thinking of the Coot Club.

The old man laughed. 'Gunners,' he said.

'What about buttles?' said Pete.

'Shot many a score of 'em I have,' said the old man.

'Oh I say. . . . Not bitterns,' said Tom.

'Many a score. There was plenty of 'em then, and then they get fewer till there ain't none. Coming back, they tell me, they are now. If I was up Hickling way with my old gun . . .'

'But you can't shoot bitterns,' said Pete, horrified.

'And why not?' asked the old man. 'In old days we shoot a plenty and there were a plenty for all to shoot.'

'But that's why they disappeared,' said Tom.

'Don't you believe it,' said the old man. 'They go what with the reed cutting and all they pleasure boats. . . .'

Tom looked at the faces of the other Coots, to see how they were taking these awful heresies.

'But they're coming back,' said Joe. 'And no one's allowed to shoot 'em. And there'll be more every year. We found two nests last spring.'

'Who buy the eggs?' asked the old man.

'Nobody,' said Joe. 'We didn't sell 'em. We didn't take 'em. But they would have been taken if we hadn't have watched.'

'Some folk are rare fools,' said the old man. 'Now if I'd have knowed where them nests was, it'd have been money in my pocket and tobacco in my old pipe.'

The Coots looked at each other. It was no good arguing with old Harry, but, after all, it was one thing for an old Broadsman to talk about taking bitterns' eggs and quite another for somebody like George Owdon who had plenty of pocket money already without robbing birds.

The old man caught the look on Pete's face.

'Old thief. Old Harry Bangate,' he said. 'That's what you think. And I say, No. What was them birds put there for? Why, for shooting.'

'But if you shoot 'em, they won't be there,' said Joe.

'When we was shooting there were always a plenty.'

It was clear that the old man would never understand why the members of the Coot Club spent their days and nights in the spring guarding nests and watching birds, and Tom was wise enough to change the subject.

Arthur Ransome, 1940

The broads had for long been the scene of jolly outings, as when the mayor of Yarmouth organized a municipal beano on Breydon Water.

The bus'ness thus settled, the mayor gave the word   40
To open the Hampers and cover the board;
How they ripp'd up the pastries, and scrambled for crust,
Dismember'd the turkies, the capons untrussed,
And unbuttoned their waistcoats, for fear they should burst.

Then how briskly they cleared away dishes and spoons,
How the Dons clapp'd a match to their pipes in platoons;
How refin'd was their wit, and how brilliant each joke
Though the atmosphere round 'em was all in a smoke;
How, with infinite judgement, distinctly, and loud,
'Rule Britannia', was sung by a voice from the crowd;
Now the Mayor stood up and commanded the fleet
To drop from their moorings, and sound a retreat;
When each flute, fife and fiddle, was instantly play'd on,
And so they sailed sweetly again over Braydon.

Norfolk Chronicle, 1777

*In time the attractions of the broads became ever more appreciated. Arthur
Patterson was another local enthusiast, who eased around them in a punt.*

Why go to the Alps or hanker after the Mediterranean, or think of   41
Germany – pshaw! – when a sort of Eden by the Yare winds around the
bends, displaying natural beauties, and revealing the charms of our
wholesome English cherubim and water-loving nymphs? I am glad the
Norwich people patronise their own river in increasing numbers
annually; and it is so easy of access, and such a washer-out of weariness
and fag. Flowers in their season smile to the passer-by, refreshing foliage
adorns the outlook, and even weeds are floating, to remind us of the
curse of Eden's Garden. Yet not all weeds are unlovely.

Arthur Patterson, 1920

*Small rowing-boats were the perfect means of exploring the upper reaches of
rivers such as the Yare. This scene opens within the private boathouse at Earlham.*

Within there was thudding and bumping and lurching, splashes of   42
echoing water, shafts of green twilight; the boat swayed and smacked its
lips (so you might say) as we bundled in and disposed ourselves.
Somebody stood in the bows to unlock the gate; and it burst open, caught
by the stream outside, and the boat pushed forth into the blaze of light,
the water-cool breezes, the clean smell of the draggled weeds. Light and
air, the silent movement, the wild and nameless fragrances – they make a
penetrating experience. The water talked beneath us as the boat swung
round into the stream; and immediately the familiar landscape was
changed before our eyes, the fields and woods beyond the low banks
seemed to have drawn apart with a new character. Committed to the
flow of the stream, one looks back on the green world as though one had
left it; to float upon water is as detaching, as liberating as to soar in air.
Those woods, that flat marshland, now belong to another sphere; I
survey it with curiosity, almost wishing to return to it already, so inviting
it seems to enterprise and discovery. But here meanwhile is the sphere of
the water-world, with its strange and lovely treasures; trailing my hands
in its delicious chill, I can soon be lost in the landscape of the river-floor.

Shallow and pool, pool and shallow, the river coiled its way through the hollow land. Outside the boat-house the gravelly bottom was full in view, only blurred a little by the twist and swirl in the clear glass of the water. Do you know that broad-leaved plant, bright green, translucent, that grows in thick drifts along the bed of the stream, never touching the surface? – and the fine feathery thing, a darker green, eternally pulled by the current, like a thicket through which a wind never ceases to blow? – and the stalks of the arrowhead, that climb to the upper air and are shaken there by a constant little breeze, it would seem, which is not really a breeze but the same secret tug of the stream below? – and the perpetual flitting of tiny shadows over the gravel and sand, as the minnows dart from under our monstrous hull, the leviathan that pushes among their cressy islets? The only sound in the quiet valley was the measured cluck of our clumsy old rowlocks; the reedy pastures were deserted, there wasn't a house or a cottage in sight; the tawny cows stood stock-still, solemnly eyeing us as we passed. And then, as we steered round a swinging bend of the river, the sunlit floor had disappeared and there was nothing but blackness beneath us, thick darkness of water unbroken by reed or rush – a deep pool, and you could plunge the oar down and down, further and further into the bottomless mud; and the next moment, perhaps, the boat was almost scraping the clean gravel again, and the smooth bottle-green reed-stems stood out into the water away from the bank; and so the river went winding on its leisurely way, and after ever so long you still saw the boat-house within easy hail, just across the breadth of a single meadow.

Percy Lubbock, 1922

Everything was so delightfully small-scale, even where cabin-boats could penetrate.

Oh, Ludham Bridge! Ludham Bridge! Temple Bar of this aquatic Fleet   43
Street, humping your mean back, blocking a free river with your ugly narrow arch. Who could have built you – *pons asinorum?*

'Can we get through?'

'I will try, master,' said the Gipsy, as she folded her sail smoothly down, and laid her mast very low.

'Now hold her straight for the very centre, skipper! Gently there with the quants.'

She pokes her nose into the dark hole; the edges of the cabin top scrape on both sides against bricks – her bows are through. Again scrape, scrape, scrape, as from the foredeck we foot it slowly aft, pushing, with our hands above our heads, against the bridge; and inch by inch the long craft squeezes out into the light of day.

'Through it is, sir, but a wonderful close shave.'

'That's so, Sam, but we've done it. Ring the bell, someone, we will have luncheon now before we hoist.'

We did, and two silly calves stood on the bank and watched us as we ate it.

The wind fell light and lighter as the afternoon wore on, and but just wafted us along the pretty stream. As the sun went down the scene grew exquisitely beautiful – hues, lustrous as some ethereal opal, overspread the western sky with glory; flaming red on the horizon, translucent ruby, pink, tender green, blending and dying towards the zenith into blue – there never could have been a lovelier sunset – against this background wheeled and gyrated clouds of starlings. Two clamorous armies of them seemed to be manoeuvring, now flying, now pursuing – black squadrons of innumerable birds gaining, losing, each in turn, the weather gage of air. We watched them, wondering, till at last they swooped down to roost in the safe shelter of a trackless reed bed.

Evening was closing in, we could not get to Barton, so we lowered and brought up against the bank, under the high land of How Hill, and near a farm, whence we had hopes of eggs and butter. We could just discern a black ghostly mill stand straddling its three legs upon the marsh, holding up a dark warning finger – one of two only sails – against the sky.

H. M. Doughty, 1899

Cabin cruisers provided comforts on the rainiest of days, even though – then, as now – cruiser comforts cannot eliminate boredom, nor music necessarily bring solace.

Although Norfolk is one of the driest counties in England because of its extreme Eastern position, still it does have rain, and when it is in earnest, it *does* come down, too. 44

It is rather a fine sight to see the rain come on, and gradually blot out the trees, and shores, and at length to beat down so furiously upon the water, as to make it hiss and bubble again. Then sky and water melt into one leaden-coloured haze, and not a sound is heard but the steady falling raindrops, which descend upon the surface of the water in a seeming hot state, each tiny drop to be cooled with a hiss and a splash. The reeds which are near enough to be seen, appear to wring their heads from side to side, and toss about as if in pain from the great cruel raindrops; but presently the clouds break, the sun and the birds come forth again, and the air seems fresher and purer than ever. This kind of rain storm is of short duration, and before one is tired of watching its various effects it is over; but it sometimes happens that the morning breaks red and angry, like a waking child, and presently it begins to cry, and keeps at it all day, sometimes without intermission. The sky is grey, the water grey, and grey the atmosphere; in fact, everything wears a grey and sombre aspect. What is to be done? Why, make a day of it in the cabin! Yes, but what shall a cabin full of people do all day? First, let the ardent fishermen, who will brave anything, don their waterproofs and mackintoshes, provision the jolly boat, and depart with their traps, and we will then see what can be done with those who remain behind.

After a time they shove off, amid the hearty wishes for 'good luck' from their friends, and the 'prisoners' cast about for recreation.

Some immediately clear the tables and commence cards, and with an occasional glass and pipe or cigar, while away the time merrily enough. 'Nap' or whist seem to be the favourite games, and bursts of hearty laughter and loud vociferation shew that the players are at all events not so dull as the weather.

The young ladies will, of course, have the latest novel with them, or better still, their fancy needlework, and thus for a time they also are happy, contented, and busy.

The large yachts and wherries carry a small piano, that is if the additional charge of about 15s. per week is not objected to, and it seldom is, so that music may shed its soothing influence over the rain-beleaguered party; but somehow, on a rainy morning, music does not seem to possess the same charm as it does in the twilight, or even later in the day, and is usually for this reason somewhat neglected.

Frequently one of the party brings along his banjo, and if he does he is usually one of those good-tempered, high-spirited fellows that nothing in the way of weather or a flying slipper seems to daunt; he is irrepressible, and he and his banjo are at it morning, noon, and night. He is usually the funny man of the party, the buffoon, the human ass. But he is happy, even if his instrument causes his neighbour (with a nervous disposition) to feel as if a worm were crawling up his spinal cord, each time a fresh attack takes the banjoist, and causes him to twang out the latest negro comicality.

Ernest Suffling, 1899

For the brave it was all very exhilarating, especially when flouting social convention, as in this action-packed story in which the three boys themselves build the boat as well as sail her. Christopher Davies' books did much to popularize the broads and also contained many handy facts about natural history.

'Let us go slap-dash into that. We shall be sure to find some nests,' said   45
Frank.

'All right,' said both Jimmy and Dick. So Frank put the helm up, and the yacht drove on before the wind, surging through the rustling reeds, which bowed and bent before her, until she came to a standstill well into the heart of the rond.

'Down with the sails,' said Frank, and the halyards were let go and the sails came down with a run. As the yacht crashed into the rond there was quite an explosion of birds from it. Water-hens, coots, and marsh-tits flew out on both sides, and from the centre of it rose a little duck with a bright, chestnut-coloured head and neck.

'That is a teal,' said Frank, 'we shall find her nest here, so look carefully.'

They jumped into the shallow water, having first taken off their shoes and stockings, and began to hunt about for nests. They speedily found several coots' and water-hens' nests, and also a dab-chick's; but they wanted none of these, and continued their search for the teal's nest. At last –

'Here it is,' said Dick delightedly, and sure enough there the nest was, in a small bush which grew in the very centre of the rond, where the soil was pretty firm. The nest was large and thickly lined with feathers, and it contained twelve cream-coloured eggs. They took six of them, and then, satisfied with their spoil, they went back to their yacht, and tried to push her off again. But this was no easy task. They pushed and pushed, until they were exhausted, and the only effect their pushing seemed to have was to push their own legs deeper into the mud. The yacht refused to be moved.

'Well, this is a pretty go, to be wrecked at the very beginning of our cruise! We have run her almost high and dry. How they will laugh at us at home!' said Jimmy.

'They sha'n't have the chance of doing that. We will get her off somehow or other. We ought to have gone to leeward of the rond, and run her up in the wind's eye into it, and then we could have backed her off with the sails,' said Frank.

'Live and learn,' said Dick. 'I vote we strip and go overboard again and try to lift her off. We can get the oars from the boat, and use them as levers.'

This was undoubtedly the best thing to do, and although the water was not over warm, they took off their clothes and worked and pushed away, until they made the mud around the yacht as soft as a pudding, and themselves as black as negroes. Then the yacht moved a little, and putting forth all their strength they shoved her back into deeper water. Not waiting to dress themselves, they ran the sails up and steered away for the Kendal Dyke at the south-east end of the Broad. They meant to stay at the mouth of the Broad to bathe and dress. There was no one to see them, so it did not matter. As they neared the mouth of the dyke, to their great dismay a yacht with several people on board came out of it. The people stared in blank astonishment at the strange double-bodied yacht and her still stranger crew. Jimmy and Dick dived at once into the cabin. Frank could not leave the helm, and yet could not stay where he was; so without further thought he plunged into the water at the stern of the yacht, and, holding on by the rudder, he contrived to keep her on her course until Jimmy reappeared with something thrown over him, and took hold of the tiller. When they came to an anchorage in a secluded spot among the reeds, they bathed and dressed.

'Well,' said Dick, 'if we go on having adventures at this rate, we shall have plenty to tell when we get home.'

'I like adventures, but these are not the sort I like,' said Jimmy.

'Well, never mind, better luck next time,' said Frank, soothingly.

Christopher Davies, 1889

Even braver actions were sometimes needed (BPS stands for Bird Protection Society).

'Here they are,' said Port.   46

There was a splash of oars, a rustling of reeds, and the old black ship's boat came pushing her way into the dyke. Under their gaudy handkerchiefs the faces of her crew looked much more worried than ever pirates' faces ought to be.

'You're jolly late,' said Starboard.

'Look here,' said Tom, 'what's the use of fixing up a Coot Club meeting if you three go off pirating and don't come back till nearly dark?'

'No, but listen,' said Joe, at the tiller. 'It ain't pirating.'

'It's BPS business,' said one of the rowers, Bill. 'It's No. 7. . . . Something got to be done.'

'What?'

'No. 7?'

'What's happened?'

All thoughts of plans proposed or rejected were gone for the moment. No. 7 nest. The club's own coot. The coot with the white feather.

'Everything was all right when we went by,' said Port.

'It's since then,' said Joe. 'One o' them big motor-cruisers o' Rodley's go an' moor right on top of her.'

Tom ran into the shed for their plan of the river, which hung from a nail on the wall. There was no need of it, for every one of the six members of the Coot Club knew exactly where No. 7 nest was to be found.

'What did you do?' Starboard asked.

'We let Pete do the talking,' said Joe. 'As polite as he know how. "If you please" and "Do you mind" an' all that.'

'Well?'

Pete, a small, black-haired boy, the owner of the enormous telescope, spoke up.

'I tell 'em there's a coot's nest with eggs nigh hatching,' he said. 'I tell 'em the old coots dussen't come back.'

'We see her scuttering about t'other side of the river,' said Bill, forgetting his handkerchief was a turban and taking it off and wiping his hot face with it. 'She'll never go back if that cruiser ain't shifted.'

'And didn't they go?' said Starboard.

'Just laugh. That's what they do,' said Peter. 'Say the river's free to all, and the birds can go nest somewhere else, and then a woman stick her head out o' the cabin and the rest of 'em go in.'

'What beasts!' said Port.

'I try again,' said Joe. 'I knock on the side, and some of 'em come up, and I tell 'em 'twas a beastly shame, just when eggs is going to hatch.'

'And I tell 'em there's a better place for mooring down the river,' said Bill.

'They tell us to clear out,' said Joe.

'And mind our own business,' put in Peter.

'I tell 'em 'twas our business,' said Joe. 'I start telling 'em about the BPS.'

'They just slam off down below. Makin' a noise in them cabins fit to wake the dead,' said Bill.

'Let's all go down there,' said Starboard.

'I'll deal with them,' said Tom. 'The fewer of us the better. Much easier for one.' He looked at the *Titmouse* in her neat awning. 'I'll take the punt.'

'Can't we come, too?' said Joe.

'We could skip across and tell Ginty we're going to be late,' said Port.

'What about the meeting?' said Bill.

'No,' said Tom. 'Meeting's closed. Plan's gone bust, anyhow. I'm going down the river at once.'

Already he had untied the old *Dreadnought*, pulled her paddle free and was working her out of the dyke.

'Look here,' he said. 'If it's as bad as you say, I may have to do something pretty tough.'

Arthur Ransome, 1934

Though the ultimate test of bravery is being chased by an angry bull.

Bulls are always a hazard on the Norfolk marshlands, and many and   47
dreadful are some of the tales that are told about them. Flea Barber, of Yarmouth, came near to being gored by a bull one day while after mushrooms on the Berney Arms marshes, in the days when the Berney Arms was an inn. Flea had come up Breydon in his wherry and moored alongside the quay heading, and gone ashore with a basket. 'Reckon I'll get some mushrooms,' he said to grandfather Hewitt, who was the landlord. 'There's a tidy few in that there marsh, I reckon – reckon I'll get them.' 'Reckon you won't,' said Hewitt. 'There's an old bull in that there marsh that'll have your guts for garters.' 'I ain't afraid of no bull,' replied Flea, and off he went.

The bull was at one end of the marsh before it came roaring up, tail out straight, slavering and foaming and all ready for business. Flea ran like a demented hare, but missed his way to the plank (ligger in Norfolk) across the dyke. The old bull was just about to give him a quick lift on its horns, and there was no time to spare, so Flea dropped the basket and jumped and landed up to his middle in mud and water, while the bull did a war dance on the bank with the basket stuck on its head and squashed mushrooms ('mushroom ketchup') running down its foam-flecked muzzle. Some time later, Flea said to Hewitt, 'I reckon, bor, yew were right about that there bull!'

Alan Savory, 1953

Fenland and Breckland

A great stretch of wetland once covered most of Cambridgeshire: an area of refuge, and of natural mystery. At the time he wrote this brilliant description of fenland, Charles Kingsley was Professor of Modern History at Cambridge.

They have a beauty of their own, these great fens, even now, when they are dyked and drained, tilled and fenced – a beauty as of the sea, of boundless expanse and freedom. Much more had they that beauty eight hundred years ago, when they were still, for the most part, as God had made them, or rather was making them even then. The low rolling uplands were clothed in primaeval forest; oak and ash, beech and elm, with here and there, perhaps, a group of ancient pines, ragged and decayed, and fast dying out in England even then; though lingering still in the forests of the Scotch highlands.

Between the forests were open wolds, dotted with white sheep and golden gorse; rolling plains of rich though ragged turf, whether cleared by the hand of man or by the wild fires which often swept over the hills. And between the wood and the wold stood many a Danish 'town', with its clusters of low straggling buildings round the holder's house, of stone or mud below, and of wood above; its high dykes round tiny fields; its flocks of sheep ranging on the wold; its herds of swine in the forest; and below, a more precious possession still – its herds of mares and colts, which fed with the cattle and the geese in the rich grass-fen.

For always, from the foot of the wolds, the green flat stretched away, illimitable, to an horizon where, from the roundness of the earth, the distant trees and islands were hulled down like ships at sea. The firm horse-fen lay, bright green, along the foot of the wold; beyond it, the browner peat, or deep fen; and among that, dark velvet alder beds, long lines of reed-rond, emerald in spring, and golden under the autumn sun; shining 'eas', or river-reaches; broad meres dotted with a million fowl, while the cattle waded along their edges after the rich sedge-grass, or wallowed in the mire through the hot summer's day. Here and there, too, upon the far horizon, rose a tall line of ashen trees, marking some island of firm rich soil. In some of them, as at Ramsey and Crowland, the huge ashes had disappeared before the axes of the monks; and a minster tower rose over the fen, amid orchards, gardens, cornfields, pastures with here and there a tree left standing for shade. 'Painted with flowers in the spring', with 'pleasant shores embosomed in still lakes', as the monk-chronicler of Ramsey has it, those islands seemed to such as the monk terrestrial paradises.

Overhead the arch of heaven spread more ample than elsewhere, as over the open sea; and that vastness gave, and still gives, such cloudlands, such sunrises, such sunsets, as can be seen nowhere else within these isles. They might well have been star worshippers, those Girvii, had their sky been as clear as that of the East: but they were like to have worshipped the clouds rather than the stars, according to the too universal law, that mankind worship the powers which do them harm, rather than the powers which do them good. Their priestly teachers, too, had darkened still further their notion of the world around, as accursed by sin, and swarming with evil spirits. The gods and fairies of their old mythology had been transformed by the Church into fiends, alluring or loathsome, but all alike destructive to man, against whom the soldier of God, the celibate monk, fought day and night with relics, Agnus Dei, and sign of Holy Cross.

And therefore the Danelagh men, who feared not mortal sword or axe, feared witches, ghosts, Pucks, Wills o' the Wisp, Werewolves, spirits of the wells and of the trees, and all dark, capricious, and harmful beings whom their fancy conjured up out of the wild, wet, and unwholesome marshes, or the dark wolf-haunted woods. For that fair land, like all things on earth, had its darker aspect. The foul exhalations of autumn called up fever and ague, crippling and enervating, and tempting, almost compelling, to that wild and desperate drinking which was the Scandinavian's special sin. Dark and sad were those short autumn days, when all the distances were shut off, and the air choked with foul brown fog and drenching rains from off the eastern sea; and pleasant the bursting forth of the keen north-east wind, with all its whirling snow-storms. For though it sent men hurrying out into the storm, to drive the cattle in from the fen, and lift the sheep out of the snow-wreaths, and now and then never to return, lost in mist and mire, in ice and snow; – yet all knew that after the snow would come the keen frost and bright sun and cloudless blue sky . . .

Charles Kingsley, 1866

The fenland had been formed by the inundations of the sea over areas of primeval forest, as William Dugdale describes in his scholarly topographical history.

That this vast level was, at first, a firm dry land, and not annoyed with   49
any extraordinary inundation from the sea, or stagnation of the fresh

waters, I shall now endeavour to manifest; which may, perhaps, seem strange to many; but when it is well considered, that timber-trees will not grow and thrive where water, for the most part, stands; or in moor, which by tract of time is bred and increased in such moist places, both the one and the other may with much probability be granted. The case being then thus stated, it now remains for me to prove, that such have heretofore been bred, and prospered in sundry parts of this now fenny country: which is no hard matter to do, divers persons, yet living, being able to testify, that in the late digging of those chanels and drains, as have been made for the exsiccation thereof, great numbers of such trees, of several kinds, have been found; most of oak and firr, and few of them severed from their roots: but of such as be so severed, the roots are observed to stand in the firm earth below the moor; of which sort I myself have seen some, that were taken up in the fens near Thorney; and have had credible information of multitudes found in other places; whereof some were digged up at the cutting of that large chanel, called Downham Ea, which extendeth itself from Salters-lode, about four miles north-wards, towards Linne.

Moreover, in Marshland, about a mile westward from Magdalen bridge, at the setting down of a sluice, very lately, there was discovered at xvii feet deep, divers furze bushes, as also nut-trees, pressed flat down, with nuts sound and firm lying by them; the bushes and tres standing in solid earth, below the silt, which hath been brought up by the inundations of the sea, and in time raised to that great thickness. Add hereunto what I have already observed in the Isle of Axholme, touching the trees of oak and firr found in such great numbers, at the making of those ditches and sewers for draining of that fen: which, though it lie not contiguous to this, out of all doubt is on the like level, and was apparently a woody country at the first. To give farther instance, therefore, to demonstrate so evident a truth, there will be no need; so that I shall hence proceed, and in the next place manifest upon what occasion this great alteration grew.

William Dugdale, 1662

Small oases of fen can still be searched out, and even plunged into at midnight.

Happily the country round Cambridge, especially towards the north-east where the fens are, is wonderfully well provided with wild pools. To such places one may go off for a whole day, carrying two or three books, and with fair confidence that no one, except a few farm-workers, perhaps, will be met with. One of these pools lies very difficult to find in what is practically a piece of untouched fen. It is surrounded with reeds whose stems are almost white, but bear at the top their long green blades which stream unanimously out in one direction if there is a little wind. If you lie flat on the bank of the diving-place and look along the pool, you see a picture of reeds in the best Chinese manner. Then if you dive in, you find the water absolutely clear and beautifully brown, contrasting marvel-lously with the brilliant blue of the surface, reflecting the sun. Or at

50

midnight, on one of those few nights of the year when the air and water are warm enough, it is lovely to swim through the moon and stars glittering on the water. Nor are excellent smells wanting, for the water-peppermint is about, and there is always a slight unidentifiable smell of fresh waters which delights those bathers, who, like myself, find nothing but disadvantages in the sea. Growing all round the pool you get ragged robin, purple loosestrife, scabious, and what Scottish friends call mouse's pea. And there in some convenient place you may lie, reading and swimming alternately, with your cells hard at work manufacturing vitamin D, and storing it, you hope, for your advantage in the coming gloomy Cambridge winter, abounding in cold and rain.

Joseph Needham, 1946

Others were also out at night – like these moth-catchers at Wicken Fen, the only surviving relic of the undrained Cambridgeshire fenland.

A successful night's work entails a good deal of trouble. Towards sunset the moth-catcher will start for the Fen wheeling a barrow heavily laden with such articles as he may require. These include a stout wooden box (inside which is carried a big lamp measuring about 18 in. high, 12 in. wide, and 10 in. deep, a 'killing' bottle of cyanide, and a number of pill boxes of various sizes): three 8 ft poles; a white sheet some 10 ft long by 5 ft wide; a pot of treacle (called 'sugar' by the moth-catcher) a lantern, a moth-trap, and the indispensable net.

51

He makes his way somewhat laboriously over the marshy ground, along narrow paths, which he picks out as though they had been clearly defined, though to the stranger there would appear to be nothing to distinguish them from the marshy soil on either side. After a walk of about fifteen minutes he arrives at a nice open space, where the sedge has been cut.

Quickly fixing in the ground two of the long poles, the moth-hunter stretches out the big white sheet between them. Ten feet or so away he fixes his lamp on the third pole, so that the light will fall full on the sheet. Conveniently near, he arranges a number of the pill boxes, the lantern, and the 'killing' bottle, and hangs the moth-trap on an adjacent tree to take its share of the night's spoil. This moth-trap, though regarded as of secondary importance, is a very ingenious contrivance, so designed that when the moths, attracted by a light inside, once enter, they cannot escape.

After the trap has been 'set', a third snare for the moths is prepared, the sinewy, young branches of the low sallow shrubs, which grow profusely hereabouts, being twisted and tied together in knotty bunches, which are liberally smeared with treacle, with a dash of rum in it. This 'sugar' is certainly not very appetising in appearance, especially as a pot full is made to last a considerable time, but it is quite good enough for the moths. When it is sufficiently dark for the moths to fly, the big lamp is lit, and its strong light is thrown upon the sheet, so that it is easy to see the smallest moth that may come within range.

The moth-catcher takes his stand, net in hand, slightly behind the lamp, and in this position he is ready to rush forward and take any moth which may settle on the sheet or fly in the lighted space. Should it be a hot, dry night, with heavy clouds banked over the set sun, as often happens, particularly in July, the moth-catcher will have a very warm time of it. The perspiration will soon be streaming down his back, his pipe will grow hot between his teeth, and it will only be kept there to repel the attacks of the flies and gnats which will soon be singing and buzzing in his eyes and ears.

But the moths are there – Crambites, Noctuae, Pearls, Tortrices, and Tineae. There is no waiting for them; the difficulty is to wade through them and get at the good ones. Flop! flop! come big Lappets, Drinkers, Eggars, and Tigers – which have probably flown rapidly up from a considerable distance across the fen – and strike the sheet or lamp with such force that they fall into the grass and lie where they fall. Two smaller moths – the Lackeys and the Ruby Tigers – are not so easily subdued, and they bustle about, hitting the entomologist smartly in the face.

On most nights the fun is all over by twelve o'clock, but on a good night it will last until one or two o'clock, and in the early part of July the moth-catcher will sometimes wait for the sun, and then stalk about to catch a beautiful little Geometer called Hyria auroraria, which is itself the colour of the rising sun, and only flies from 3 to 8 a.m.

The Cambridge Graphic, 1901

Early Christian hermits sought out the fenland islands; Guthlac's hermitage grew and in time became the great monastery of Crowland.

There is in the middle reaches of Britain a fearful morass of wide extent which begins at the banks of the Grant River not a great way from the castle which they call Grant and extends from south to north in a long marshy waste, now marish, now swampy, with here and there black vaporous pools and island outcroppings, interspersed with circuitous meadowland bordering tortuous river courses. When our hero Guthlac of blessed memory learned of these wild spots in that vast solitude, quickened by the heavenly ministry he searched out the straightest and most direct road to it. It happened that after he had inquired from those living near that vast wasteland and from their tales had learned of the many savage spots in the tremendous wilderness, lo, one standing nearby named Tatwine privily let him know of still another island in the further stretches of those waste regions which many had tried to settle but had abandoned because of the unknown monsters and terrors of other guise frequenting the solitude. On hearing of it our blessed hero Guthlac earnestly requested that the spot be shown to him. The man assented to our hero's overtures and, taking a small fishing boat, conveyed Christ's wayfarer through trackless bogs between the borders of the gloomy fen to the agreed spot. The island, called Crowland, is situated in the middle of the fen, and until a short time ago was widely

52

known for its savageness because of its remote isolation. Not a single settler had been able to live there before Guthlac, the servant of Christ – apparently because of the vagaries of the infesting demons. There the man of God Guthlac, spurred on by heavenly favor to disdain for such a foe, began his life alone on the gloomy solitary heath.

Felix the monk, eighth century (translation, Charles W. Jones)

Of these islands, Ely was the finest, and was teeming with natural life.

The isle is within itself plentifully endowed, it is supplied with various   53
kinds of herbage, and for its richer soil surpasses the rest of England. Most delightful for its charming fields and pastures, it is also remarkable for its beasts of chase, and is in no ordinary way fertile in flocks and herds. Its woods and vineyards are not worthy of equal praise, but it is beset by great meres and fens as though by a strong wall. In this isle there is an abundance of domestic cattle and a multitude of wild animals; Stags, Roes, Goats, and Hares are found in its groves and by these fens. Moreover there is a fair plenty of Otters, Weasels and Polecats, which in a hard winter are caught by traps, snares, or by any other device. But what am I to say of the kind of fishes, and of fowls, both those that fly and those that swim? In the eddy at the sluices of these meres are netted innumerable Eels, large Water-wolves – even Pickerels, Perches, Roaches, Burbots and Lampreys, which we call Water-snakes. It is indeed said by many men that sometimes *Isicii* [?salmon], together with the royal fish, the Sturgeon, are taken. As to fowls, let us, if it be not troublesome to you, recount those which abide there and thereabout, as we have done with the rest. There are numberless Geese, *Fiscedulae*, Coots, Didappers, Water-crows, Herons, and Ducks, of which the number is very great. At midwinter or when the birds moult their quills I have seen them caught by the hundred, and even by three hundreds more or less; sometimes they are taken in nets and snares as well as by bird-lime.

'Liber Eliensis', twelfth century (translation, nineteenth century)

Ely was also rich in pasture.

Of all the Marshland isles, I Ely am the queen,   54
For winter each where sad, in me looks fresh and green.
The horse, or other beast, o'erweigh'd with his own mass,
Lies wallowing in my fens, hid over head in grass;
And in the place where grows rank fodder for my neat,
The turf which bears the hay, is wondrous needful peat:
My full and batt'ning earth needs not the ploughman's pains,
The rills which run in me, are like the branched veins
In human bodies seen; those ditches cut by hand,
From the surrounding meres to win the measur'd land,

To those choice waters I most fitly may compare,
Wherewith nice women use to blanch their beauties rare.

Michael Drayton, 1622

The draining of the fens in the seventeenth century spelt the end of the fenmen's way of life.

The north part of this county is lately much improved by draining,   55
though the poorest sort of people will not be sensible thereof. Tell them
of the great benefit to the public, because where a pike or duck fed
formerly, now a bullock or sheep is fatted; they will be ready to return,
that if they be taken in taking that bullock or sheep, the rich owner
inditeth them for felons; whereas that pike or duck were their own
goods only for their pains of catching them. So impossible it is that the
best project, though perfectly performed, should please all interests and
affections.

Thomas Fuller, 1662

Their skills in wildfowling were remarkable. (A 'coy' is a decoy; 'clapper claw' means clawing and scratching; 'slake' is mud; a 'hingle' is a hinge, a 'sprink' a sprinkle, and a 'trammel' a long, narrow fishing-net.)

Born in a coy, and bred in a mill,   56
Taught water to grind, and Ducks for to kill;
Seeing coots clapper claw, lying flat on their backs
Standing upright to row, and crowning of jacks;
Laying spring nets for to catch ruff and reeve,
Stretched out in a boat with a shade to deceive.
Taking geese, ducks, and coots, with nets upon stakes,
Riding in a calm day for to catch moulted drakes;
Gathering eggs to the top of one's wish,
Cutting tracks in the flags for decoying of fish.
Seeing rudds run in shoals 'bout the side of Gill sike,
Being dreadfully venom'd by rolling in slake;
Looking hingles and sprinks, trammels, hoop-nets and teamings,
Few persons I think can explain all their meanings.

Anon., early nineteenth century

No wonder they wanted to protect their precious habitat.

Come, Brethren of the water, and let us all assemble,   57
To treat upon this matter, which makes us quake and tremble;
For we shall rue it, if't be true, that Fens be undertaken,
And where we feed in Fen and Reed, they'll feed both Beef and
    Bacon.

They'll sow both beans and oats, where never man yet thought
    it,
Where men did row in boats, ere undertakers bought it:
But, Ceres, thou behold us now, let wild oats be their venture,
Oh let the frogs and miry bogs destroy where they do enter.

Behold the great design, which they do now determine,
Will make our bodies pine, a prey to crows and vermine:
For they do mean all Fens to drain, and waters overmaster,
All will be dry, and we must die, 'cause Essex calves want pasture.

Away with boats and rudder, farewell both boots and skatches,
No need of one nor th'other, men now make better matches;
Stilt-makers all and tanners shall complain of this disaster;
For they will make each muddy lake for Essex calves a pasture.

The feather'd fowls have wings, to fly to other nations;
But we have no such things, to help our transportations;
We must give place (oh grievous case) to horned beasts and cattle,
Except that we can all agree to drive them out by battle.

Anon., seventeenth century

*After the draining a much less skilful type of work was called for. These women
have been weeding the couch-grass (or 'twitch') from the arable fields.*

Fenland is bare and colourless, and these women-workers attune their   58
dress to the surroundings. It is well suited to their occupation, however,
and as they presently file out of the yards with the barking dogs about
them, they look quite as well equipped for the dirty, arduous labour
before them as the men. Even the most ardent reformers of feminine
attire could find little fault with them in their short kirtles, their high
leather-top boots that meet the abbreviated petticoats, and the sensible
headgear that protects them equally well from rain and sun. They are
tanned, of course, a fine rich brown, and their arms and hands are as rough
and as sinewy as those of the husbands, fathers, and brothers; but, by-and-
bye, when the day's work is done, when the horses are groomed and
stabled, and the great heaps of twitch have been duly burnt, these sun-
burnt agricultural labouresses will come home and discard the rough boots
for fashionable buttoned ones, and lay aside the kirtles and the sun-bonnets
for gaudy stuff gowns with high sleeves, and hats of more or less fashionable
shape, adorned with bright ribbons and plush and impossible flowers. To be
at liberty to parade the village all the evening in their finery is their reward
for the long hours of labour in the fields. It is better to rise up early, they
argue, to toil all day beneath the sun, to drive the cart across the hard fields
in harvest time, than to go to 'sarvice', where the hours of work are longer
and those of freedom so limited.

Annie Berlyn, 1894

The mysterious fenland had been transformed into a monotonous plain.

To Crowland, I went, as before stated, from Wisbeach, staying two nights   59
at St Edmund's. Here I was in the heart of the Fens. The whole country as
level as the table on which I am now writing. The horizon like the sea in a
dead calm: you see the morning sun come up, just as at sea; and see it go
down over the rim, in just the same way as at sea in a calm. The land
covered with beautiful grass, with sheep lying about upon it, as fat as
hogs stretched out sleeping in a stye. The kind and polite friends, with
whom we were lodged, had a very neat garden, and fine young orchard.
Every thing grows well here: earth without a stone so big as a pin's head;
grass as thick as it can grow on the ground; immense bowling-greens
separated by ditches; and not the sign of dock or thistle or other weed to
be seen.

   William Cobbett, 1830

This plain was not without its own particular beauty, at any rate in the days
before electricity poles and wires.

The vast height and width of the sky-arch, as seen from those flats as   60
from an ocean – the grey haze shrouding the horizon of our narrow
land-view, and closing us in, till we seemed to be floating through
infinite space, on a little platform of earth; the rich poplar-fringed farms,
with their herds of dappled oxen – the luxuriant crops of oats and beans –
the tender green of the tall-rape, a plant till then unknown to me – the
long, straight, silver dykes, with their gaudy carpets of strange floating
water-plants, and their black banks, studded with the remains of buried
forests – the innumerable draining-mills, with their creaking sails and
groaning wheels – the endless rows of pollard willows, through which
the breeze moaned and rung, as through the strings of some vast Aeolian
harp; the little island knolls in that vast sea of fen, each with its long
village street, and delicately taper spire; all this seemed to me to contain
an element of new and peculiar beauty.

   Charles Kingsley, 1850

As part of the bewildering change, the first train journey was an unnerving
experience for simple country folk. Here is a scene on the halt at Warboys.

You stand on it at six o'clock on a bright morning and wait with   61
impatience and a certain nervousness. You have not absolutely mastered
the intricacies of steam transit yet, you are in your heart of hearts a trifle
frightened of these new-fangled things in which your grandfather would
never have ridden – no, not to save his life, he wouldn't – till, with a
distant puff of smoke and an ear-splitting whistle, the 'Mail' signals its
approach.
   You gather your parcels together – you are about to take a long
journey – you have taken a ticket to Ely to attend the market there, and it

is a red-letter day to you. Presently, with a roar and a mighty display of machinery, a monster comes thundering into the station and pulls up as if by a miracle. The stationmaster-porter-collector-postman-gardener-water-attendant, and whatever other duties he may fancy, stalks leisurely out of the booking shed, where he has been vainly endeavouring to calculate the difference between five shillings, which you have given him, and the two and fourpence-halfpenny which is the fare. However, he has given you some change and hopes it will be all right. In the fluster of departure you do not stop to count it. You rush for the nearest compartment – there are only four altogether – and clamber up the steps provided for you. You sink down breathlessly on to the cushions and once again count your parcels, in spite of the fact that you know perfectly well the train will not start till the engine has taken in water, the driver has had his accustomed cup of tea with the stationmaster, and the tickets have been duly examined and punched. These rites accomplished, the engine gives another long shriek, the guard waves his flag, and off you go, leaving, on the deserted platform, a mail bag and a couple of milk cans.

Christopher Morley, 1925

Dorothy Sayers, whose father had been vicar of Bluntisham, possessed an intimate knowledge of fenland which she put to good use in The Nine Tailors.

'Thaw's coming, Bunter.'   62
    'Yes, my lord.'
    'Ever seen this part of the country when the floods are out?'
    'No, my lord.'
    'It looks pretty desolate; especially round about the Welney and Mepal Washes, when they let the waters out between the Old and New Bedford Rivers, and across the fen between Over and Earith Bridge. Acres of water, with just a bank running across it here and there or a broken line of willows. Hereabouts I think it's rather more effectively drained. Ah! look – over to the right – that must be Van Leyden's Sluice that turns the tide up the Thirty-foot Drain – Denver Sluice again on a smaller scale. Let's look at the map. Yes, that's it. See, here's where the Drain joins the Wale, but it meets it at a higher level; if it wasn't for the sluice, all the Drain water would turn back up the Wale and flood the whole place. Bad engineering – but the seventeenth-century engineers had to work piecemeal and take things as they found 'em. That's the Wale, coming down through Potter's Lode from Fenchurch St Peter. I shouldn't care for the sluice-keeper's job – dashed lonely, I should think.'
    They gazed at the ugly little brick house, which stood up quaintly on their right, like a pricked ear, between the two sides of the Sluice. On the one side a weir, with a small lock, spanned the Thirty-foot, where it ran into the Wale six feet above the course of the river. On the other, the upper course of the Wale itself was spanned by a sluice of five gates, which held the Upper Level waters from turning back up the river.
    'Not another house within sight – oh, yes – one cottage about two

miles further up the bank. Boo! Enough to make one drown one's self in one's own lock. Hullo! what happens to the road here? Oh, I see; over the Drain by the bridge and turn sharp right – then follow the river. I do wish everything wasn't so rectangular in this part of the world. Hoops-a-daisy, over she goes! There's the sluice-keeper running out to have a look at us. I expect we're his great event of the day. Let's wave our hats to him – Hullo-ullo! Cheerio! – I'm all for scattering sunshine as we pass. As Stevenson says, we shall pass this way but once – and I devoutly hope he's right. Now then, what's this fellow want?'

Along the bleak white road a solitary figure, plodding towards them, had stopped and extended both arms in appeal. Wimsey slowed the Daimler to a halt.

Dorothy L. Sayers, 1934

Meanwhile the flat landscape around Cambridge could be a source of inspiration for undergraduates – as it was for John Cowper Powys, whose writings are otherwise mainly concerned with Devon and Somerset.

But if I did not gain much from Cambridge I gained all the world from   63
Cambridgeshire! Oh how can I express my deep, my indurated, my passionate, my unforgettable, my *eternal* debt, to that dull, flat, monotonous, tedious, unpicturesque Cambridgeshire landscape? How those roads out of Cambridge – and it seems as if all my most heavenly roads have been out of, rather than into somewhere – come back to my mind now! Those absurd little eminences known as the Gog and Magog hills: that long interminable road that leads to some pastoral churchyard that once claimed precedence of Stoke Pogis as the site of the Elegy: that more beguiling, but not *very* beguiling road that led in the Ely direction, past the place where my father's father, when a fellow of Corpus, used to go courting: those meadows towards Grandchester where there is that particular massive and wistful effect about the poplars and willows that always makes me think of Northwold: these are my masters, my fellows, my libraries, my lecture-halls; these are my Gothic shrines! And not only these in their large aspects, but every swamp-pool, every rushy brook, every weedy estuary, every turnip-field, every grey milestone, every desolate haystack became part of my spirit.

John Cowper Powys, 1934

Many undergraduates realized their affection for the Cambridge countryside only after they had gone down. Revelation came to Rupert Brooke (despite his mock-castigation of various villages) when sitting in the Café des Westens, Berlin.

God! I will pack, and take a train,   64
And get me to England once again!
For England's the one land, I know,
Where men with Splendid Hearts may go;

And Cambridgeshire, of all England,
The shire for Men who Understand;
And of *that* district I prefer
The lovely hamlet Grantchester.
For Cambridge people rarely smile,
Being urban, squat, and packed with guile;
And Royston men in the far South
Are black and fierce and strange of mouth;
At Over they fling oaths at one,
And worse than oaths at Trumpington,
And Ditton girls are mean and dirty,
And there's none in Harston under thirty,
And folks in Shelford and those parts
Have twisted lips and twisted hearts,
And Barton men make Cockney rhymes,
And Coton's full of nameless crimes,
And things are done you'd not believe
At Madingley, on Christmas Eve.
Strong men have run for miles and miles,
When one from Cherry Hinton smiles;
Strong men have blanched, and shot their wives,
Rather than send them to St Ives;
Strong men have cried like babes, bydam,
To hear what happened at Babraham.
But Grantchester! ah, Grantchester!
There's peace and holy quiet there,
Great clouds along pacific skies,
And men and women with straight eyes,
Lithe children lovelier than a dream,
A bosky wood, a slumbrous stream,
And little kindly winds that creep
Round twilight corners, half asleep.
In Grantchester their skins are white;
They bathe by day, they bathe by night;
The women there do all they ought;
The men observe the Rules of Thought.
They love the Good; they worship Truth;
They laugh uproariously in youth;
(And when they get to feeling old,
They up and shoot themselves, I'm told) . . .
　　Ah God! to see the branches stir
Across the moon at Grantchester!
To smell the thrilling-sweet and rotten
Unforgettable, unforgotten
River-smell, and hear the breeze
Sobbing in the little trees.
Say, do the elm-clumps greatly stand
Still guardians of that holy land?
The chestnuts shade, in reverend dream,
The yet unacademic stream?

Is dawn a secret shy and cold
Anadyomene, silver-gold?
And sunset still a golden sea
From Haslingfield to Madingley?
And after, ere the night is born,
Do hares come out about the corn?
Oh, is the water sweet and cool,
Gentle and brown, above the pool?
And laughs the immortal river still
Under the mill, under the mill?
Say, is there Beauty yet to find?
And Certainty? and Quiet kind?
Deep meadows yet, for to forget
The lies, and truths, and pain? . . . oh! yet
Stands the Church clock at ten to three?
And is there honey still for tea?

Rupert Brooke, 1912

Dons, too, were imbued with the spirit of the countryside. The Master of Magdalene College describes the pleasures of his regular brisk afternoon 'constitutional'.

Then, too, I must confess to a lamentably feeble pleasure in mere country 65
sights and sounds. I love to watch the curious and beautiful things that go
on in every hedgerow and every field; it is a ceaseless delight to see the
tender uncrumpling leaves of the copse in spring, and no less a pleasure
to see the woodland streaked and stained with the flaming glories of
autumn. It is a joy in high midsummer to see the clear dwindled stream
run under the thick hazels, among the rich water-plants; it is no less a joy
to see the same stream running full and turbid in winter, when the banks
are bare, and the trees are leafless, and the pasture is wrinkled with frost.
Half the joy, for instance, of shooting, in which I frankly confess I take a
childish delight, is the quiet tramping over the clean-cut stubble, the
distant view of field and wood, the long, quiet wait at the covert-end,
where the spindle-wood hangs out her quaint rosy berries, and the
rabbits come scampering up the copse, as the far-off tapping of the
beaters draws near in the frosty air. The delights of the country-side grow
upon me every month and every year. I love to stroll in the lanes in
spring, with white clouds floating in the blue above, and to see the glade
carpeted with steel-blue hyacinths. I love to walk on country roads or by
woodland paths, on a rain-drenched day of summer, when the sky is full
of heavy inky clouds, and the earth smells fresh and sweet; I love to go
briskly homeward on a winter evening, when the sunset smoulders low
in the west, when the pheasants leap trumpeting to their roosts, and the
lights begin to peep in cottage windows.

Arthur Christopher Benson, 1906

A perceptive and poetic child could appreciate the landscape also.

The stacks, like blunt impassive temples, rise   66
Across flat fields against the autumnal skies.
The hairy-footed horses plough the land,
Or as in prayer and meditation stand
Upholding square, primeval, dung-stained carts,
With an unending patience in their hearts.

Nothing is changed. The farmer's gig goes by
Against the horizon. Surely, the same sky,
So vast and yet familiar, grey and mild,
And streaked with light like music, I, a child,
Lifted my face from leaf-edged lanes to see,
Late-coming home, to bread-and-butter tea.

Frances Cornford, 1954

In August the great Sturbridge Fair was held in some fields outside Cambridge.

It is kept in a large cornfield near *Casterton* [Chesterton], extending from   67
the side of the river Cam, towards the road for half a mile square.

If the husbandmen who rent the land do not get their corn off
before a certain day in August, the fair-keepers may trample it under foot
and spoil it to build their booths or tents; for all the fair is kept in tents and
booths. On the other hand, to balance that severity, if the fair-keepers
have not done their business of the fair and removed and cleared the field
by another certain day in September, the ploughmen may come in again
with plough and cart and overthrow all and trample it into the dirt, and
as for the filth, dung, straw, etc., necessarily left by the fair-keepers, the
quantity of which is very great, it is the farmers' fees and makes them full
amends for the trampling, riding and carting upon, and hardening the
ground.

It is impossible to describe all the parts and circumstances of this fair
exactly; the shops are placed in rows like streets, whereof one is called
Cheapside, and here, as in several other streets, are all sorts of trades who
sell by retail and who come principally from *London* with their goods;
scarce any trades are omitted, goldsmiths, toyshops, brasiers, turners,
milliners, haberdashers, hatters, mercers, drapers, pewterers, china-
warehouses and in a word all trades that can be named in *London*, with
coffee houses, taverns, brandy-shops and eating-houses innumerable,
and all in tents and booths, as above.

This great street reaches from the road, which as I said goes from
Cambridge to *New-Market*, turning short out of it to the right towards the
river, and holds in a line near half a mile quite down to the riverside; in
another street parallel with the road are like rows of booths, but larger,
and more intermingled with wholesale dealers, and one side, passing out
of this last street to the left hand, is a formal great square formed by the
largest booths, built in that form, and which they call the Duddery;

whence the name is derived and what its signification is, I could never yet learn, though I made all possible search into it. The area of this square is about 80 to 100 yards where the dealers have room before every booth to take down and open their packs, and to bring in waggons to load and unload.

This place is separated and peculiar to the wholesale dealers in the woollen manufacture. Here the booths or tents are of a vast extent, have different apartments and the quantities of goods they bring are so great that the insides of them look like another *Blackwell-Hall*, being as vast warehouses piled up with goods to the top. In this Duddery, as I have been informed, there have been sold one hundred thousand pounds worth of woollen manufactures in less than a week's time besides the prodigious trade carried on here by wholesalemen from *London* and all parts of *England*, who transact their business wholly in their pocket books and meeting their chapmen from all parts and take orders; these they say exceed by far the sales of goods actually brought to the fair, and delivered in kind, it being frequent for the *London* wholesale men to carry back orders from their dealers for ten thousand pounds worth of goods a man, and some much more. This especially respects those people who deal in heavy goods, as wholesale grocers, salters, braziers, iron-merchants, wine merchants, and the like, but does exclude the dealers in woollen manufactures, and especially in mercery goods of all sorts, the dealers in which generally manage their business in this manner.

Daniel Defoe, 1724

To the east of fenland lay a sandy area of heath known as breckland, today largely covered with softwood plantations. William Gilpin was an inquisitive traveller, always on the lookout for the 'picturesque'; but he was not the only one to compare parts of breckland – in this case the stretch between Soham and Mildenhall – to the Sahara desert.

We soon however found, that we were in the neighbourhood of a   68
country still more disagreeable, at least for travelling, than the fenny one. This was a vast tract of sand. At Soham, which is a considerable village, we *landed*, if I may so speak, from the fens; and hoped we had now gotten upon stable ground. But we soon found our mistake. We had scarce left it, when we entered upon the sands; and only changed the colour of the landscape; both of them being equally wild, open, and dreary. Not a tree was to be seen. The wildness was in some degree lessened by a few patch-faced sheep, and a few struggling cattle grazing in the greener parts. But this little appearance of herbage soon went off. In a few miles the country became an absolute desert. Nothing was to be seen on either side, but sand, and scattered gravel, without the least vegetation; a mere African desert: ager arenosus, une specie aqualis, nudus gignentium. In some places this sandy waste occupied the whole scope of the eye: in other places, at a distance, we could see a skirting of the green, with a few straggling bushes, which being surrounded by sand, appeared like a stretch of low land, shooting to the sea. The whole country indeed had

the appearance of a beaten sea-coast; but without the beauties, which adorn that species of landscape. In many places we saw the sand even driven into ridges; and the road was totally covered; which indeed was everywhere so deep, and heavy, that four horses, which we were obliged to take, could scarce in the slowest pace, drag us through it. It was a little surprizing to find such a piece of *absolute desert* almost in the heart of England. To us it was a novel idea. We had not even heard of it.

William Gilpin, 1809

Very different was the impression of breckland in a storm, as seen by a much more receptive traveller. James Hissey conceived the admirable idea of touring with his wife in a phaeton (a light open carriage drawn by two horses) at the height of the railway age, braving the rough roads and run-down coaching inns. They had many happy little adventures.

The little town of Watton left behind, we soon entered upon a wild wooded country, a country where the signs of human habitations were few and far between. Trees bounded our roadway on either side, the wind stirred and rustled their branches and leaves with a continual 'sur, sur, sur'. A wild warm wind it was, blowing in fitful gusts, now just bending the tops of the trees, now roaring and whistling through the stems, now falling almost altogether away. The dark, drifting, lowering clouds foreboded rain; all Nature seemed in a state of unrest. There was a kind of mild excitement in driving on such a day through a strange country; the air was so invigorating, the effects of light and shade over the landscape were so peculiar and powerful. Away in front of us the horizon was of the darkest indigo, just above it the sky was of a wan yellow, and towards us great grey clouds drooping with aqueous vapour travelled apace. Now and again slanting lines of rain revealed where a storm was sweeping along, and now and again the distance would be sponged out by a passing shower. Rain storms (to parody the poet laureate) to the right of us, rain storms to the left of us, rain storms in front of us, but so far, by curious good fortune, we had escaped without a single drop, and as we drove along we watched with unabated interest the ever changing cloud forms, great banks of cumulus, gathering fold upon fold in ominous grandeur, their forms and outlines ever changing; anon a momentary gleam of sunlight would gild their wreathing crests, then all would be grey and gloom again, and a dreariness would be cast over the landscape. As the wind freshened an extra gust would ever and again drive a fir cone or a portion of a branch right into the phaeton. One great piece of dead wood crashed down on to the road just after we had passed; had we been a few seconds earlier, it might have brought our journey to an unpleasant ending; and we were not sorry in time to get away from the trees into a more open heath land, though the further we progressed the rougher became our way. The surface of the road was of soft sand, making travelling heavy, and there was a plentiful supply of stones about, of all sizes and shapes, from that of a miniature boulder to a moderate-sized flint. But though the road was bad – wretchedly bad, to

69

use no worse an adjective – we felt that we could hardly complain, as it was really the only bit of bad road we had experienced since we left home, and what better had we a right to expect over a bleak untravelled moorland?

We had escaped the wandering storms so far in a wonderful manner, but as we progressed the road showed signs of heavy rain; great pools of water stood in the ruts, the surface was soft and running with moisture, on either side the streams were swollen into tiny torrents. Just as we were congratulating ourselves upon our escaping the wet, down came the rain in a regular deluge, or rather a combination of rain and hail; it rebounded from off the road, and the horses, stung by the icy darts, pranced about so that, what with the blinding rain and our struggling steeds, it was as much as we could manage to keep on the road. The water ran off our aprons on either side of the phaeton in miniature cascades, and tested the weatherproof qualities of our mackintoshes to the utmost. It was a wild wet drive – we were passing through a vast unenclosed heath, of shelter there was none, a few wind-blown trees here and there, and that was all – but because of its very wildness we enjoyed the drive exceedingly. It was worth even the risk of a wetting to watch the storm sweep along, bending the trees before it. The landscape had a dark dreary look, brightened only by lonely pools on the moorland; then as the storm spent its fury, the cloud above us seemed to lift, the horizon in front grew lighter, the air became warmer, the sun suddenly burst forth, and the long grasses and fir trees seemed as though they were sprinkled with diamonds, as the sun's rays caught the countless raindrops thereon and converted them into glowing jewels.

James John Hissey, 1889

For close examination of the country, however, nothing can beat the solitary naturalist travelling on foot. Edward Thomas set out to walk the Icknield Way, starting at Thetford; he made it that night to Newmarket, but not without painful blisters.

My road was now an ordinary white road between hedges, but with a   70
furzy heath on both sides beyond the hedges. It had no grassy borders, but at the turning to Lackford manor-house there was a little triangular common on the left, of grass, gorse, hawthorns, and an ash tree. On the right there was a larger common, called Clamp's Heath. On my left I saw corn and a field of pale sainfoin extending to the edge of a dark oak wood. The road was, if anything, slightly embanked over this level ground. After passing the Heath it had grassy borders and low hedges and corn on both sides, and then, after a short distance, no border, and on the right no hedge. Where it descended towards the woods of Cavenham it was sunk a little and had a left-hand border of grass. Just before this I saw the first chalk pit under the road on my left, with wild rose and elder on its floor. At Cavenham a new flat bridge of two arches crossed a tiny tributary of the Lark; but on the left of this was an old single arch about seven feet broad of narrow bricks, still firm but all grass-grown over its high curved

crown which passengers used to mount like a barrel. The new bridge probably took the ford's place. At Cavenham the road went under the trees of Cavenham Park – oak, beech, elm and sycamore, ash and aspen. Turtle-doves were cooing unseen. The house was some way off, the church farther, the village yet farther along a by-road. At each turning there was an open space for trees and men, for example, at the two ways down to Lark Hall. Beyond the second of these the road was lined by beech trees and wych elms standing in grass: it was cool, but gave a view of sunlit barley between the trunks, and soon afterwards of an undulating lowland, heath and corn, and wooded ridges on the right; while on the left the land fell away and I felt the curve of the earth, the wooded horizon being lower than the road. Before reaching Tuddenham Corner the bank of bird's-foot trefoil was wide enough for a path; only on the left was there a hedge, on the right was tall barley. Past Tuddenham Corner the road was narrow and shaded by beech trees of half a century's growth; it had hedges and grassy borders, and down the middle two lines of grass between the ordinary course of the horses' feet and the wheels. On both sides were many long, straight plantations of trees, but in a low, cultivated country where they gave little offence. Presently the road touched a tumulus on the left, and drew near another on the right. Then it was crossed by the Great Eastern Railway, and turning sharper to the right than probably it used to, went due west towards Kentford. Being now a highway between Newmarket and Bury St Edmunds, it was broader, and had also grassy margins of twice its own width, and beeches in the hedgerows.

Edward Thomas, 1913

Dawn in breckland.

No human eye sees millions of the flowers that bloom; no human ear   71
hears the song of thousands of birds. Yet each flower gives something of its fragrance to the passing wind; each bird adds to the flood of melody which surges through the land – a throbbing of life, a chorus of joy, an uprising of the elemental forces. New beauties are perceptible with each succeeding dawn, – a tinge of green here, a richer purple there, sun and cloud weaving the warp and woof of the panorama of colour in the landscape, flashing on the silver trunk of a birch or the ruddy richness of a Scots pine or plunging the distant woodland into a haze of blue.

W. G. Clarke, 1925

In his evocative account of breckland as seen through the eyes of a child, Michael Home has disguised the place-names. His home was at Great Hockham, where his father was a tenant-farmer.

I wish I had the words to convey to you that utter remoteness of our   72
western hinterland. No sooner did one pass West Farm than one had a

choice of tracks that led through Cranberry to the great heaths of Topleigh and Tottley. The continuation of the Wortley Road past Gallows Hill led the same way. If one took the Illboro track there were the great heaths towards Rudgham and Ouseland, and even if one took the Hareborough Road and then one of the numerous lanes or tracks that led west, one could tramp for a day and more and still be in the brecklands. When on a Wednesday in my holidays I rode all day with Walter Addis in his cart, we were never out of the sight of brecks and heaths. As Punch jogged his way across the marled and flinty roads, the bracken brushed the wheels of the cart, and between the oases of hamlets would be the quiet and lonely miles. Between hamlet and hamlet it was rare to meet another cart or a living soul; indeed the only living things might be the crying peewits, aloof protected pheasants, or, if it were towards evening, the innumerable rabbits that rose at our approach and scattered to their sandy burrows as if the earth itself had moved in flight.

I wish, too, that I could convey to you the incredible beauty of that vast and lonely country. For all its quietude there was in it nothing forbidding. It had space and freedom and the friendliness of growing things. The heaths and brecks had their gentle undulations so that in lanes and tracks one never saw too far ahead. And then again there would be great sweeps of open country. And even there the miles of bracken or heather would have no monotony for they would be broken by ancient woods or clusters of gnarled pines, and mossy pools with their silver birches, or the oases of silver sand which were the burrows of the teeming rabbits. Above would be the open sky, and across the clear stretches it would be hard to tell where the faint blue of the horizon ended and that sky began. Then there were the meres, as varying as the heath itself. Ringmere and Langmere lay open while Fowlmere and Topleigh Watering were embowered in trees, though Topleigh was open on one side to the brecks. Everywhere was a prodigality of colour that somehow blended and harmonized, so that the golden flare of massed canker-weed seemed to merge into green bracken, and that again into the madders and lakes of the squat heather. And then when that colouring of the heaths seemed endless, one would suddenly be at a vast stretch of breck, the bare grey soil showing a sheen of dwarf flowers and always the silver-grey of the rabbit burrows.

Michael Home, 1946

Coast and Sea

At low tide the great sands along the north coast of Norfolk are revealed, their colours changing with the light.

The Great Barrier Sand to which the geese were flying is the counterpart in our island of the Great Barrier Reef guarding the east Australian shore. From the Lynn Deeps eastward it swells and grows, until the myriad particles, compacted by tide and current, rise into the bank marked in the charts as the High Sand, which lies between wind and water, from Hunstanton to Yarmouth Roads. From Wells to Blakeney its summit caps all but the highest tides, soft in outline like golden snow, built up of matter as homogeneous as snowflakes, but less fantastic in contour than the snowdrifts, because water-soaked sand is heavier than an equal mass of clay. In the dark winter days the contrast of colours between the region of the sand and the parallel line of cultivated land marks and emphasises the wide difference in kind between those adjacent tracts of earth. The contrast extends from earth to sky, for the salt sands invite the wind and repel the clouds, while the sodden uplands, with their lines of wood, suck in the water and hug the mists in every hollow. Thus each region keeps its own scheme of colour, and covers this with an appropriate sky. Dull clouds brood in smoke and heaviness above the fields, and steam and mist rise from the earth to meet them, suggesting the origin of the late-Roman myth that here lay the land of everlasting twilight, to whose verge the ghostly ships were ever busy transporting the souls of the departed. But the edge of the bright sand marks the limit of these clinging vapours. As the leaden clouds drift seawards, they are sucked outwards and upwards by ascending currents, the solid masses are drawn out, torn, and carded into flakes, as if by invisible fingers; the 'rack dislimns', and whitens into drift and scud; lakes and splashes of azure broaden between the whitening clouds; tall shafts of light stalk across the plain and along the margin of the bank whence comes the everlasting thunder of the sea. Under such shifting skies the tawny sand changes with every gleam of light, or shadow of cloud, or change of level in the bank. Where the mass rises like a turtle's back, or has beset the black timbers of the wrecks, it takes the colour of red-gold; where the shafts of light traverse it, or the wet flats lie, it pales and fades. When the clouds darken and descend, then the sand flushes and reddens, and the darkness, which kills all colour on the land, only brings out by contrast the warmth and glow of the limitless levels of the bank. When the tide is at its lowest, the sands seem more extensive even than the levels of the sea. Northwards the shallow sea itself seems to rise abruptly to the horizon, the lines of breakers appearing superimposed each upon the other, like a wall of faced grey flint with the white edges shining. But right and left the sand runs on, its surface unbroken by wave or ridge, but marked from distance to distance by the wrecks, the beacons, and the dim outline of the fowlers' nets, hanging like giant cobwebs, or the sails of phantom ships.

Charles Cornish, 1897

On bright days the light on the beach is dazzling, the sea-birds brilliant, and the comments of the visitors to Blakeney Point typically mundane.

It is the view over the far side of the dunes which always astonishes – that   74
immense view over sand and breakers into the clean blue north where sea meets sky. It draws the footsteps down to the beach. Here is a wide but secret place, for the hills cut out the familiar man-altered mainland. What the Norfolk inland scene lacks in luxury of herbage, it makes up for in brightness, and as for the shore, it must be the most brilliant place in Britain. Amidst the ecstasy of colouring, somebody, with the local tendency to deprecation was heard to remark 'This old beach hurt my eyes'. Certainly there is a glare, and on bright summer days there is no shade. The sand-valleys amongst the dunes, into which an occasional tide has flooded and left its jetsam, are parched and dazzling. There is an aromatic scent. Overhead, a pair of gaily coloured shell-drake are attracting attention. Above their nests on the powdery beach is a storm of white sea-swallows. The air is full of the birds' protective clamour. The eggs look neater than pebbles which give them camouflage, the chicks, mobile soon after hatching, speed along like mechanical toys. For the noisy nursery is still dangerous in spite of the Keeper. How long have tern been using Blakeney Point as a breeding ground, nobody knows. They are partly responsible for drawing human visitors there from all parts of the country. Yet there are people living in the immediate neighbourhood who have never seen the birds or set foot on the Point. For as one old man remarked upon his first visit 'There isn't much here except for the eye-sight'.

Jane Hales, 1969

The crumbling cliffs, as seen around Sidestrand, spell danger for clamberers.

Rough and yielding as were the paths, called 'gangways', connecting the   75
cliffs with the endless reaches of sand below, they were not rough
enough, or yielding enough, or in any way dangerous enough for me.

So I used to fashion 'gangways' of my own; I used to descend the
cliff at whatsoever point it pleased me, clinging to the lumps of sandy
earth with the prehensile power of a spider-monkey. Many a warning
had I had from the good fishermen and sea-folk, that some day I should
fall from top to bottom – fall and break my neck. A laugh was my sole
answer to these warnings; for, with the possession of perfect health, I had
inherited that instinctive belief in good luck which perfect health will
often engender.

However, my punishment came at last. The coast, which is yielding
gradually to the sea, is famous for sudden and gigantic landslips. These
landslips are sometimes followed, at the return of the tide, by a further
fall, called a 'settlement'. The word 'settlement' explains itself, perhaps.
No matter how smooth the sea, the return of the tide seems on that coast
to have a strange magnetic power upon the land, and the *débris* of a
landslip will sometimes, though not always, respond to it by again falling
and settling into new and permanent shapes.

Now, on the morning after a great landslip, when the coastguard,
returning on his beat, found a cove where, half-an-hour before, he had
left his own cabbages growing, I, in spite of all warnings, had climbed the
heap of *débris* from the sands, and while I was hallooing triumphantly to
two companions below – the two most impudent-looking urchins,
barefooted and unkempt, that ever a gentleman's son forgathered with –
a great mass of loose earth settled, carrying me with it in its fall. I was
taken up for dead.

It was, however, only a matter of broken ribs and a damaged leg.
And there is no doubt that if the local surgeon had not been allowed to
have his own way, I should soon have been cured. As it was I became a
cripple. The great central fact – the very pivot upon which all the wheels
of my life have since been turning – is that for two years during the
impressionable period of childhood I walked with crutches.

Theodore Watts-Dunton, 1900

But they provide a secure habitat for wild flowers. Agnes Strickland lived at
Reydon Hall, near Southwold.

The wild sea-cliff, though rude it be,   76
   Is wreathed with many a flower
That blossoms there, unscathed and free,
    Through storm and shower.

There, bright as gems of fairy lore,
   Or eastern poet's dream,
The horned poppies gild the shore
    With sunny gleam.

The threatening clouds and tempests dark
  No terrors have for them,
When billows 'whelm the gallant bark
    From stern to stem;

When men who've braved the cannon's roar
  Are pale with speechless dread,
The stonecrop calmly mantles o'er
    Her rugged bed.

The red-bind to the barren soil
  Clings safe, 'midst all alarms,
While drowning seamen vainly toil,
    With fainting arms.

The burnet there securely grows,
  And scorns to turn away,
When o'er her hardy bosom blows
    The drifting spray.

Agnes Strickland, 1850

William Dutt was a prolific writer about East Anglia, producing at least a dozen books on the subject. Here he is, on foot, observing the farming land just behind the dunes of the coast.

I can remember walking through this sparsely populated district on my   77
way to Happisburgh late in the afternoon of a day in early spring. All day
the fresh furrows of the hedgeless fields had been white with seagulls; for
near the coast more gulls than rooks or grey crows follow the plough. All
day, too, dun clouds had been coming up from the south-west and
passing swiftly overhead and out to sea. There had been no rain, but the
air was laden with moisture, which clung to the lichen-stained field-
gates and the trunks of the stunted oaks, making them clammy to the
touch. The earth also was saturated with it, and where the plough had
lately passed, the ridges were wet and smooth, ready to gleam in the
sunlight if the sun had shone. But from daybreak to dusk there was no
ray of sunlight, and after midday the aspect of the countryside was
sullenly sombre. All the while a buffeting, gusty wind was blowing – a
wind that whistled shrilly amongst the sapless stems of last year's
knapweeds and tansies, and made the sturdy but stunted oaks by the
roadside strain and creak and groan.
  The night came on with surprising suddenness. From any slight
eminence you could watch it approaching; its advance was swift but
stealthy; it seemed bent on coming upon you unawares. After watching
in a field corner a labourer repairing a bank the rabbits had undermined,
I looked elsewhere for a moment, and on seeking him again I could not
find him. He was still there, but the night was there too, and the night hid
him. Over the newly ploughed fields the darkness gathered as though it

were some enshrouding exhalation of the earth. There seemed, in the transition hour, no obvious reason for its presence there; for the sky was still grey, and against it some rooks could be seen flying inland to some distant woodland. It was that time of the day which the country-folk of East Norfolk call 'shutting-in time', and in the comparatively quiet intervals between the wind-gusts I could hear the thudding of hooves and the clinking of chain harness – the ploughmen had left the fields and were on their way back to the farm stables. As I drew near Happisburgh, several of the small birds that had spent the day in the stubble betrayed the places where, in this hedgeless country, they spend the night. Startled by my footsteps, they darted from little holes in the banks, and I caught just a glimpse of them before they vanished in the gloom.

William Dutt, 1909

Here, just inland, the influence of the sea is always felt.

As on the highway's quiet edge   78
He mows the grass beside the hedge,
The old man has for company
The distant, grey, salt-smelling sea,
A poppied field, a cow and calf,
The finches on the telegraph.

Across his faded back a hone,
He slowly, slowly scythes alone
In silence of the wind-soft air,
With ladies' bedstraw everywhere,
With whitened corn, and tarry poles,
And far-off gulls like risen souls.

Frances Cornford, 1948

And here the colours can be more varied, and no less brilliant, than on the beach.

Across Toll's Hill, where in former days the smugglers, who flourished   79
hereabouts, hid their goods, lies Northrepps, a village of flowers; and Northrepps Wood, always charming, is most beautiful in June, when, in the deep valley opening to the sea, the rhododendrons are in bloom, and the picturesque Hermitage is almost hidden by the dazzling masses of these beautiful flowering trees. Like children in a wood gay with wild flowers, one is thus tempted further and further along the coast. The influence of the poppy may be strong, and it is sweet to lie on these purpling hills overlooking the green and blue and pink sea; but there are always allurements beyond. Climb to the hill-top, and look down on the scene, and wide stretches of orange sands, and the tiny village of red houses clustering on the cliff's edge, and so surely will you be tempted to go further along up the ever-ascending cliffs to the dreamy little fishing hamlets that lie yonder.

So exquisitely clear is the atmosphere that every spot of colour stands out vivid and distinct. The impression is never blurred. And what great rolling waves of colour there are in this land! Under the pink slopes of the purple heathery hills the corn gleams like copper and gold, from which the eye finds rest in the cool sage-green of the great patches of mangolds. The red admirals flitting by, the green and grey and sapphire waves, fringed with white, the great brown bees buzzing over the red and white clover, all add to the mass of dazzling tints that catch the eye. Under the shady hollow of the hills, a group of roan horses form a picturesque knot. It is almost a relief to turn into a lane where there are only masses of blue-grey 'smoke-Jack' and cool feathery grasses.

Annie Berlyn, 1894

Some places along the coast are less propitious for agriculture. The Aldeburgh sandlings were the inspiration for Crabbe's portrayal of a blighted landscape.

Lo! Where the heath, with withering brake grown o'er,   80
Lends the light turf that warms the neighbouring poor;
From thence a length of burning sand appears,
Where the thin harvest waves its wither'd ears;
Rank weeds, that every art and care defy,
Reign o'er the land, and rob the blighted rye:
There thistles stretch their prickly arms afar,
And to the ragged infant threaten war;
There poppies nodding, mock the hope of toil;
There the blue bugloss paints the sterile soil;
Hardy and high, above the slender sheaf,
The slimy mallow waves her silky leaf;
O'er the young shoot the charlock throws a shade,
And clasping tares cling round the sickly blade;
With mingled tints the rocky coasts abound,
And a sad splendour vainly shines around.

George Crabbe, 1783

The coastline also evokes thoughts of death, especially at places where the sea has encroached into graveyards, as here at Sidestrand. Clement Scott's haunting poem gave the countryside around Cromer a new name – 'Poppy-Land'.

On the grass of the cliff, at the edge of the steep,   81
God planted a garden – a garden of sleep!
'Neath the blue of the sky, in the green of the corn,
It is there that the regal red poppies are born!
Brief days of desire, and long dreams of delight,
They are there when my Poppy-Land cometh in sight.
In music of distance, with eyes that are wet,
It is there I remember, and there I forget!

O! heart of my heart! where the poppies are born,
I am waiting for thee, in the hush of the corn.
    Sleep! Sleep! From the Cliff to the Deep!
    Sleep, my Poppy-Land, Sleep!

In my garden of sleep, where red poppies are spread,
I wait for the living, alone with the dead!
For a tower in ruins stands guard o'er the deep,
At whose feet are green graves of dead women asleep!
Did they love as I love, when they lived by the sea?
Did they wait as I wait, for the days that may be?
Was it hope or fulfilling that entered each breast,
Ere death gave release, and the poppies gave rest?
O! life of my life! on the cliffs by the sea,
By the graves in the grass, I am waiting for thee!
    Sleep! Sleep! In the Dews by the Deep!
    Sleep, my Poppy-Land, Sleep!

Clement Scott, 1886

The geese on their evening flight over the marshes at Holkham.

The stream of gulls had hardly ceased when our old gunner, eager, acute
and vigilant, exclaimed, 'I see the geese', and pointed to the west,
whence in the distance he had spied them flying up the marsh. When
opposite the bay they turned, and, flying backwards, pitched in a long
line in the marsh, and there waited for the dusk before taking their final
flight. From a hollow on the summit of a sandhill, sheltered by fringes of
marrum grass and cushioned on soft sand, we watched the night set in
over marshes, sands and sea. Landwards, as the light faded and the
after-glow died out, the line of woods formed a wall of blackness next the
sky. At their feet the marsh levels still held light, and even the mass of the
grey geese was visible for a time. A sheet of greenish cloud still lit up the
west, and when the marshes were at last wrapped in the blanket of
twilight, the pools and dykes shone bright with its reflected glow. Behind
and seawards were the fast-narrowing line of sands and the ever-
growing sea, as the tide crept up in infinite lines of dark water and white
breakers, with a continuous moaning roar – now louder, now softer – as
the land wind freshened or fell. As colour died here also, and the ducks
began to come in, like bullets, from the sea, a sound came across the flats
like the sound of a ship passing in the night. It was the rising of the whole
body of the geese, and the measured beats of their four hundred pairs of
wings. When once in mid-air they came on 'singing' – *jubilantes ordine* –
with calls as if a band of musicians with flutes and oboes were passing
across the sky. As they reached the sandhills and rose high above their
crests, the dusky lines were just discernible against the darkened sky.

82

Charles Cornish, 1897

The coastline also comprises a very different environment – the muddy river estuaries. Sabine Baring-Gould was at one time rector of the remote parish of East Mersea.

Between the mouths of the Blackwater and the Colne, on the east coast of Essex, lies an extensive marshy tract veined and freckled in every part with water. It is a wide waste of debatable ground contested by sea and land, subject to incessant incursions from the former, but stubbornly maintained by the latter. At high tide the appearance is that of a vast surface of moss or Sargasso weed floating on the sea, with rents and patches of shining water traversing and dappling it in all directions. The creeks, some of considerable length and breadth, extend many miles inland, and are arteries whence branches out a fibrous tissue of smaller channels, flushed with water twice in the twenty-four hours. At noontides, and especially at the equinoxes, the sea asserts its royalty over this vast region, and overflows the whole, leaving standing out of the flood only the long island of Mersea, and the lesser islet, called the Ray. This latter is a hill of gravel rising from the heart of the Marshes, crowned with ancient thorntrees, and possessing, what is denied the mainland, an unfailing spring of purest water. At ebb, the Ray can only be reached from the old Roman causeway, called the Strood, over which runs the road from Colchester to Mersea Isle, connecting formerly the city of the Trinobantes with the station of the count of the Saxon shore. But even at ebb, the Ray is not approachable by land unless the sun or east wind has parched the ooze into brick; and then the way is long, tedious and tortuous, among bitter pools and over shining creeks. It was perhaps because this ridge of high ground was so inaccessible, so well protected by nature, that the ancient inhabitants had erected on it a *rath*, or fortified camp of wooden logs, which left its name to the place long after the timber defences had rotted away.

A more desolate region can scarce be conceived, and yet it is not without beauty. In summer, the thrift mantles the marshes with shot satin, passing through all gradations of tint from maiden's blush to lily white. Thereafter a purple glow steals over the waste, as the sea lavender bursts into flower, and simultaneously every creek and pool is royally fringed with sea aster. A little later the glass-wort, that shot up green and transparent as emerald glass in the early spring, turns to every tinge of carmine.

When all vegetation ceases to live, and goes to sleep, the marshes are alive and wakeful with countless wild fowl. At all times they are haunted with sea mews and royston crows, in winter they teem with wild duck and grey geese. The stately heron loves to wade in the pools, occasionally the whooper swan sounds his loud trumpet, and flashes a white reflection in the still blue waters of the fleets. The plaintive pipe of the curlew is familiar to those who frequent these marshes, and the barking of the brent geese as they return from their northern breeding places is heard in November.

Sabine Baring-Gould, 1880

Here the tide exhibits its elemental force. The scene is the Orwell at Pin Mill.

But the eye wanders as the sunshafts lower.   84
Here is a wash of oyster-coloured ooze
Tongued with the turquoise thrusting of the flood,
The insinuating seas that, twisting wry
In a Suffolk tideway, spill their strength and lose
The aspiring water welling in a sigh.
Here is the press of an insistent blood,
    The pulse of power.

It vivifies; it fills. Here in the bay
The leaning masts, awakening, ride upright.
As jewels move upon a breathing breast
So gently sway the little coloured craft
On this resurgent bosom. Lifting light
They swing to the stream. Landward a voice has laughed
Out of the huddle of homes that proffer rest
    At the close of the day.

Francis Engleheart, 1965

And here the continuity of the land is split (for Whitewater read Blackwater, and for Maychester read Colchester).

The Whitewater estuary stretches far and wide beyond the meadow, and   85
at times of the year like the present, when 'longen folk to gon on
pilgrimage', I am filled with a keen desire to travel. Not to go abroad, not
to journey to some sun-stricken town in a far-off land where the
civilisation we know best is not, but to cross the shining estuary and
explore the villages on the far side of the river. I have travelled, have been
north and south and east and to the isles of the sea; certain far lands and
wild peoples are no longer strange to me, but the mysterious country
across the estuary enshrines more possibilities than Tibet. The sun lights
up tiny villages set amid prosperous fields, a telescope brings them
seemingly within reach, but I am no nearer. Villagers who have passed
more than eighty years on this side of the Whitewater have never been
across the estuary; there are strong tides, dangerous currents, sandbanks,
impediments innumerable. Though the river narrows rapidly a mile or
two further inland, the only bridge across it is nearly fifteen miles away
amid the peaceful streets of the market-town. At the waterside down
here, where the barges come and go, riding high beneath their burden of
ripened grain or weighed down with stone for the sea wall, the half-
dozen fishermen do not respond readily to suggestions that they should
cross the water. There is a feud between the river-men of Maychester
and those of the village on the other side; nobody living knows or cares
about the cause of it. Last summer a big boatload of villagers decided to
cross; their light vessel was carried along by an irresistible current in the
direction of the open sea. A Customs boat went to the rescue after the

seafarers had been out for some hours, and were tired, hungry, and frightened.

S. L. Bensusan, 1907

Natural life on the marshes of Mersea Island.

'Otters, now,' said John, as we sat on the sea-wall, with the gulls   86
quarrelling on the tide-edge and all the flats shining like opals. 'Otters.
I've laid in those reeds an' watched the young playin' like kittens in the
water, goin' head over heels down the bank, pushin' each other under
an' boxin' each other like tomboys. Mother would pop up now and then
with an eel an' whistle to 'em – just like a train whistle in the distance –
an' then there'd be a rare scramble an' spittin' an' scratchin' before they
settled down to feed. No, I never shoot 'em. We can spare the eels, an' I
like watchin' 'em.'

He has seen wild ducks mob a fox which tried to stalk them. They
swam wildly up the fleet after him, quacking abuse at the top of their
voices and flapping their wings. Reynard, discomfited, slunk off.

He has seen a whale come ashore on the mud-flats and thrash off
again in a mighty cloud of spumy froth when the tide flowed, and he has
watched the schools of porpoises playing under the September moon,
jumping high out of the water and falling back with reports like cannon-
shots. 'Sink a boat they would, if they hit it. . . .'

And he has seen, winter after winter for sixty years, the wild geese
come and go in their clanging thousands, heard the springtime carillon of
the redshank ringing their million bells, and seen the coots, massed in
hundreds on the big pool, dive like a flash in unanimous confusion and
throw up a mighty sheet of spray which confounded even the peregrine
falcon when he swooped from the clouds like a thunderbolt at eighty
miles an hour.

'Yes, I was born on this owd marsh an' I'm a-goin' to live to a
hundred, the good God willin'. An' I hope they bury me under the sea-
wall when I die . . . they can have London! That ain't our country, sir.'

J. Wentworth Day, 1946

*The shoreline was frequently the scene for smuggling affrays. This incident took
place at Hollesley Bay in 1797.*

Night now began to draw on, and the sea-birds left off their screaming;   87
the tern and the dottrell hastened to their resting-places; and the last of
all the feathered sea-shore tribe, the one which goes to roost the latest,
the grey curlew, bent his rapid wing toward Havergate Island, and gave a
mournful note as he flapped over the head of the young watchman. As
the moon arose the wind began to blow a little fresh, and the ocean to
roar upon the beach. The smugglers rejoiced at this, as it would enable
them to land their cargo with less chance of being heard. The flag still

streamed and flapped in the wind; the light shone like a star in the shepherd's cot; and the time drew near for the contest.

Not a sound could be now heard save that of the wind. The vessel, however, might be seen in the moonlight, approaching the shore; and now a heavy eight-oared boat was seen to leave her: she was heavily laden, even to the gunwale. The boat lurched through the breakers like a log. On she came, with her helmsman, John Luff, who laid her broadside on to the shore. Now for an anxious moment. Not a word was spoken. The wind preventing any sound along the shore, nothing could be heard even of the grounding of the boat's keel upon the beach. Dark figures of men were seen getting out of the boat. They were expert sailors, up to their work; as the sea heaved the boat up they dragged her higher on the shore, until they could more conveniently unload her. This was done as expeditiously as possible; each man carried a sack heavily laden. They went to the very spot that Barry had named, deposited their load, and again returned to their boat. Twice they performed this work; and now the two last men, carrying the eight oars, brought up the rear. The eight quietly seated themselves on the sacks, whilst the other two went forward with the oars; they returned, and, as young Edward concluded, must have said, 'All's right.'

By this time the coast-guard were drawing their lines closer to the spot, each man taking up his brother, or calling on him as he passed him, until the whole fourteen were within the space of ten yards from the flag; breathless, on their knees, did they await the shrill whistle which, like the trumpet's sound, was to give the word for the charge.

Young Catchpole saw the smugglers emerge from the dell, with each man his sack upon his shoulder; for an instant he thought he ought to wait until they came the second time, but as his orders did not say so, and he judged that if they once stowed away half their cargo they would make quickly for the river, he deemed it best to give the signal at once; so drawing in his breath, he gave the whistle such a long, shrill blast, that had the wind lay that way it might have been heard to Orford. He did not raise himself up, and it was well he did not, for over his head whizzed a ball, and flash–flash–flash went the pistols. As was predicted the men dropped their cargoes, and ran for the pit, but here stood the coast-guard ready to receive them, young Barry having brought his men down below the horizon of the sea, that they might not be exposed to the sight of the smugglers, whilst the river lying lower, and they ascending from it, became a visible mark against the moonlit water for their fire.

Dreadful was the contest that ensued.

Richard Cobbold, 1846

The marshy estuaries were the havens of fishermen such as Peter Grimes of Aldeburgh, whose story, created by Crabbe, has been immortalized by Benjamin Britten.

Thus by himself compell'd to live each day,
To wait for certain hours the tide's delay;

At the same times the same dull views to see,   88
The bounding marsh-bank and the blighted tree;
The water only, when the tides were high,
When low, the mud half-cover'd and half-dry;
The sun-burnt tar that blisters on the planks,
And bank-side stakes in their uneven ranks;
Heaps of entangled weeds that slowly float,
As the tide rolls by the impeded boat.
   When tides were neap, and, in the sultry day,
Through the tall bounding mud-banks made their way,
Which on each side rose swelling, and below
The dark warm flood ran silently and slow;
There anchoring, Peter chose from man to hide,
There hang his head, and view the lazy tide
In its hot slimy channel slowly glide;
Where the small eels that left the deeper way
For the warm shore, within the shallows play;
Where gaping muscles, left upon the mud,
Slope their slow passage to the fallen flood; –
Here dull and hopeless he'd lie down and trace
How sidelong crabs had scrawl'd their crooked race;
Or sadly listen to the tuneless cry
Of fishing gull or clanging golden-eye;
What time the sea-birds to the marsh would come,
And the loud bittern, from the bull-rush home,
Gave from the salt-ditch side the bellowing boom:
He nursed the feelings these dull scenes produce,
And loved to stop beside the opening sluice;
Where the small stream, confined in narrow bound,
Ran with a dull, unvaried, sadd'ning sound;
Where all, presented to the eye or ear,
Oppress'd the soul with misery, grief, and fear.

George Crabbe, 1810

*Their principal catch was the herring, the source of the prosperity of Yarmouth;
'hosted, rosted and tosted' it was pickled or kippered, to the evident benefit of
everybody, rich and poor.*

On no coast like ours is it caught in such abundance, no where drest in his   89
right cue but vnder our Horizon; hosted, rosted, and tosted heere alone it
is, and as well poudred and salted as any Duchman would desire. If you
articulate with me of the gaine or profit of it, without the which the newe
fanglest raritie, that no body can boast of but our selues, after three dayes
gazing is reuerst ouer to children for babies to play with; behold, it is
euery mans money, from the King to the Courtier; euery housholder or
goodman *Baltrop*, that keepes a family in pay, casts for it as one of his
standing prouisions. The poorer sort make it three parts of there suste-

nance; with it, for his dinnier, the patchedest *Leather piltche laboratho* may dine like a Spanish Duke, when the niggardliest mouse of biefe will cost him sixpence. In the craft of catching or taking it, and smudging it Marchant and chapmanable as it should be, it sets a worke thousands, who liue all the rest of the yeare gayly well by what in some fewe weekes they scratch vp then, and come to beare office of Questman and Scauinger in the Parish where they dwell; which they could neuer haue done, but would haue begd or starud with their wiues and brattes, had not this Captaine of the squamy cattell so stoode their good Lord and master: Carpenters, Shipwrights, makers of lines, roapes, and cables, dressers of Hempe, spinners of thred, and net weauers it giues their handfuls to, sets vp so many salt-houses to make salt, and salt vpon salt; keepes in earnings the Cooper, the Brewer, the Baker, and numbers of other people, to gill, wash, and packe it, and carrie it and recarrie it.

Thomas Nash, 1598

In the past the quantity and variety of sailing-boats must have looked superb on a calm sea; 'sublime' (as indicating natural magnificence) was the buzzword at the time of James Ford's classic guide to Aldeburgh.

The view, which the eye commands from this eminence, embraces many 90 features both of the sublime and the beautiful.

To the admirers of the first, the boundless expanse of Aldborough and of Hollesley Bays, richly studded with their moving treasures, and separated from each other by the well-known Promontory of Orford-Ness, affords a banquet which can never satiate. Sometimes thirty or forty fishing-boats are seen within a mile of the shore; and fleets of three hundred colliers and other large trading vessels pass so near, that, with the naked eye, may be discovered the men on board. Owing, indeed, to the immense trade, which is carried on with the Baltic and the northern parts of England, the sea is, on this coast, constantly enriched by fleets of merchantmen, passing and repassing; the variety and gallant trim of whose appearance always excite ideas congenial to every thing that a Briton esteems and values. At low water the beach also is enlivened by numbers of fishermen either drying their nets, hauling up their boats, repairing their tackle, or landing their fish.

James Ford, 1815

In the modern world shipping is equally fascinating, if less elegant. At this time Arthur Ransome was living at Broke House, on the opposite bank of the Orwell from Pin Mill, where the Goblin's *voyage began.*

The *Goblin* had left the river now and was sailing out into the wide waters 91 of Harwich harbour where the Stour and the Orwell meet before pouring out into the sea. Far away over blue rippled water they could see tall mills by Felixstowe Dock, and the green sheds which Jim told them were for seaplanes, and a huge gantry for lifting the planes out of the water, and a low fort of stone and earthwork on a sandy point. On the other side was another low point, and the houses of Harwich, and a white lighthouse on the water's edge, and dark wooden jetties, and barges at anchor. Three big vessels were lying quite near them, near enough for them to see the flags on the jackstaffs. Jim pointed out a Dutch motor vessel, a Norwegian timber-ship with a tremendous deck cargo of golden sawn planks, and a rusty-sided Greek with a tattered flag of blue and white stripes.

'But where are the boats that go to Holland?' asked Titty.

Jim pointed away up the Stour, where, on the Harwich side, they could see the masts and funnels of the mailboats along the Parkeston quays.

A small dumpy steamboat came hurrying out from the Harwich jetties. Its deck was crowded with people.

'That's the ferry,' said Jim. 'It runs between Shotley and Harwich and Felixstowe.'

'We'll be going by it,' said Roger. 'We'll be going to Harwich to meet Daddy's steamer as soon as we know which day he's coming.'

They sailed on as far as the first of the big anchored steamships, and then swung round to work their way up into the Stour.

'We're hardly moving,' said Roger.

'Tide's against us,' said Jim. 'But it's all right. She's creeping over it.'

Slowly, though the water was swirling past the *Goblin*'s sides, they drove up, past the Spit buoy, past Harwich town, past the Trinity House steamer, past a group of anchored barges.

'See those vessels?' said Jim. 'The red ones, with lanterns half-way up the mast, lightships in for repairs. There's the *Galloper*. Her place is thirty miles out. . . . There's the *Outer Gabbard*. Each one shows a light of its own, you know, flashes so that you can tell which it is, and each has its own fog signal.'

Arthur Ransome, 1937

The surf and the breakers on a stormy day: there could hardly be a wilder scene than this in the whole of East Anglia. Crabbe's exactitude is the antithesis of the wilder style adopted by his contemporary, Coleridge, to describe the moods of the sea.

View now the Winter-storm! above, one cloud,   92
Black and unbroken, all the skies o'ershroud;
Th' unwieldy porpoise through the day before
Had roll'd in view of boding men on shore;
And sometimes hid and sometimes show'd his form,
Dark as the cloud, and furious as the storm.
    All where the eye delights, yet dreads to roam,
The breaking billows cast the flying foam
Upon the billows rising – all the deep
Is restless change; the waves so swell'd and steep,

Breaking and sinking, and the sunken swells,
Nor one, one moment, in its station dwells:
But nearer land you may the billows trace,
As if contending in their watery chase;
May watch the mightiest till the shoal they reach,
Then break and hurry to their utmost stretch;
Curl'd as they come, they strike with furious force,
And then re-flowing, take their grating course,
Raking the rounded flints, which ages past
Roll'd by their rage, and shall to ages last.

George Crabbe, 1810

A dreadful storm wreaked havoc on the shipping at Lowestoft in 1770.

The dreadful storm on Wednesday the 19th instant, began about one   93
o'clock in the morning, and continued with increasing violence till five;
when the wind suddenly changed from the south-west to the north-
west, and for two hours raged with a fury that was hardly ever equalled.
Anchors and cables proved too feeble a security for the ships, which
instantly parting from them, and running on board each other, produced
a confusion, neither to be described nor conceived: not a few immediately foundered; others were dismasted, and none escaped unhurt. At
daylight a scene of the most tragic distress was exhibited. Those who first
beheld it assert, that no less than eighteen ships were on the sand before
this place at one and the same time; and many others were seen to sink.
Of those on the sand, one-half were entirely demolished with their
crews, before nine o'clock; the rest were preserved a few hours longer:
but this dreadful pause served only to aggravate the destruction of the
unhappy men who belonged to them, who betook themselves to the
masts and rigging. These continually breaking, eight or ten were not
unfrequently seen to perish at a time, without the possibility of being
assisted. Fifteen only, about two in the afternoon, were taken off one of
the wrecks; and about as many more were saved by taking to their boats,
or getting on board other ships when they boarded each other. It is
impossible to collect with certainty how many lives, or how many ships,
were lost in this terrible hurricane. Twenty-five at least, perhaps thirty
ships, and two hundred men, do not seem to be an exaggerated account.

Robert Reeve, 1770

*In time the coast became a pleasure ground. Some went boating; one of the first to
do so was Edward Fitzgerald, then living at Woodbridge. His boat at this time
was the 'Waveney'.*

My chief Amusement in Life is Boating, on River and Sea. The Country   94
about here is the Cemetery of so many of my oldest Friends: and the
petty race of Squires who have succeeded, only use the Earth for an

Investment: cut down every old Tree: level every Violet Bank: and make the old Country of my Youth hideous to me in my Decline. There are fewer Birds to be heard, as fewer Trees for them to resort to. So I get to the Water: where Friends are not buried nor Pathways stopt up: but all is, as the Poets say, as Creation's Dawn beheld. I am happiest going in my little Boat round the Coast to Aldbro, with some Bottled Porter and some Bread and Cheese, and some good rough Soul who works the Boat and chews his Tobacco in peace. An Aldbro Sailor talking of my Boat said — 'She go like a Wiolin, she do!' What a pretty Conceit, is it not? As the Bow slides over the Strings in a liquid Tune. Another man was talking yesterday of a great Storm: 'and, in a moment, all as calm as a Clock'.

Edward Fitzgerald, 1861

Others went swimming, some reluctantly. John Betjeman's father kept a boat on the broads; at Horsey Mere it was only just behind the dunes of the coast.

Oh when the early morning at the seaside   95
   Took us with hurrying steps from Horsey Mere
To see the whistling bent-grass on the leeside
   And then the tumbled breaker-line appear,
On high, the clouds with mighty adumbration
   Sailed over us to seaward fast and clear
And jellyfish in quivering isolation
   Lay silted in the dry sand of the breeze
And we, along the table-land of beach blown
   Went gooseflesh from our shoulders to our knees
And ran to catch the football, each to each thrown,
   In the soft and swirling music of the seas.

There splashed about our ankles as we waded
   Those intersecting wavelets morning-cold,
And sudden dark a patch of sea was shaded,
   And sudden light, another patch would hold
The warmth of whirling atoms in a sun-shot
   And underwater sandstorm green and gold.
So in we dived and louder than a gunshot
   Sea-water broke in fountains down the ear.
How cold the bathe, how chattering cold the drying,
   How welcoming the inland reeds appear,
The wood-smoke and the breakfast and the frying,
   And your warm freshwater ripples, Horsey Mere.

John Betjeman, 1945

Others just wandered along the coast. One of these children was Benjamin Britten, and it was from scenes such as this that he enriched his musical inspiration.

The children spent their summer holidays in a farmhouse belonging to   96
their nurse's uncle. It was near Butley, about thirty miles south of
Lowestoft. Here the walks were across the marshes, with the wind
blowing from the sea. As they went on their way, the tall reeds and
rushes moved with them, leaning over with a swishing sound, while
high overhead the curlews and redshanks called to each other. Beyond
the marshes, the farthest walks led to Shingle Street, a small row of
cottages on a pebbly beach, where there was nothing in sight except a
vast expanse of sea and sky. Shingle Street has altered very little since
those Augusts at the end of the First World War. The stony shelf of
pebbles stretches for mile after mile into the distance. On a still day, the
light can have the delicate outlines of a Japanese picture. On a stormy
day, even in summer, the grey sea batters itself against the shelf, dragging
the shingle down with a scrunching, grating, slithering sound. To anyone
who lives on the Suffolk coast, this sound means home.

Imogen Holst, 1966

The coastal towns became places of summer resort, initially for a select few. The
General Evening Post *for 30 September 1804 announced that Aldeburgh had
'this year become quite a new place' with a promenade, bathing-machines,
circulating library and so on; and that among the visitors were the Earl of Bristol,
Dr Charles Burney, and Mr Nichols with two daughters.*

Permit me, dear sister, to greet you once more,   97
Not from shady retreats, but from Aldeburgh's rough shore.
Thro' Woodbridge and Wickham our post horses rattled,
Whilst the ride we enjoy'd, and incessantly prattled.
'Twas a custom in Suffolk, I've heard trav'llers tell,
To drink health to all friends who live round Wickham well;
But I'm sure sister Sarah was ready to jump,
When she found the old well was transform'd to a pump.
At last passing Snape church, on Snape common, believe me,
A friend in the coach with intent to deceive me,
To a number of sticks my attention directed,
Which for May-poles, she said, had been lately erected.
But that this was mere joking, I very well knew,
For presently many tall ships pass'd in view;
And you cannot but guess how my heart was in motion,
When at length we obtain'd a full view of the ocean.
The first moment I could, to the shingles I stalk'd,
And close to the loud-sounding billows I walk'd,
Where astonish'd indeed for some moments I stood,
Admiring the wonderful strength of the flood;
But quickly found out it was time to be walking,
Being caught by a wave as I only stood talking;
And one of my legs got so copious a dipping,
That I speedily hopp'd away, laughing, but dripping;
And thought myself happy so snug to retreat,

For, like cats, I dislike to be wet in my feet.
But, although from the surges we steer'd far away,
I got pretty well sous'd with the splash of the spray.

Anne Nichols, 1804

In later years many more visitors came to the seaside.

Oh Lowestoft! Your pier bathed in an atmosphere of delicious summer   98
dreaminess, the distant music of a band, the sunlit red-brown sails of
trawlers, your harbour's sleeping water which flanks you, oh you
fisherman's Venice, on the one side; while on the other, the masts of
many boats and ships wing the air, and such air, and the towering
pinnacles of hotels, presenting to the imaginative eye the illusion of fairy
palaces; all these, and much besides, start one wondering why the
crowds that flock each summer to your shores are not even yet more
dense than they are − like those of comparatively languid southern
watering-places.

Alfred James Swinbourne, 1912

Finally, some of the seaside towns became the resorts of the masses.

The first time I ever gorged myself with Yarmouth rock on Yarmouth   99
beach the ancient monuments in which I was most interested were the
bathing machines. Out of them came dozens of the fattest women I have
ever seen, in frilly bathing costumes that came down to their knees. They
clung to ropes that stretched out into the sea and they ducked themselves
under the waves, and every time a wave came they shrieked in unison
and Cockney. On the beach their men folk, in shirt sleeves and enormous
waistcoats spanned with watch chains and medals for billiards and
Buffaloism, roared themselves hoarse with laughter, and belched out
great whiffs of beer and twopenny cigar. I don't suppose I was more than
five years old then, and I was awestruck at the masses of flesh and
hilarity. England does not seem to breed such people now, and if it did, I
doubt whether it could feed them. They were on the Pleasure Beach, too,
with their sons and daughters, shrieking again on the scenic railway, and
sprawling and sliding all over an affair called the Joy Wheel, with a great
display of petticoats and elephantine legs, and with roars of laughter at
jokes I wish I could remember, even if I could not print them. The same
immense people rolled along the Front, rode on the staggering donkeys,
were weighed on a massive pair of brass scales whose weights went up to
twenty stone, ate mountainous shrimp teas, and refreshed themselves in
the evening with gallons of beer, or stout for the ladies, and plate after
plate of shell-fish soused in vinegar. What a place it was, and in my eyes
has been ever since, for jollity; though I'm blowed if I have ever found
the match of my original East Enders for corpulence!

Eric Fowler, 1947

To get to the coast, virtually everyone came by train. Southwold, one of the smallest resorts, appropriately had the smallest railway line.

The sight which greeted main-line passengers at Halesworth in the years   100
immediately before World War I was unique in East Anglia. A tiny blue locomotive, immaculate paintwork and burnished brass, stood bunker-first at the head of a mixed train of goods wagons, vans, and a couple of maroon coaches. Goods transferred from the main line were heaved bodily across a transshipment platform at the rear of the Southwold Railway station. Passengers from the GER trains crossed by footbridge onto the island platform to join the little train. After running parallel with the main line for a few hundred yards, crossing the main road by separate bridges, the Southwold train swung eastwards through woods and fields, under the road bridge at Holton (which still exists), over the Blyth at Wenhaston Mill and across the sole level-crossing on the line before drawing into Wenhaston station, delightfully rustic apart from its corrugated iron roof. The Blyth valley widens from here onwards to the sea and broad vistas of water and marsh came closer as Blythburgh was approached. The church on the hill dominated the local scene and the railway respected this eminence by skirting around it in a wide loop, avoiding earthworks and gradients. Blythburgh station was a passing loop, tokens were exchanged here, goods wagons were frequently shunted into the sidings. The train then passed under the only other road bridge on the line, now part of the A12 embankment, and emerged to give a fine view of the ever-widening estuary. Sandy heath and hills now dominated the scene south of the river, the diminutive locomotive working as hard as possible; despite the low speed it always seemed much faster, as the train was so much nearer the rails than a standard-gauge train. Walberswick was a brief halt, a small isolated station, even after its 1902 enlargement, almost out of view of human habitation at the approaches to the great swing bridge into Southwold. This had been renewed in 1907 at great cost as part of a programme aimed at widening and strengthening the line sufficiently to allow conversion to standard gauge. A long-planned harbour branch was also built just before World War I and included a weighbridge with a few yards of standard gauge line on it. Southwold station with its locomotive and carriage sheds, toilets, bookstall and electric lighting was the most elaborate on the line. With its long, tree-shaded platform piled with luggage, produce baskets and hampers it was the miniature epitome of the Edwardian station in its heyday. The railway company even managed a 2 per cent dividend between 1911 and 1913, only a point behind the GER at its best!

    R. S. Joby, 1977

Momentous and Magnificent Events

In AD 62 the Iceni tribe, who inhabited what is now Norfolk, revolted against the rule of Imperial Rome. The revolt spread to the Trinovantes, who were governed from the Roman colony at Camalodunum (Colchester).

Prasutagus, king of the Icenians, a prince long renowned for opulence, had by will appointed the emperor joint heir with his own two daughters: judging that by such an instance of loyalty, he should place his kingdom and family out of the reach of harm; a design which turned out so contrary to his anticipations, that his realm was ravaged by the centurions, and his house by slaves; as if they had been the spoils of war. First of all Boadicea his wife was subjected to stripes, and his daughters ravished: and, as though the entire region had been a donation to the plunderers, all the principal Icenians were spoiled of their hereditary possessions, and the relations of the king were made slaves of. Enraged by these indignities, and dreading oppressions still more severe, for they were reduced into the form of a province, they flew to arms; having roused the Trinobantes to join in the revolt; as well as all others who, not yet broken by the yoke of servitude, had secretly covenanted to recover their liberty, from their implacable antipathy to the veterans. For those who had been recently planted in the colony of Camalodunum had thrust the people out of their houses, and driven them from their lands, calling them captives and slaves. These outrages of the veterans were encouraged by the common soldiers, from similarity of occupation and the hope of enjoying the same privilege.

Tacitus, first century (Oxford translation)

The revolt was led by Boàdicea (Boudicca), Queen of the Iceni. Here is Henty's stirring account of the declaration of war.

'Why come you here, woman?' the chief priest asked, addressing the   102
queen.

'I come as a supplicant to the gods,' she said; 'as an outraged queen, a dishonoured woman, and a broken-hearted mother, and in each of these capacities I call upon my country's gods for vengeance.' Then in passionate words she poured out the story of the indignities that she and her daughters had suffered, and suddenly loosening her garment, and suffering it to drop to her waist, she turned and showed the marks of the Roman rods across her back, the sight eliciting a shout of fury from the chiefs around her.

'Let all retire to the woods,' the Druids said, 'and see that no eye profanes our mysteries. When the gods have answered we will summon you.' The queen, followed by all the chiefs, retired at once to the forest, while the Druids proceeded to carry out the sacred mysteries. Although all knew well what the decision would be, they waited with suppressed excitement the summons to return and hear the decision that was to embark them in a desperate struggle with Rome. Some threw themselves down under the trees, some walked up and down together discussing in low tones the prospects of a struggle, and the question what tribes would join it. The queen and her daughters sat apart, none venturing to approach them. Parta and three other female chiefs sat a short distance away talking together, while two or three of the younger chiefs, their attitude towards Beric entirely altered by the report of the Druids' predictions concerning him, gathered round him and asked questions concerning the Romans' methods of fighting, their arms and power. An hour after they had retired a deep sound of a conch rose in the air. The queen and her daughters at once moved forward, followed by the four female chiefs, behind whom came the rest in a body. Issuing from the forest they advanced to the sacred oak and stood in an attitude of deep respect, while the chief Druid announced the decision of the gods.

'The gods have spoken,' he said. 'Too long have the Iceni stood aloof from their countrymen, therefore have the gods withdrawn their faces from them; therefore has punishment and woe fallen upon them. Prasutagus is dead; his queen and his daughters have suffered the direst indignities; a Roman has seized the wealth heaped up by inglorious cowardice. But the moment has come; the gods have suffered their own altars to be desecrated in order that over the whole length and breadth of the land the cry for vengeance shall arise simultaneously. The cup is full; vengeance is at hand upon the oppressors and tyrants, the land reeks with British blood. Not content with grasping our possessions, our lives and the honour of our women are held as nought by them, our altars are cold, our priests slaughtered. The hour of vengeance is at hand. I see the smoke of burning cities ascending in the air. I hear the groans of countless victims to British vengeance. I see broken legions and flying men.

'To arms! the gods have spoken. Strike for vengeance. Strike for the gods. Strike for your country and outraged queen. Chiefs of the Iceni, to arms! May the curse of the gods fall upon an enemy who draws back in the day of battle! May the gods give strength to your arms and render you invincible in battle! The gods have spoken.'

A mighty shout was raised by his hearers; swords were brandished, and spears shaken, and the cry 'To arms! the gods have spoken,' was repeated unanimously. As the Druids closed round their chief, who had been seized with strong convulsions as soon as he had uttered the message of the gods, Boadicea turned to the chiefs and raised her arm for silence.

G. A. Henty, 1893

In 870 Edmund, the Christian king of the East Angles, defied a marauding army of pagan Danes, but was captured and lynched. He later became East Anglia's patron saint.

The tyrant Hinguar then commanded the king and all his followers to be   103 surrounded, that not one of them might escape alive; whereupon the most holy king Edmund, perceiving himself to be hedged in by his enemies, by the advice of Humbert, bishop of Helmham, fled to the church that he might show himself a member of Christ, and there exchanging his temporal for celestial weapons, he humbly prayed the Father, the Son, and the Holy Ghost to grant him fortitude in suffering. The most merciful king Edmund was then forcibly bound by the ministers of iniquity, and led forth from the church before their wicked chief, as was Christ before the governor Pilate; at whose command he was tied to a neighbouring tree; after which he was scourged for a long time, and insulted with every species of mockery. But the undaunted champion of Christ, by continuing to call on him between every lash, provoked to fury his tormentors, who then in their mockery using his body as a mark, shot at him with their bows till he was entirely covered with arrows, so that there was not a place in the martyr's body in which a fresh wound could be inflicted, but it was as completely covered with darts and arrows as is the hedgehog's skin with spines. And so the fierce executioner Hinguar, not being able to make the holy martyr Edmund relinquish his faith in Christ and the confession of the Trinity, so as at all to yield to his wicked persuasions, ordered one of his attendants to cut off the martyr's head with his bloody sword; whereupon the executioner, with one fierce stroke, severed his holy head from its trunk on the 20th day of November, as he was praying and confessing the name of Christ.

Roger of Wendover, thirteenth century (translation, J. A. Giles)

Eleven centuries after the event, the story was still told, though in quite another way.

These ere Deens they had marder in em, they din't giv a cat's ear fer   10 nobuddy, they landed up in the noth o' Britten, Yorksher way somewheres, an they whully med sech a mess up there that was five year afore they come down these parts at all. Little ould Edmund he was riddy for em, good boy, he come out of is pallis at Thetford an he fot em a whull day thru, but that warn't na good, he han't got the min an he warn't strong enuf altogether. So he then went to Framlingem but they shuffed im out o' that an he come up ere to Hoxon all by isself pore chap, he was so done up he went an crulled in under th'ould Goldbrook Bridge an was pretty sune asleep. Them Deens was a comin up be'ind roight enuf, but they'd lorst im, that was whully luck what hoped em dew they woulden ha ketched im at all.

By'nby there come a chap an a gal, orf to be marrerd they was, they come 'long ower the bridge, they was a scroogin an a noodlin one nuther like willy-oh, silly young fules, so they stopped on the Goldbrook a bit cause they din't think there was nobuddy about. Time they was a noodlin together yew woulden ha thot as they'd ha nottissed much would yew, but dret if she din't then goo an sing out, 'Whoi, John boy,' she say, 'stop tittlin me will yew, whativer's that down there, there's suthen a glistin in the watter d'yew see?' 'Whoi, thass roight, Meery,' he say, 'there's suthen down under th'ould bridge, that look like a cupple o' sparrs on't yew think so? There's ony one chap has gowld sparrs like that,' he say, 'an thass King Edmund, the Deens is arter im,' he say, 'less goo an tell em.' Now I dew think that was the wustest trick of all, pore young faller he niver ad na luck did he?

Oh ah, that surely was a rotten trick, this ere cupple they went orf an fitched the Deens, ould Luddy's two sons an the whull blessed army, they come a runnin up an took ahowd o' young Edmund an hulled im out from under the little ould bridge. 'Oho, me little King-o,' they say, 'yew're ketched now an yew're a goin to be kilt an no mistake. But ere's one thing,' they say, 'will yew give up yer Chrisheranity afore yew're kilt, y'know kind o' change yer relijun like, cause thass the wrong un yew got there, boy.' But young Edmund he was a werry kerajus chap, he whully stuck by what he thot was roight, dew they moight ha let im orf. 'I ain't a goin to give up nuthen fer yew,' he say, 'yew're a rotten lot o' barstids the whull bloody bag of ye.' 'Thass all roight, boy,' they say, 'we on't waste na more time then,' they hulled im orf to a fild an tied im to a owk tree an they took the whip to im, like a lot o' savidges they was, han't no marcy fer the pore boy. Howsever, they din't kill im that way, they shot all their arrers into im an they then cut is hid orf, an thass how they left im under that ould tree an then went orf arter a lot more daviltry all ower the country.

Julian Tennyson, 1939

By the end of the first millennium the Anglo-Saxons had gathered strength against the Danes, who narrowly avoided defeat at Thetford in 1004.

In this year Swein came with his fleet to Norwich and completely ravaged and burnt the borough. Then Ulfcetel with the councillors in East Anglia determined that it would be better to buy peace from the   105 army before they did too much damage in the country, for they had come unexpectedly and he had not time to collect his army. Then, under cover of the truce which was supposed to be between them, the Danish army stole inland from the ships, and directed their course to Thetford. When Ulfcetel perceived that, he sent orders that the ships were to be hewn to bits, but those whom he intended for this failed him; he then collected his army secretly, as quickly as he could. And the Danish army then came to Thetford within three weeks after their ravaging of Norwich, and remained inside there one night, and ravaged and burnt the borough. Then in the morning, when they wished to go to their ships, Ulfcetel arrived with his troops to offer battle there. And they resolutely joined battle, and many fell slain on both sides. There the flower of the East Anglian people was killed. But if their full strength had been there, the Danes would never have got back to their ships; as they themselves said that they never met worse fighting in England than Ulfcetel dealt to them.

Anglo-Saxon Chronicle, eleventh century (translation, Dorothy White-lock)

Hugh Bigod was the most powerful East Anglian magnate of his day, and he defied the authority of Henry III in the thirteenth century. The Bramfield oak, now a mere stump, was then a mighty landmark.

The King has sent for Bigod bold, 　　　　　　　　　　　　106
　　In Essex, whereat he lay,
But Lord Bigod laugh'd at his Poursuivant,
　　And stoutly thus did say:
　　'Were I in my Castle of Bungay,
　　Upon the river of Waveney,
I would ne care for the King of Cockney.'

Hugh Bigod was Lord of Bungay tower,
　　And a merry lord was he;
So away he rode on his berry-black steed,
　　And sung with license and glee:
　　'Were I in my Castle of Bungay,
　　Upon the river of Waveney,
I would ne care for the King of Cockney.'

At Ipswich they laugh'd to see how he sped,
　　And at Ufford they star'd, I wis;
But at merry Saxmundham they heard his song,
　　And the song he sung was this:
　　'Were I in my Castle of Bungay,
　　Upon the river of Waveney,
I would ne care for the King of Cockney.'

The Baily he rode and the Baily he ran,
   To catch the gallant Lord Hugh,
But for every mile the Baily rode,
   The Earl he rode more than two;
   Says, 'Were I in my Castle of Bungay,
   Upon the river of Waveney,
I would ne care for the King of Cockney.'

When the Baily had ridden to Bramfield oak,
   Sir Hugh was at Ilksall bower;
When the Baily had ridden to Halesworth cross,
   He was singing in Bungay tower –
   'Now that I am in my Castle of Bungay,
   Upon the river of Waveney,
I will ne care for the King of Cockney.'

Anon., fifteenth century (?)

The Black Death devastated East Anglia, as it did most of Europe; its effect on one small village in one single year – 1349 – was chilling enough.

In the Valley of the Stour, a mile or two from Sudbury, where the stream   107
serves as the boundary between Suffolk and Essex, the ancestors of Lord
Walsingham had two manors in the township of Little Cornard – the one
was called Caxtons, the other was the manor of Cornard Parva. At this
latter manor a court was held on March 31; the number of tenants of the
manor can at no time have exceeded fifty, yet at this court six women
and three men are registered as having died since the last court was held,
two months before. This is the earliest instance I have yet met with of the
appearance of the plague among us, and as it is the earliest, so does it
appear to have been one of the most frightful visitations from which any
town or village in Suffolk or Norfolk suffered during the time the
pestilence lasted. On May 1 another court was held: fifteen more deaths
are recorded – thirteen men and two women. *Seven of them without heirs.*
On November 3, apparently when the panic abated, again the court met.
In the six months that had passed thirty-six more deaths had occurred,
and *thirteen more households* had been left without a living soul to
represent them. In this little community, in six months' time, twenty-
one families had been absolutely obliterated – men, women, and
children – and of the rest it is difficult to see how there can have been a
single house in which there was not one dead. Meanwhile, some time in
September, the parson of the parish had fallen a victim to the scourge,
and on October 2 another was instituted in his room. Who reaped the
harvest? The tithe sheaf too – how was it garnered in the barn? And the
poor kine at milking time? Hush! Let us pass on.

Augustus Jessopp, 1884

The Peasants' Revolt of 1381 began with success for the rebels, as with the murder of John de Cavendish at Lakenheath.

We may suppose that the justice was travelling on his round of duty in   108
the district, but with too weak an escort, and being surprised by a band of
rioters was compelled to fly for his life. Chief among his pursuers were
Stephen Martyn and Richard Rond, who, as the scribe has noted,
followed him 'usque ad mortem'. Perhaps thinking of Ely as a refuge he
directed his steps for the river, hoping that by boat his chance of escape
thither would be considerably enhanced, or that, could he even manage
to put that barrier between himself and his pursuers he might yet
manage to elude them.

At the water's edge, however, his object was cruelly frustrated, and
that too by a woman, for against the name of Katharine Gamen, of
Lakenheath, stands the following note – 'liberavit batellam de terra,
perquod dictus Johannes de Cavendish non potuit evadere mortem'.
From which we may gather that, seeing the pursuit, and divining the
object the unhappy man was straining every nerve to obtain, she rushed
for the boat, and by pushing it off into mid-stream rendered escape in
that direction impossible. The final scene in the tragedy probably
followed immediately. The justice was soon seized by one John Pedder,
of Fordham, and on the arrival of the mob was beheaded forthwith, one
Matthew Miller, we are told, performing the horrid office of executioner.
Cavendish's head was then carried back by the mob to Bury, and placed
over the pillory there.

It has been often stated that the murder of John de Cavendish was
committed by the insurgents in revenge for the death of Wat Tyler, who
is said by some to have been finally dispatched by the justice's younger
son. This I think can hardly have been the reason, as, on examining the
evidences of the dates, it appears that Tyler's death did not take place till
after that of Cavendish.

The real clue to the justice's unpopularity among the peasant class
is, I think, given on the rolls of Parliament, where it appears he was
granted extra salary as a justice for enforcing the Statutes of Labourers in
the counties of Suffolk and Essex.

Edgar Powell, 1896

But it ended with victory for the authorities, as when Henry le Despenser, Bishop of Norwich, captured Jack Litster, leader of the Norfolk rebels.

But this Henry, a good bishop and pastor, who seeing the wolf, fled not,   109
but exposed himself to danger, enquired of the citizens where the head of
all the evil and of all this infamy might be found. And they said that he
was wandering about the neighbourhood of Walsham-market, and of
Gimingham, where he had the largest number of rustics and ribald
fellows. Thereupon the bishop commanded his domestics to transfer
themselves to those parts, and with them he himself was always
foremost. For the bishop had said to those who were with him: 'It is

better that one evil and wicked man should die, than that the whole people perish, for they, taking license from him, commit assaults and robberies, killing those who are unconscious of crime.'

And saying this he came to the town called Felmingham, where the said ringleader had a mansion. And those who resided there, being questioned where he was, said that on the previous day he was at Thorp-market, where he had caused it to be publicly proclaimed that all who desired the welfare of the kingdom and of the community should follow him to Walsham; where he intended, as he said, to defend the people against the tyranny of the approaching bishop by military force. And on this, all the able-bodied of the adjacent villages had followed him, and were there. To his informant the bishop said: – 'Blessed be thou, my son, since thou hast not mingled with wicked men, nor with a mischievous people.'

And thus hastening on to Walsham, he found the openings of the roads blocked with timbers, and towers, and other impediments. But by the good management of the bishop, and of other men who had assembled there, the whole people surrendered, rejoicing that they might withdraw in peace. Jack Litster himself, leaping over a wall, hid himself in a corn-field. And one of the people, perceiving this, announced it to the bishop. The traitor was sought and found; he was captured and beheaded; and, divided into four parts, he was sent through the country to Norwich, Yarmouth, and Lynn, and to the site of his mansion; that rebels and insurgents against the peace might learn by what end they will finish their career.

These are the acts of this venerable bishop.

John Capgrave, fifteenth century (translation, Francis Hingeston)

The grievances that inspired the rebellion in Norfolk in 1549 (under Robert Kett) included the construction of the hedges and ditches that are today so much admired.

The common pastures left by our predecessors for the reliefe of vs, and   110 our children, are taken away. The lands which in the memory of our fathers, were common, those are ditched and hedged in, and made seueral; the pastures are inclosed, and we shut out: whatsoeuer fowles of the aire, or fishes of the water, and increase of the earth, all these doe they deuoure, consume and swallow vp; yea, nature doth not suffice to satisfie their lusts, but they seeke out new deuices, and as it were, formes of pleasures, to imbalme and perfume themselues, to abound in pleasant smells, to powre in sweete things to sweete things: finally, they seeke from all places, all things for their desire, and prouocation of lust: while we in the meane time, eate hearbs and roots, and languish with continu-all labour, and yet enuie that we liue, breathe, and inioy common ayre. Shall they, as they haue brought hedges about common pastures, inclose with their intolerable lusts also, al the commodities and pleasure of this life, which, Nature, the parent of vs all, would haue common, and bringeth foorth euery day, for vs, as well as for them? We can no longer beare so much, so great, and so cruell iniurie, neither can wee with quiet minds behold so great couetousnesse, excesse, and pride of the nobilitie; we will rather take armes, and mixe Heauen and Earth together, then indure so great crueltie. Nature hath prouided for vs, as well as for them; hath giuen vs a body, and a soule, and hath not enuied vs other things. While we haue the same forme, and the same condition of birth together with them, why should they haue a life so vnlike vnto ours, and differ so farre from vs in calling? We see that now it is come to extremitie, wee will also prooue extremitie: rend downe hedges, fill up ditches, make way for euery man into the common pasture: finally, lay all euen with the ground, which they no lesse wickedly, then cruelly and couetously haue inclosed.

Alexander Neville, 1615 (translation, Richard Woods)

On the premature death of Edward VI in 1553 the succession was disputed. Mary Tudor, his half sister, fled into East Anglia.

The fugitive heiress of England bent her flight in the direction of   111 Cambridgeshire, as the nearest way to her seat of Kenninghall, through Bury St Edmunds. As the soft shades of a July night fell round her hasty course, over those desolate plains which are intersected by the eastern road, (once so familiar to the pilgrims bound to the Lady shrine of Walsingham, and since as much traversed by the frequenters of Newmarket,) the ladies and cavaliers of her faithful retinue began to discuss the unexpected death of the young king. They were all catholics of the ancient ritual, and, of course, viewed the changes of the eventful times wholly according to their prejudices. They recalled with awe that the only heir male of the line of Henry VIII had expired on the very anniversary of the lawless execution of sir Thomas More. It was in vain that king Henry had overthrown all existing impediments, and set at nought the lives of thousands in his wilfulness; for his frantic desire of continuing his name and sceptre, by heirs male, was now as much blighted, as if the divorce of Katharine of Arragon, and the awful bloodshed which stained his latter years, had never taken place. Wearied and worn, the whole party arrived at the gate of Sawston Hall, in the neighbourhood of Cambridge, and craved the hospitality of Mr Huddleston, its owner. That gentleman, like his descendant, who watched the royal oak at Boscobel so well, was a zealous Roman Catholic. He knew, though she did not, how inimical his neighbours of the town of Cambridge were to the cause of the lineal heiress. Huddleston was, nevertheless, too true a gentleman to refuse shelter to the way-wearied princess and her harassed retinue, though there can be little doubt but that he must have foreseen the perilous consequences which threatened himself, and his Lares and Penates.

Mary lodged that night under the hospitable roof which was never more to shelter a human being. She was astir with her ladies and retinue before sunrise, but commenced not the arduous journey before her till she had offered up her devotions according to the rites of her religion.

Very early in the morning she set out on her journey to Kenninghall; when she and her party gained the rise called the Gogmagog-hills, she drew her bridle-rein, and paused to look back on Sawston Hall. At that moment it burst into flames, for a party from Cambridge, adverse to her cause, had heard of her arrival, and had mustered early in the morning to attack the house that harboured her; if they had not amused themselves with plundering and burning Sawston Hall, they might have seized Mary, so close were they on her traces.

She gazed on the flaming pile undauntedly. 'Let it blaze,' she said, 'I will build Huddleston a better.'

She kept her word – the present Sawston Hall was built by her order, and at her expense.

Agnes Strickland, 1842

During the period of religious conflict both sides incurred persecution. In 1557 the Puritan John Noyes suffered martyrdom at Laxfield.

Now being condemned, he was sent again from Norwich to Eye-prison; 112 and upon the 21st day of September, in the year aforesaid, about midnight, he was brought from Eye to Laxfield, to be burnt; and on the next-day morning was brought to the stake, where were ready against his coming the foresaid justice, master Thurston, one master Waller, then being under-sheriff, and master Thomas Lovel, being high-constable, as is before expressed; the which commanded men to make ready all things meet for that sinful purpose. Now the fire in most places of the street was put out, saving a smoke was espied by the said Thomas Lovel proceeding out from the top of a chimney, to which house the sheriff and Grannow his man went, and brake open the door, and thereby got fire, and brought the same to the place of execution. When John Noyes came to the place where he should be burnt, he kneeled down and said the 50th Psalm, with other prayers; and then they, making haste, bound him to the stake. And being bound, the said John Noyes said, 'Fear not them that can kill the body, but fear him that can kill both body and soul, and cast it into everlasting fire.'

When he saw his sister weeping, and making moan for him, he bade her that she should not weep for him, but weep for her sins.

Then one Nicholas Cadman, being hastler, a valiant champion in the pope's affairs, brought a faggot and set against him; and the said John Noyes took up the faggot and kissed it, and said, 'Blessed be the time that ever I was born to come to this.'

Then he delivered his Psalter to the under-sheriff, desiring him to be good to his wife and children, and to deliver to her that same book and the sheriff promised him that he would, notwithstanding he never as yet performed his promise. Then the said John Noyes said to the people, 'They say, they can make God of a piece of bread: believe them not!'

Then said he, 'Good people, bear witness that I do believe to be saved by the merits and passion of Jesus Christ, and not by mine own deeds.' And so the fire was kindled, and burnt about him. Then he said,

'Lord have mercy upon me! Christ have mercy upon me! Son of David have mercy upon me!'

And so he yielded up his life. And when his body was burned, they made a pit to bury the coals and ashes, and amongst the same they found one of his feet that was unburnt, whole up to the ankle, with the hose on; and that they buried with the rest.

Now while he was a burning, there stood one John Jarvis by, a man's servant of the same town, a plain fellow, which said, 'Good Lord, how the sinews of his arms shrink up!' And there stood behind him one Grannow, and Benet, being the sheriff's men, and they said to their master, that John Jarvis said, 'What vile wretches are these!' And their master bade lay hand on him, and they took him and pinioned him, and carried him before the justice that same day; and the justice did examine him of the words aforesaid; but he denied them, and answered that he said nothing but this, 'Good Lord, how the sinews of his arms shrink up!' But, for all this, the justice did bind his father and his master in five pounds a-piece, that he should be forthcoming at all times.

And on the Wednesday next he was brought again before the justices, master Thurston and master Kene, they sitting at Fressingfield in Hoxne hundred; and there they did appoint and command, that the said John Jarvis should be set in the stocks the next market-day, and whipt about the market, naked. But his master, one William Jarvis, did after crave friendship of the constables; and they did not set him in the stocks till Sunday morning. And in the afternoon they did whip him about the market with a dog-whip, having three cords; and so they let him go. – Some do give out, that John Jarvis was whipt for saying that Nicholas Cadman was Noyes's hastler; that is, such an one as maketh and hasteth the fire.

John Foxe, 1559

During the Civil War East Anglia was a Parliamentarian power-base. The Puritan iconoclasts smashed their way through churches, as at Ufford in 1643.

UFFORD, Aug. 31st. Where is set down what we did, Jan. the 27th. '30 superstitious Pictures; and left 37 more to break down'; and some of them we brake down now. In the Chancel, we brake down an Angel; 3 *orate pro anima*, in the Glass; and the Trinity in a Triangle; and 12 Cherubims on the Roof of the Chancel; and nigh a 100 JESUS–MARIA, in Capital Letters; and the Steps to be levelled. And we brake down the Organ Cases, and gave them to the Poor. – In the Church, there was on the Roof, above a 100 JESUS and MARY, in great Capital Letters; and a Crosier Staff to be broke down, in Glass; and above 20 Stars on the Roof. There is a glorious Cover over the Font, like a Pope's Tripple Crown, with a Pelican on the Top, picking its Breast, all gilt over with Gold. And we were kept out of the Church above 2 hours, and neither Churchwardens, *William Brown*, nor *Roger Small*, that were enjoyned these things above three months afore, had not done them in May, and I sent one then to see it done, and they would not let him have the key. And now, neither the

113

Churchwardens, nor *William Brown*, nor the Constable *James Tokelove*, and *William Gardener* the Sexton, would not let us have the key, in 2 hours time. New Churchwardens, *Thomas Stanard*, *Thomas Stroud*. And *Samuel Canham*, of the same Town, said, 'I sent men to rifle the Church;' – and *Will. Brown*, old Churchwarden, said, 'I went about to pull down the Church, and had carried away part of the Church.'

William Dowsing, 1643

Also at Norwich Cathedral in 1644, as recounted by the bishop, an impotent spectator and prisoner in his palace.

There was not that care and moderation used in reforming the cathedral   114
church bordering on my palace. It is no other than tragical, to relate the carriage of that furious sacrilege, whereof our eyes and ears were the sad witnesses, under the authority and presence of Linsey, Toftes the sheriff, and Greenwood. Lord, what work was here! what clattering of glasses! what beating down of seats! what wrestling out of irons and brass from the windows and graves! what defacing of arms! what demolishing of curious stone-work, that had not any representation in the world, but only of the cost of the founder, and the skill of the mason! what tooting and piping on the destroyed organ pipes! and what a hideous triumph on the market-day before all the country; when, in a kind of sacrilegious and profane procession, all the organ pipes, vestments, both copes and surplices, together with the leaden cross which had been newly sawn down from over the Green-yard pulpit, and the service-books and singing-books that could be had, were carried to the fire in the public market place; a lewd wretch walking before the train, in his cope trailing in the dirt, with a service-book in his hand, imitating in an impious scorn the tune, and usurping the words of the litany used formerly in the church. Near the public cross, all these monuments of idolatry must be sacrificed to the fire not without much ostentation of zealous joy, in discharging ordnance, to the cost of some, who professed how much they had longed to see that day. Neither was it any news upon this Guild-day, to have the cathedral, now open on all sides, to be filled with musketeers, waiting for the Major's return; drinking and tobacconing as freely, as if it had turned alehouse.

Joseph Hall, 1647

The Royalists held Colchester till 1648. They delayed their surrender too long for the patience of Generals Fairfax and Ireton, who broke the code of military conduct by shooting three Royalist leaders.

The total defeat of the Scottish army lately mentioned succeeded this,   115
and when those noble persons within Colchester were advertised of both, they knew well that there was no possibility of relief, nor could they subsist longer to expect it, being pressed with want of all kind of

victual, and having eaten near all their horses. They sent therefore to Fairfax, to treat about the delivery of the town upon reasonable conditions; but he refused to treat, or give any conditions, if they would not render to mercy all the officers and gentlemen; the common soldiers he was contented to dismiss. A day or two was spent in deliberation. They within proposed 'to make a brisk sally; and thereby to shift for themselves, as many as could'. But they had too few horse, and the few that were left uneaten were too weak for that enterprise. Then, 'that they should open a port, and every man die with their arms in their hands'; but that way they could only be sure of being killed, without much hurting their adversaries, who had ways enough securely to assault them. Hereupon, they were in the end obliged to deliver themselves up prisoners at mercy; and were, all the officers and gentlemen, led into the public hall of the town; where they were locked up, and a strong guard set upon them. They were required presently to send a list of all their names to the general; which they did; and, within a short time after, a guard was sent to bring sir Charles Lucas, and sir George Lisle, and sir Bernard Gascoigne to the general, being sat with his council of war. They were carried in, and in a very short discourse told, 'that after so long and so obstinate a defence until they found it necessary to deliver themselves up to mercy, it was necessary, for the example of others, and that the peace of the kingdom might be no more disturbed in that manner, that some military justice should be executed; and therefore, that council had determined they three should be presently shot to death'; for which they were advised to prepare themselves; and without considering, or hearing what they had a mind to say for themselves, they were led into a yard there by; where they found three files of musketeers ready for their despatch.

Edward Hyde, Earl of Clarendon, seventeenth century

The battle of Sole Bay (off Southwold) in 1672 was a major engagement during the Anglo-Dutch wars; James II (then Duke of York) fought in it.

The English fleet were at anchor in Solebay, on the twenty-eighth of   116
May, when the Dutch fell in with them, and if they had not spent too much time in council, had certainly surprised them. As it was, many of the English captains were forced to cut their cables, in order to get time enough into the line of battle. The engagement began between seven and eight in the morning, when De Ruyter attacked the red squadron in the centre, and engaged the admiral, on board of which was his royal highness the duke of York, for two hours, forcing his highness at last to remove to another ship. The Dutch captain, Van Brakell, attacked the earl of Sandwich in the Royal James: and while they were engaged, almost all the squadron of Van Ghent fell upon the earl's ships. His lordship behaved with amazing intrepidity, killed Admiral Van Ghent himself, sunk three fire-ships and a man of war, that would have laid him on board; but then having lost all his officers, and two thirds of his men, his battered ship was grappled, and set on fire by a fourth fire-ship. Some

of his men escaped; yet the earl continued on board till the flames surrounded him, where he perished; but left behind him an immortal name which will ever be revered by such as esteem the valour of an officer, the capacity of a statesman, or the integrity of a patriot.

The death of their admiral, with the furious attack of part of the blue squadron, coming in, though too late, to the earl of Sandwich's assistance, threw this part of the Dutch fleet, which had been commanded by Van Ghent, into very great confusion, and forced them to stand off. This gave an opportunity for the blue squadron to join the red, and to assist the duke of York; who, deserted by the French, was in the utmost danger of being oppressed by the two squadrons of De Ruyter and Bankert. About this time Cornelius Evertz, vice-admiral of Zealand, was killed, and De Ruyter and Allemond narrowly escaped being burnt by fire-ships; but, when the English thought themselves secure of victory, the scattered squadron of Van Ghent came in to the assistance of their countrymen, and again rendered doubtful the fortune of the day.

All this time the French, who composed the white squadron, instead of seconding the continued efforts of the English, kept as far out of danger as they could, and left our fleet to sustain the whole force of the enemy, at a disadvantage of three to two. But, notwithstanding this vast inequality of numbers, the fight continued with inexpressible obstinacy till towards the evening, when victory declared for the English. Five or six of the enemy's fire-ships were sunk by an English man of war, and Sir Joseph Jordan, of the blue squadron, having the advantage of the wind, pierced the Dutch fleet, and thereby spread through it the utmost confusion; while a fire-ship clapped their Admiral De Ruyter on board, and it was not without the utmost difficulty that he escaped being burnt or taken. As it grew dark, De Ruyter, collecting his fleet in the best order he could, fought retreating; and, as the most authentic of the Dutch historians say, quitted the place of fight, and steered northwards.

John Campbell, 1818

Civic violence was endemic in the early nineteenth century, and two Whig grandees (Thomas Coke and Lord Albemarle) narrowly escaped the mob in Norwich in 1815.

In the month of March, 1815, he and my father attended a Cattle Show   117 in the Norwich Castle Ditches. On the same day, an Anti-Corn-Law mob paraded the streets preceded by a man bearing a small loaf on a pole. Mr Coke was immediately recognised. 'Let us seize the villain,' cried some of the weavers, 'and before night we will have his heart on a gridiron.' At the same moment they made a rush towards their intended victim. In the crowd, a stalwart poacher, whom my father had once befriended, formed with his body a temporary barrier between the mob and the object of their resentment. Coke and my father took advantage of the momentary respite, and amidst a shower of stones, scrambled over some cattle-pens. A butcher named Kett, seeing their danger, opened the door of one of his pens, and having first twisted the tail of a large bull, let him loose on the crowd. The beast, maddened with pain, went bellowing and galloping down the hill. The mob dispersed in a trice, but quickly reassembled in greater force. The Riot Act was read, and the military – a regiment of Black Brunswickers (soon to deal with a more formidable foe) – was called out. One trooper was wounded by a stone.

In the meanwhile the two fugitives made their escape to the 'Angel', now the 'Royal' Hotel. The gates were closed; the Anti-Corn-Law rioters assembled round the inn. It was whispered that Coke would be found in the boot of the London night coach, now about to take its departure. The gates were opened, the coach was searched, – no Coke was to be found. He and my father, having escaped by the back way, were on their road to Quidenham, where they arrived safely the same evening.

George Thomas Keppel, Earl of Albemarle, 1876

The hungry labourers staged a revolt at Littleport in 1816.

Then Beamish sprang on a bench and entreated the men to attend to   118 what he had to say.

'We want no words,' said one of the rioters. 'We are dry, we want drink. We've empty pockets, and want to fill them. Our ears have been stuffed with words. Keep them for chapel on Sundays.'

'I will speak,' cried Beamish. 'I am your leader. You have sworn to follow and obey me. You elected me yourselves.'

'Lead us to liquor and sovereigns, and we'll follow sharp enough.'

'You are wasting time. You are damaging a righteous cause. Have we not to march to Ely? Have we not to visit the farmers on the way, and impose our terms there?'

'There's plenty of time for that, Pip.'

'There is not plenty of time. The Mildenhall men are on their way under Cutman, five hundred strong.'

'How do you know that?'

'It was so planned. The Isleham men are marching under Goat, the Soham men under Gotobed. Who will be first in Ely? Is Littleport, that should lead the way, to come in at the tail?'

'There is something in that, mates,' shouted one of the rioters. 'Stand in order, you chaps. To Ely! Bring along the waggon.'

The idea that, if looting were to be done, they of Littleport might come in merely to glean where others had reaped, and the consciousness that a far richer harvest was awaiting them in Ely than could be garnered in Littleport, acted as a stimulus, and the mob desisted from further violence, and roughly organised itself into marching order. All were armed after a fashion, with guns, pitchforks, cudgels, leaping-poles, and cleavers; and as the day was declining, there was a cry for torches.

'We shan't want them,' called one of the men. 'We'll light bonfires on our way.'   .

Then a waggon was drawn out. In it were stationed some fowlers with duck-guns. The object of the waggon was to serve as a sort of fortress. Those in it were above the heads of the rest, and, in the event of resistance or an attack, could fire over their heads. Moreover, the waggon would be serviceable to carry the spoil taken on the way, or gathered in Ely.

Then the mob rolled along the great drove or highway to the city, with shouts, and oaths, and laughter, and trampled the snow as it advanced, leaving a black slush behind it.

Many of the men were half intoxicated with the ale and spirits they had already imbibed, and all were wholly drunk with lust of gain and love of destruction.

Then one in the waggon shouted, 'To Crumbland!' Another shouted, 'No, no! Young Runham is not bad. He has sold his wheat cheap and thrashed out all his stacks. And the old woman is a widow.'

'That's nought,' exclaimed a third, 'if there's any liquor to be had there!'

'To Gaultrip's!' was the cry.

'Gaultrip is my cousin!' shouted another.

'That's nought,' called one of the mob. 'I suppose he has money.'

'Ely way!' roared Beamish, scrambling into the waggon. 'Drive ahead. What's the use of being the commander, if nobody listens to the word of command, and nobody thinks of obeying it, if he does hear it?'

Sabine Baring-Gould, 1893

The impotence felt by civilians during the air attacks on East Anglia in the Second World War was gracefully expressed by this farmer near Cromer.

My father once shot at a V-1, but did it no damage. He was out on the   119
lawn one windy chill afternoon, flattening mole hills and shooting at the
moles. I don't know if he had damaged any of the moles, but he was doing his best. I was out there with him, and I looked up and saw, silent above the trees, long and silver, a great gleaming fish passing over the garden. It made no sound at all, and it looked beautiful and not at all dangerous. It seemed to be going quite fast, cleaving the air. I don't know if I cried out – it was certainly a surprising and unexpected sight. My father, as if sensing from me, from some movement, or arrested movement I made, the passage of something strange, also looked up and saw it. He stood there, his straddled legs in leather gaiters one on each side of the little mound of flattened earth, feet firm on the grass, looking up at this extraordinary apparition. I had no idea what it was. Certainly I did not know that it was dangerous. Then, without warning, my father suddenly flung up his gun to his shoulder and fired both barrels straight into the air at the passing monster. It did not falter or waver in its course. I am sure that neither of us expected it to do so. It had been a token, a gesture of defiance, no more. It passed on, over the trees, and out of sight. We waited, in an absolute, tingling silence. I did not know what to expect. But I saw from my father's attitude of strained attention that something was about to happen. The thing passed over the trees, behind the line of the hills, and blew itself up, quite harmlessly, in the middle of a

pine plantation. It was quite a shock – I had not imagined that it menaced us in any way. My father, firing at it, had seemed rather to salute, than to assault it. I think it must have been wildly off course. We never saw another, never even heard of one coming down anywhere near us. It was our own particular V-1, beautiful, strange, something from a war that we, in our remote corner of England, sometimes seemed hardly to be engaged upon at all.

Jane White, 1973

From momentous events to magnificent events. Elizabeth I toured the country as a matter of policy. The climax of her progress through East Anglia in 1578 was her arrival at Norwich, especially since Norfolk had not been included in her earlier progress of 1561. (Gurgunt was an entirely mythical personage.)

Sir Robert Wood, then Esquire, and nowe Knight, Maior of the same Citie, at one of the clocke the same happy day, sette forwarde to meete with hir Majestie in this order: firste, there roade before him, wel and seemely mounted, three-score of the most comelie yong men of the Citie, as Bachelers, apparelled all in blacke sattyn doublets, blacke hose, blacke taffata hattes and yeallowe bandes, and their universall liverie was a mandylion of purple taffata, layde aboute with silver lace; and so apparelled, marched forwardes, two and two in a rank.

120

Then one whiche represented King Gurgunt, sometyme Kyng of Englande, whiche buylded the Castle of Norwich, called *Blanch Flowre*, and layde the foundation of the Citie. He was mounted uppon a brave courser, and was thus furnished: his body armed, his bases of greene and white silke; on his head a black velvet hat, with a plume of white feathers. There attended uppon him three henchmen in white and greene: one of them did beare his helmet, the seconde his tergat, the thirde his staffe. After him a noble companie of Gentlemen and wealthie Citizens, in velvet coates and other costly furniture, bravely mounted. Then followed the Officers of the Citie, every one in his place. Then the Sword-bearer, with the sworde and hatte of maintaynaunce. Then the Maior, and foure and twentie Aldermen, and the Recorder, all in scarlette gownes, whereof, so many as had bin Maiors of the Citie, and were Justices, did weare their scarlet cloakes. Then followed so many as had bin Sherifs, and were no Aldermen, in violet gownes, and satten tippets. Then followed divers other, to keepe the people from disturbyng the array aforesayde.

Thus every thing in comely order, they all (except Gurgunt, whiche stayed hir Majesties commyng within a flight shotte or two of the Citie, where the Castle of Blaunche Flowre was in moste beautifull prospect) marched forwarde to a bridge, called Hartforde Bridge, the uttermoste lymit that way, distant from the Citie two miles or thereabouts, to meete with hyr Majestie: who, within one houre or little more after their attendaunce, came in suche gratious and princely wise, as ravished the hartes of all hir loving subjects, and might have terrified the stoutest heart of any enemy to beholde. Whether the Majestie of the

Prince, whiche is incomparable, or joy of hir subjectes, whiche exceeded measure, were the greater, I thinke, woulde have appalled the judgement of Apollo to define. The acclamations and cries of the people to the Almighty God for the preservation of hir Majesty ratled so loude, as hardly for a great tyme coulde any thinge be hearde: but at last, as every thyng hath an ende, the noyse appeased; and the Maior saluted hir Highnesse with the Oration following; and yeelded to hir Majestie therewith the sworde of the Citie, and a fayre standing cuppe of silver, and guilt, with a cover; and in the cup one hundreth poundes in golde.

Bernard Goldringham, sixteenth century

St Blaise was the patron saint of the wool trade. The traditional procession in his honour that took place at Norwich was specially magnificent in 1783, in celebration of the end of the war with France. James Woodforde, rector of Weston Longville, tops and tails his account of it with typical details of his personal life.

Mar: 24. . . . About 6 o'clock this Morning we all got up to go to Norwich   121 and after breakfast we set forth at 8 o'clock, Mrs Davy and Nancy in the Chaise, myself on Horseback, Will, Ben and Lizzy on horseback, Jack went behind the Chaise as I was willing that all shd go that could. Betty, my Upper Maid stayed at home being Washing Week. We all got to Norwich about 10 o'clock – The Road we went was filled with People on Horseback and foot, going to see the fine Sight – Ben carried Lizzy behind him on Phyllis and the first Time she ever carried any one, double, and she carried her very well and safe, to Norwich and back again. I put up my Horses at the Kings Head – Mrs Davy and Nancy were at Mr Priests. The grand Procession began about 11 o'clock this morning – I saw them first beyond Black Friars Bridge near St Saviours Church and a very pretty and grand Sight it was. The Order of the Procession was as follows.

Four Trumpeters
Marshal-Man
Peace
Orator
Banner of Brittania
Plenty
Drums and Fifes
20 Argonauts
Hercules
The Golden Fleece

Lynceus { borne on a grand Palanquin } Tiphy[s]
Zetes   {   by four Men   } Calais

Castor { Jason drawn in a Phaeton } Pollux
        {   by four Horses   }

Standard of the Argonauts
20 Argonauts
Militia Band
Standard of the City

Two Vergers
Orator
{ Bishop's Chaplain }
{ in a Phaeton and Pair }
{ Bishop Blaize }
{ in a Phaeton drawn by 6 Horses }
{ Standard of the City }

The book-keepers, Shepherds and Shepherdesses belonging to the different Societies of Combers 12 Companies – Seven Companies on foot – Five Companies on Horseback.

    Mr and Mrs Custance, Sr Edmund Bacon and Lady at the Kings Head, I called on them about 11 o'clock, and gave them an Account of the grand Sight and left with them a Paper of the Procession. I never saw so great a Multitude of People in my Life collected together, the Market-Place was as full as it could be, both in the area, at the Windows and on the Tops of the Houses – and every Street besides full of People from all Parts of the County. The Procession proceeded thro' every principal Street of the City and it lasted till 4 in the Afternoon. We eat some cold Ham and Veal at Mr Priests about 2. A Mrs Goddard an old Maid, Du Quesne's Maid Betty and a Miss High with her in Du Quesne's Chaise were at Mr Priests, as was Miss Priest of Reepham. About ½ past 4 we all set forth for Weston and got home about 7 o'clock, rather fatigued. Mem: Just without the Gates Mr Howes's Chaise broke down, one of the Axle-Trees being broke, which my Servant Boy Jack, behind the Chaise, found out – but luckily for it we were near Mr Howes's Coach Maker, a Mr Baldwin, who lent them a carriage leaving the old Shatterdan behind to be mended. Paid and gave to day at Norwich abt 2.6. We were all highly delighted indeed with this Days Sight – it far exceeded every Idea I cd have of it. Hercules, Jason, and Bishop Blaize, were exceedingly well kept up and very superbly dressed. All the Combers were in white ruffled Shirts with Cross-Belts of Wool of divers Colours – with Mitred Caps on their heads – The Shepherds and Shepherdesses were little Boys and Girls on horseback, very handsomely and [with] great Propriety dressed. Orations spoke in most of the principal Streets. I never saw a Procession so grand and well conducted.

James Woodforde, 1783

The annual Colchester Oyster Feast has been held for centuries, but it took an enterprising mayor to transfer the ceremonial on to a boat, in 1970.

The Town Clerk, his wig clearly secure by Divine intervention, declaimed   122 to sea and saltings:
    'Be it known the Several Fishery of the River Colne and waters thereof hath, from time beyond which memory runneth not to the contrary, belonged and appertained to the Corporation of the Borough of Colchester by whatsoever name or designation called or known; and this in virtue and pursuance of the divers Royal Charters, Grants, Liberties and Franchises to the same Borough conceded.

'And be it further known the Several Oyster Fishery of the said River and Waters is at this time present closed, in accord with ancient usage, and so must remain until it be willed that the same shall be opened.'

At that moment Neptune pursed his lips and blew a frightful blast. The hat of Mr Webb, the Mayor's secretary, lifted gloriously and floated with regal calm into the sea. They fished it out with a broom. ('What a do!')

The Town Clerk, safe in his God-fixed wig, rolled on resonantly with splendid imperturbability.

'And be it further known the will now is that the same several Oyster Fishery may be and continue opened and open until such time as hereafter it may to the Contrary be ordained *now therefore it is hereby publicly proclaimed and declared* that the said Several Oyster Fishery is this day opened, and that the same shall be and continue open henceforth until such other day as may, in like accord with ancient usage, be fixed and determined as proper and appropriate for the further customary closing thereof.

'Ordered this tenth day of September in the year of our Lord, One thousand nine hundred and seventy.

'The following are the words of the Ancient Proclamation made in the Colne Water in the year 1256, and in subsequent years, by the Bailiffs of the Borough of Colchester, on behalf of the Corporation of the Borough:

(A passing seagull baptised a town councillor. The Town Clerk, with legal calm, turned a blind eye.)

'Whereas many of the noble Kings of England before time or memory, progenitors of our very excellent lord King who now is, by their special charters have granted and confirmed to the Burgesses of Colchester, and to their heirs and successors, to have and to hold the Borough of Colchester in fee farm freely, with all the franchises and privileges contained in the said charters.

'Also that the said Burgesses, their heirs and successors, may have their fishery from the North Bridge of Colchester, as far as Westnesse on the one side and the other, with their easements whatsoever, franchises, and customs, belonging to such persons to whom franchise of water and river is granted, and notwithstanding all those who have lands adjacent, on the one side or other of Water or River.'

Something grey and grisly surfaced fifty yards to starboard. 'Ooh! There's the Loch Ness Monster,' quacked a young girl.

''Tain't. Thass on'y an owd porpuss arter a bellyfull o' fish,' said a sea-dog of 16 brusquely. The porpoise subsided.

'Also that no man nor other person may place piles, weirs, nor other works of hand nearer to our said water than is necessary for the maintenance of their properties.

'Nor that any dredgers of oysters may dredge broods in the water of our said fishery nor in any of the creeks of the same, nor at any time except in the time limited, under pain of forfeiture and grievous amerciaments.'

The Town Sergeant roared: 'God Save the Queen, The Mayor, and this Corporation.' The heron squawked: 'Fra-aank! Fra-aank!'

The Mayor took the hint and ordered: 'Three Cheers for Her Majesty The Queen.'

We roared it out like all the marsh bulls of Lagenhoe. Curlew took off with scandalised skirlings. White-waistcoated ringed plover, decent little bodies, fled along the tide line.

James Wentworth Day, 1970

Apparitions and Marvels

Woolpit was the scene of what might have been an early visitation from Martians.

In East Anglia there is a village, distant, as it is said, four or five miles from the noble monastery of the blessed king and martyr, Edmund; near this place are seen some very ancient cavities, called 'Wolfpittes', that is, in English, 'Pits for wolves', and which give their name to the adjacent village. During harvest, while the reapers were employed in gathering in the produce of the fields, two children, a boy and a girl, completely green in their persons, and clad in garments of a strange colour, and unknown materials, emerged from these excavations. While wandering through the fields in astonishment, they were seized by the reapers, and conducted to the village, and many persons coming to see so novel a sight, they were kept some days without food. But when they were nearly exhausted with hunger, and yet could relish no species of support which was offered to them, it happened, that some beans were brought in from the field, which they immediately seized with avidity, and examined the stalk for the pulse, but not finding it in the hollow of the stalk, they wept bitterly. Upon this, one of the bystanders, taking the beans from the pods, offered them to the children, who seized them directly, and ate them with pleasure. By this food they were supported for many months, until they learnt the use of bread. At length, by degrees, they changed their original colour, through the natural effect of our food, and became like ourselves, and also learnt our language. It seemed fitting to certain discreet persons that they should receive the sacrament of baptism, which was administered accordingly. The boy, who appeared to be the younger, surviving his baptism but a little time, died prematurely; his sister, however, continued in good health, and differed not in the least from the women of our own country.

Afterwards, as it is reported, she was married at Lynne, and was living a few years since, at least, so they say. Moreover, after they had acquired our language, on being asked who and whence they were, they are said to have replied, 'We are inhabitants of the land of St Martin, who is regarded with peculiar veneration in the country which gave us birth.' Being further asked where that land was, and how they came thence hither, they answered, 'We are ignorant of both those circumstances; we only remember this, that on a certain day, when we were feeding our father's flocks in the fields, we heard a great sound, such as we are now accustomed to hear at St Edmund's, when the bells are chiming; and whilst listening to the sound in admiration, we became on a sudden, as it were, entranced, and found ourselves among you in the fields where you were reaping.'

William of Newburgh, twelfth century (translation, Joseph Stevenson)

But the strange visitor at Orford Castle was surely a seal.

In the time of Henry II, when Bartholomew de Glanville was keeper of   124
Orford castle, it happened that fishermen fishing in the sea there caught a wild man in their nets; who was taken to the aforesaid castellan as a marvel. He was entirely naked, and like a human being in all his limbs. But he had hair, though it seemed on the surface almost torn away and destroyed. His beard was full and pointed, and his chest was extremely hairy and shaggy. The aforesaid knight had him guarded day and night for a long time, so that he could not approach the sea. Whatever was brought up to him he ate greedily. He ate fish raw as well as cooked, but he wrung out the raw fish in his hands, until all the liquid had gone, and then ate them. But he would not utter a word, or rather could not, even though he was hung up by his feet and often severely tortured. When he was taken to a church, he showed not the least sign of reverence or belief, either by kneeling or bowing his head, when he saw anything holy. He always hurried to his sleeping place at nightfall and slept there until dawn. It happened that they took him once to the harbour and let him loose in the sea, having placed a triple line of very strong nets across the harbour. He soon made for the depths of the sea, passing all the nets, and repeatedly came up from the deep water, gazing at those who were watching him from the shore for a long time, often diving down and reappearing after a moment, as though he was mocking those who watched him because he had escaped from their nets. He played like this in the sea for a long while, and everyone had given up hope that he would return, but he came back of his own accord to them, swimming through the waves, and remained with them for another two months. But after this he was less carefully guarded, and he now disliked his way of life; so he secretly slipped down to the sea and never appeared again. Whether this was a mortal man or some kind of fish pretending to be a human being or some evil spirit lurking in the body of a drowned man (such as is described in the life of St Audoen) it is not easy to see, particularly because so many people tell such marvellous tales about this kind of event.

Ralph of Coggeshall, thirteenth century (Oxford translation)

In an age when fires and other calamities were thought to be the judgement of God, it seemed miraculous that great monuments should only just escape destruction. This happened to the shrine of St Edmund at Bury, as recounted by a very practical-minded monk.

In the year of grace one thousand one hundred and ninety-eight, the   125
glorious martyr Edmund willed to terrify our monastery, and to teach us
that his body should be more reverently and carefully guarded. There
was a certain wooden floor between the shrine and the high altar, on
which were two candles, which the guardians of the shrine used to
relight. And they were wont to put one candle on another, and to stick
them together carelessly. And under this floor many things were lying
together in an untidy manner, such as flax and thread and wax and
vessels of different sorts, in fact the keepers of the shrine used to put there
whatever came into their hands, behind the door with iron sides which
the place had.

On the night of St Etheldreda's day then the keepers were asleep,
and part of a candle, which had been relit, fell, as we believe, while it was
still burning, on the same floor which was covered with rags. And it
caught all things which were near it, and those above and underneath
went on fire, so that the iron walls were all white hot. And lo! the anger
of the Lord was kindled, but not without mercy, as it is written, In wrath
remember mercy. For in the same hour the clock struck before the hour
of matins, and the master of the vestry arose and perceived and knew of
the fire. Then he ran at once, and sounding the gong, as if for a dead man,
he cried with a loud voice and said that the shrine was on fire.

Then we all ran up and found the fire raging with incredible
fierceness, and surrounding the whole shrine, and almost reaching the
beams of the church. Then the young men ran for water, some to the well
and some to the clock, and some used their hoods, and with great labour
put out the fire. But first they stripped some of the altars. Then, when
cold water had been poured on the front of the shrine, the stones fell and
were reduced as it were to dust. And the nails with which the silver plates
were fastened to the shrine came out of the wood, which had been burnt
to the depth of my finger, and the plates hung one from another without
nails.

Yet the golden image of the saint at the front of the shrine, and
some stones, remained firm and unharmed, and the image was more
beautiful after the fire than it had been before, because it was of pure
gold.

Now it happened by the will of the Most High, that at this time the
great beam, which had been over the altar, had been taken away that it
might be newly carved. It happened also that the cross, and the little
Mary, and the John, and the chest with the garment of St Edmund, and
the case containing the relics, which had formerly hung from the same
beam, and other holy things which had stood on the beam, had all been
carried away beforehand. Otherwise, we believe that they would all have
been burnt, as a painted cloth was burnt, which was hanging in the place
of the beam. But what would have happened if the church had been
hung with curtains?

So when we were sure that the fire had nowhere entered the shrine, after carefully looking at the cracks and chinks, wherever they were, and after seeing that all was cold, our sorrow was greatly lessened. And lo! some of our brothers cried with much wailing that the cup of St Edmund was consumed. And when many sought the stones and metal plates in all directions among the ashes and cinders, they brought forth the cup quite unharmed. It was lying in the midst of a heap of ashes, which were now cool, and it was found covered with a linen cloth, which, however, was half-burned. The oak chest, also, in which the cup was usually placed, had been burnt to ashes, and only the iron fastenings and the iron lock were found. Then when we saw this miracle, we all wept for joy.

Then when we saw that the greater part of the front of the shrine had been ruined, and were angered at the wickedness of the cause of the fire, with common assent a goldsmith was privately summoned, and we caused him to make plates and fix on the shrine without any delay, that the scandal might be avoided, and we caused the signs of the fire to be covered up with wax or in some other way.

But the gospel bears witness, There is nothing hid which shall not be revealed. Very early in the morning there came strangers bearing gifts, and noticed nothing of the fire. Yet some of them looking round, asked where the fire round the shrine had been, of which they had already heard. And so when it was impossible to conceal it altogether, we answered those who asked that a candle had fallen and burnt three napkins, and that owing to the heat of the fire some stones on the front of the shrine had been destroyed. Yet lying rumour pretended that the head of the saint had been burnt; some said that only the hair had been consumed; but in the end the truth was known, and the mouth of them that spoke lies was stopped.

Now all this was done, by the providence of the Lord, that the places round the shrine of His saint might be more honestly cared for, and that that which the lord abbot proposed might the more quickly come and without delay come to a fitting conclusion. For he proposed that the shrine, with the body of the glorious martyr, should be placed more securely and splendidly in a more prominent position. And, before this same misfortune befell, the crest of the shrine was half finished, and the marble stones for raising and supporting the shrine had been largely prepared and polished.

Jocelin of Brakelond, thirteenth century (translation, L. C. Jane)

Fire also nearly destroyed St Margaret's Church at Lynn. This account is by a mystic who refers to herself as 'the said creature'.

On a time, there happed to be a great fire in Lynne Bishop, which fire 126 burnt up the Guild Hall of the Trinity, and in the same town, a hideous fire and grievous, full likely to have burnt the parish church dedicated in honour of Saint Margaret, a stately place and richly honoured, and all the town as well, had there been no grace or miracle.

The said creature being there present, and seeing the peril and mischief of all the town, cried full loud many times that day and wept full abundantly, praying for grace and mercy to all the people.

And, notwithstanding at other times they could not endure her to cry and weep for the plenteous grace that God wrought in her, this day, for the eschewing of their bodily peril, they could suffer her to cry and weep as much as ever she would, and no man would bid her cease but rather prayed her to continue, fully trusting and believing that through her crying and weeping, Our Lord would take them to mercy.

Then came her confessor to her, and asked if it were best to bear the Sacrament to the fire or not. She said: – 'Yes, sir, yes! For Our Lord Jesus Christ told me, it shall be right well.'

So her confessor, parish priest of Saint Margaret's Church, took the Precious Sacrament and went before the fire as devoutly as he could, and then brought It in again to the church. And the sparks of the fire flew about the church.

The said creature, desiring to follow the Precious Sacrament to the fire, went out of the church door, and, as soon as she beheld the hideous flame of the fire, anon she cried with a loud voice: –

'Good Lord! Make it well.'

These words wrought in her mind, inasmuch as Our Lord had said to her before that He should make it well. And therefore she cried: –

'Good Lord! Make it well and send down some rain, or some weather that may, through Thy mercy, quench this fire and ease my heart.'

Later on, she went again into the church, and then she beheld how the sparks came into the choir through the lantern of the church.

Then she had a new sorrow, and cried full loud again for grace and mercy, with great plenty of tears.

Soon after, there came in to her three worshipful men with white snow on their clothes, saying unto her: –

'Lo! Margery, God hath wrought great grace for us, and sent us a fair snow to quench the fire with. Be now of good cheer, and thank God therefor.'

Margery Kempe, 1436 (modern version, W. Butler-Bowdon)

The shrine of Our Lady at Walsingham was, before the Reformation, one of the greatest pilgrim destinations in England. The true pilgrim experienced a spiritual, as well as a physical, journey.

Gentle heardsman, tell to me,   127
   Of curtesy I thee pray,
Unto the towne of Walsingham
   Which is the right and ready way.

'Unto the towne of Walsingham
    The way is hard for to be gone;
And very crooked are those paths
    For you to find out all alone.'

Anon., fifteenth century

But it took an exceptionally wise visitor to Walsingham to perceive that a truly spiritual approach need not embrace superstition. Erasmus ('Ogygius') went there in 1511.

Ogygius At the north Side there is a certain Gate, not of a Church, don't   128
mistake me, but of the Wall that incloses the Church-Yard, that has a very little Wicket, as in the great Gates of Noblemen, that he that has a Mind to get in, must first venture the breaking of his Shins, and afterwards stoop his Head too.
Menedemus In Truth, it would not be safe for a Man to enter in against an Enemy at such a little Door.
O. You're in the Right on't. But yet the Verger told me, that some Time since a Knight on Horse-Back, having escaped out of the Hands of his Enemy, who follow'd him at the Heels, got in thro' this Wicket. The poor Man at the last Pinch, by a sudden Turn of Thought, recommended himself to the holy Virgin, that was the nearest to him. For he resolv'd to take Sanctuary at her Altar, if the Gate had been open. When behold, which is such a Thing as was never heard of, both Man and Horse were on a sudden taken into the Church-Yard, and his Enemy left on the out-Side of it, stark mad at his Disappointment.
M. And did he give you Reason to believe so wonderful a Relation?
O. Without Doubt.
M. That was no easy Matter to a Man of your Philosophy.
O. He shew'd me a Plate of Copper nail'd on the Door, that had the very Image of this Knight, that was thus sav'd; and in the very Habit, which was then in Fashion among the *English*, which is the same we see in old Pictures, which, if they are drawn truly, the Barbers, and Dyers, and Weavers in those Days, had but a bad Time on't.
M. Why so?
O. Why, he had a Beard like a Goat; and there was not a Wrinkle in any of his Cloaths, they were made so strait to his Body, that the very Straitness of them made his Body the more slender. There was also another Plate that was an exact Description of the Chapel, and the Size of it.
M. Then there was no Doubt to be made on't.
O. Under the little Wicket there was an iron Grate, no bigger than what a Man on Foot could just get in at. For it was not fit that any Horse afterwards should tread upon that Place, which the former Knight had consecrated to the Virgin.
M. And very good Reason.
O. From hence towards the East, there is another Chapel full of Wonders; thither I went. Another Verger received me. There we pray'd a

little; and there was shewn us the middle Joint of a Man's Finger; I kiss'd it, and ask'd whose Relick it was. He told me it was St *Peter's*; what, said I, the Apostle? He said it was. I then took Notice of the Bigness of the Joint, which was large enough to be taken for that of a Giant. Upon which, said I, *Peter* must Needs have been a very lusty Man. At this one of the Company fell a laughing; I was very much vext at it, for if he had held his Tongue, the Verger would have shewn us all the Relicks. However, we pacified him pretty well, by giving him a few Groats. Before this little Chapel stood a House, which he told us, in the Winter-Time when all Things were buried in Snow, was brought there on a sudden, from some Place a great Way off. Under this House there were two Pits Brim-full, that were fed by a Fountain consecrated to the holy Virgin. The Water was wonderful cold, and of great Virtue in curing Pains in the Head and Stomach.

Erasmus, 1524 (translation, N. Bailey)

The Black Dog of the lightning was feared throughout East Anglia, but never was its apparition so terrible as on one Sunday at Bungay.

SUNDAY, being the fourthe of this August, in ye yeer of our Lord 1577, to   129
the amazing and singular astonishment of the present beholders, and absent hearers, at a certain towne called BONGAY, not past tenne miles from the citie of NORWICHE, there fell from Heaven an exceeding great and terrible tempeste sodein and violent, between nine of the clock in the morning, and tenne of the day aforesaid.

This tempest took beginning with a rain, which fel with a wonderful force, with no lesse violence than abundance which made the storme so muche the more extrem and terrible.

This tempest was not simply of rain, but also of lightning, and thunder, the flashing of the one wherof was so rare and vehement, and the roaring noise of the other so forceable and violent, that it made not only people perplexed in minde and at their wits end, but ministered such strange and unaccustomed cause of feare to be conceived, that dumb creatures with ye horrour of that which fortuned, were exceedingly disquieted, and senselesse things void of all life and feeling shook and trembled.

Therr werr assembled at the same season, to hear divine service and common prayer, according to order, in the Parish Churche of the said towne of BONGAY, the people thereabouts inhabiting, who were witnesses of the straungenesse, the carenesse, and sodenesse of the storme, consisting of raine violently falling, fearful flashes of lightning, and terrible cracks of thunder, which came with such unwonted force and power, that to the perceiving of the people, at the time and in the place above named, assembled, the Church did as it were quake and stagger, which struck into the harts of those that were present, such a sore and sodain feare, that they were in a manner robbed of their right wits.

Immediately herrupon, there appeared in a most horrible

similitude and likenesse to the congregation, then and there present, A DOG as they might discerne it, of a BLACK COLOUR; at the sight wherof, together with the fearful flashes of fire then were seene, moved such admiration in the minds of the assemblie, that they thought doomes day was alread'y come.

This BLACK DOG, or the *Divel* in such a likenesse (God hee knoweth all who worketh all) running all along down the body of the Church with great swiftnesse, and incredible haste, among the people, in a visible forme and shape, passed between two persons, as they were kneeling upon their knees, and occupied in prayer as it seemed, wrung the necks of them bothe at one instant clene backward, insomuche that even in a moment where they kneeled they stra'gely dyed.

This is a wonderful example of God's wrath, no doubt to terrifie us, that we might feare him for his justice, or putting back our footsteps from the pathes of sinne, to love him for his mercy.

To our matter again. There was at ye same time another WUNDER wrought; for the same BLACK DOG, still continuing and remaining in one and the self-same shape, passing by an other man of the congregation in the Church, gave him such a gripe in the back, that therewith all he was presently drawen togither and shrunk up, as it were a piece of lether scorched in a hot fire; or at the mouth of a purse or bag, drawen togither with a string; the man, albeit he was in so straunge a taking, dyed not, but, as it is thought, is yet alive: whiche thing is mervellous in the eyes of men, and offereth muche matter of amasing the minde.

Anon., 1577

At least the Black Dog was a manifestation, which is more than can be said of the visions dreamt up by the wicked persecutors of lonely old women, and here brazenly described by their leader, the self-styled 'discoverer of witches'. Hopkins' activities, stimulated by the Puritanical inclination of the region, turned East Anglia into a nightmare of oppression.

Querie 4. I pray where was this experience gained? And why gained by   130 him and not by others?

Answer. The Discoverer never travelled far for it, but in *March*, 1644, he had some seven or eight of that horrible sect of Witches living in the Towne where he lived, a Towne in *Essex*, called *Maningtree*, with divers other adjacent Witches of other towns, who every six weeks in the night (being always on the Friday night) had their meeting close by his house, and had their severall solemne sacrifices there offered to the Devill, one of which this discoverer heard speaking to her *Imps* one night, and bid them goe to another Witch, who was thereupon apprehended, and searched by women who had for many yeares knowne the Devill's marks, and found to have three teats about her, which honest women have not: so upon command from the *Justice* they were to keep her from sleep two or three nights, expecting in that time to see her *familiars*, which the fourth night she called in by their severall names, and told them what shapes, a quarter of an houre before they came in, there being ten of us in the roome; the first she called was,

1. *Holt*, who came in like a white kitling.

2. *Jarmara*, who came in like a fat Spaniel without any legs at all, she said she kept him fat, for she clapt her hand on her belly, and said he suckt good blood from her body.

3. *Vinegar Tom*, who was like a long-legg'd Greyhound, with an head like an Oxe, with a long taile and broad eyes, who when this discoverer spoke to, and bade him goe to the place provided for him and his Angels, immediately transformed himselfe into the shape of a child of foure yeeres old without a head, and gave halfe a dozen turnes about the house, and vanished at the doore.

4. *Sack and Sugar*, like a black Rabbet.

5. *Newes*, like a Polcat. All these vanished away in a little time. Immediately after this Witch confessed severall other Witches, from whom she had her *Imps*, and named to divers women where their marks were, the number of their *Marks*, and *Imps*, and *Imps* names, as *Elemanzer, Pyewacket, Peckin the Crown, Grizzel, Greedigut &c.* which no mortall could invent; and upon their searches the same Markes were found, the same number, and in the same place, and the like confessions from them of the same Imps, (though they knew not that we were told before) and so peached one another thereabouts that joyned together in the like damnable practise, that in our Hundred in *Essex*, 29 were condemned at once, 4 brought 25 miles to be hanged, where this Discoverer lives. . . .

Matthew Hopkins, 1647

Witches were usually blamed for any strange phenomenon.

At St Edmund's-Bury, in Suffolk, Sep. 6, 1660, in the middle of the Broad   131
Street, there were got together, an innumerable company of Spiders of a redish colour, the spectators judged them to be as many as would have filled a Peck; These Spiders marched together, and in a strange kind of order, from the place where they were first discovered, towards one Mr Duncomb's house, a member of the late Parliament, and since Knighted; and as the people passed the street, or came near the spiders, to look upon so strange a sight, they would shun the people, and kept themselves together in a body till they came to the said Duncombe's house, before whose door there are two great Posts, there they staied, and many of them got under the door into the house, but the greatest part of them, climbing up the posts, spun a very great web presently from the one post to the other, and then wrapt themselves in it in two very great parcels that hung down near to the ground, which the servants of the house at last perceiving, got dry straw and laid it under them, and putting fire to it by a suddain flame consumed the greatest part of them, the number of those that remained were not at all considerable; all the use that the Gentleman made of this strange accident, so far as we can learn, is only this, that he believes they were sent to his house by some Witches.

Anon., 1660

But many people were prepared to use the crudest forms of black magic to attempt to cure illness.

The charm-remedies for whooping cough are, I think, more numerous   132
than for any other of the ills that flesh is heir to, and the directions of the medical attendant are often set aside in their favour. The following are among those to which my attention has been called.

It is necessary that a live flat-fish should be procured – 'a little dab' will do. Then it must be placed whilst alive on the bare chest of the patient, and kept there till it is dead. This is considered to be a certain remedy, though it must be confessed it is one somewhat difficult of accomplishment.

Then there is the spider remedy. Let the parent of the child afflicted find a dark spider in her own house, and hold it over the head of the child, repeating three times,

Spider, as you waste away/Whooping cough no longer stay.

The spider must then be hung up in a bag over the mantle-shelf, and when the spider has dried up the cough will be gone.

On the border ground of Norfolk and Suffolk the following charm has been tried. A hole was dug in a meadow, and into this the poor little sufferer was placed in a bent position head downwards. The flag cut in making the hole was then placed over him, and the child remained in the hole until he coughed. It is thought that if this charm be done in the evening, with only the father or the mother to witness it, the child will soon recover. In another parish a variation of this charm was tried. The child was laid face downwards on the turf of the meadow; the turf was then cut round the child in the shape of a coffin. The child was taken up and the flag turned roots upwards, and as the grass withered it was believed the cough wasted. This also must be done secretly or the charm will fail.

To eat a roasted mouse is said to be a certain cure for the disease. I have heard of a live frog, which had been held with its head within the mouth of the person affected, being hung up the chimney of the patient's house, in the belief that as it died the whooping cough would vanish. An instance is recorded of a woman who obtained a number of small snails. These were passed through the hands of the invalid and then suspended in a chimney on a string, in order that as they died the whooping might leave the children.

Among other remedies the following may be enumerated: – Let the patient drink some milk which a ferret has lapped; or be dragged three times, then wait three days and be dragged three times again under a gooseberry bush or bramble, both ends of which are growing in the ground; or procure hair from the cross on the back of a donkey, and having placed it in a bag hang it round the invalid's neck next the skin. If this be done secretly a speedy cure will result. The presumed efficacy in this hair is connected no doubt with the fact that the ass is the animal which was ridden by Jesus, and with the superstition that the cross was imprinted on its back as a memorial of that event.

John Glyde, 1872

Ghosts have appeared in all sorts of places, but seldom on the beach. Monty James, Provost of King's College, Cambridge, set the scene of his most famous short story at Felixstowe (he calls it 'Burnstow').

A long stretch of shore – shingle edged by sand, and intersected at short   133
intervals with black groynes running down to the water – a scene, in fact,
so like that of his afternoon's walk that, in the absence of any landmark,
it could not be distinguished therefrom. The light was obscure, conveying an impression of gathering storm, late winter evening, and slight cold
rain. On this bleak stage at first no actor was visible. Then, in the distance,
a bobbing black object appeared; a moment more, and it was a man
running, jumping, clambering over the groyne, and every few seconds
looking eagerly back. The nearer he came the more obvious it was that he
was not only anxious, but even terribly frightened, though his face was
not to be distinguished. He was, moreover, almost at the end of his
strength. On he came; each successive obstacle seemed to cause him
more difficulty than the last. 'Will he get over this next one?' thought
Parkins; 'it seems a little higher than the others.' Yes; half climbing, half
throwing himself, he did get over, and fell all in a heap on the other side
(the side nearest to the spectator). There, as if really unable to get up
again, he remained crouching under the groyne, looking up in an
attitude of painful anxiety.

So far no cause whatever for the fear of the runner had been
shown; but now there began to be seen, far up the shore, a little flicker of
something light-coloured moving to and fro with great swiftness and
irregularity. Rapidly growing larger, it, too, declared itself as a figure in
pale, fluttering draperies, ill-defined. There was something about its
motion which made Parkins very unwilling to see it at close quarters. It
would stop, raise arms, bow itself toward the sand, then run stooping
across the beach to the water-edge and back again; and then, rising
upright, once more continue its course forward at a speed that was
startling and terrifying. The moment came when the pursuer was
hovering about from left to right only a few yards beyond the groyne
where the runner lay in hiding. After two or three ineffectual castings
hither and thither it came to a stop, stood upright, with arms raised high,
and then darted straight forward towards the groyne.

   M. R. James, 1904

Borley Rectory was known as the most haunted house in England, and strange things appeared even in the garden in broad daylight.

While I was painting, and about 3 o'clock in the afternoon, I suddenly   134
noticed a sound, such as of approaching wings or rushing wind coming
towards me. Looking up, I saw the queerest object with impelling eyes
advancing towards me at about eye level. It seemed to be coming out of a
mist. It was accompanied by a wasp on its left, and this must have been
the wings I heard. I had just time to jump up and as they were quite near
my face, which seemed to be the objective, I struck at it with my

mahlstick, and seemed to hit the big object into the grass. The wasp seemed to go off on its own. With alarm I searched for the nameless object I had struck, as if I had not killed it, I thought it was possible it might attack me. I searched, but was unable to trace it and eventually gave up looking. Gradually, the unusualness of the creature dawned upon me and the more I thought of it, the less I could understand what it was.

Certainly, I had never seen anything like it before, and should describe it as being quite three inches in length, the body entirely black and composed of sections enabling it to bend and expand with ease. Its eyes were large and the colour of bloomy black grapes. The object was flattish. It was so real, that in jumping up, I had no time to put my palette down, and this resulted in upsetting medium on my skirt and ruining it. I had grasped the palette in my left hand.

As time elapsed I gathered myself together, mentally realizing that I had to catch a train and that it was useless to go on thinking as every moment was precious if I hoped to obtain what I was down here for – that is, to paint the Rectory – and I worked with renewed speed to recover lost time.

Margaret Wilson, 1940

At Sutton Hoo, near Woodbridge, England's greatest treasure-trove was uncovered in 1939 – a Saxon royal funerary ship bearing precious metal artefacts. It was indeed a genuine marvel.

The finding of the gold clasps was another wonderful moment. As always with gold objects, they were in perfect condition, without spot or tarnish. They are unique, and it was a happy chance they should be found on a day when we had visitors from the British Museum. The same evening there came, as a fitting climax to a crowded day, what was perhaps the most unexpected discovery of all. For some time we had been puzzled by a tantalizing patch of purple dust, sure harbinger of silver. It developed into a dome-shaped lump which Mr Grimes undercut and placed on a zinc tray. He deposited this on the grass outside the barrow and proceeded to take away the much corroded outer fragments. When at last he lifted the top we saw a bright silver bowl, base upwards, in perfect condition, and under this was yet another bowl. In all eight were thus uncovered, each with different ornamentation inside. That same day we removed the iron stand and silver tray, the iron-bound bucket, the gold clasps, and the sword.

O. G. S. Crawford, 1940

But a hoax, even if only in a work of fiction, can be more amusing. Here Professor Stokesay describes his astonishing find in the sandlings of east Suffolk.

'A most wonderful find,' he said. 'Now be prepared for a great shock. I can hardly believe it yet. We've discovered Eorpwald's tomb. Those loyal monks brought him here to Melpham. Stone coffin with inscription in an excellent condition. We've moved it to the outhouse. Some trace of the skeleton. . . .' And then as Gerald was about to speak, he held up his finger for attention. 'But wait a bit! That's less than half. In the coffin with its Christian inscription, the remains and the well-preserved remains of a wooden figure. I don't know what to make of it; if it wasn't too extraordinary I would say it was a pagan idol. I've only seen sketches and poor photographs of the Anglo-Saxon gods found in Friesland and on the Baltic coast, but I'd swear it was the same. After all there were many of them in the country. It might be. Nothing like it has been found in England before, it's true, but there must have been many of them, and the lucky chance of a preserving peaty soil. . . . But, in a Christian tomb! Well, I have my ideas, though it's too soon to speak yet. All I hope, my dear fellow, is that Portway doesn't rush . . .'

His voice tailed off and, in a rather artificial note, he said, 'Ah! Portway! I'm just telling this young fellow of our remarkable discoveries and adding a word of caution about rushing to conclusions. But I forgot, you don't know each other. Mr Portway, my promising pupil, Middleton.

Angus Wilson, 1956

Towns and Villages

The fine old city of Norwich. George Borrow began his career as an articled clerk in Norwich, and later lived at Oulton Broad.

A fine old city, truly, is that, view it from whatever side you will; but it shows best from the east, where the ground, bold and elevated, overlooks the fair and fertile valley in which it stands. Gazing from those heights, the eye beholds a scene which cannot fail to awaken, even in the least sensitive bosom, feelings of pleasure and admiration. At the foot of the heights flows a narrow and deep river, with an antique bridge communicating with a long and narrow suburb, flanked on either side by rich meadows of the brightest green, beyond which spreads the city; the fine old city, perhaps the most curious specimen at present extant of the genuine old English town. Yes, there it spreads from north to south, with its venerable houses, its numerous gardens, its thrice twelve churches, its mighty mound, which, if tradition speaks true, was raised by human hands to serve as the grave heap of an old heathen king, who sits deep within it, with his sword in his hand, and his gold and silver treasures about him. There is a grey old castle upon the top of that mighty mound; and yonder, rising three hundred feet above the soil, from among those noble forest trees, behold that old Norman master-work, that cloud-encircled cathedral spire, around which a garrulous army of rooks and choughs continually wheel their flight.

George Borrow, 1851

Norwich Cathedral spire. Though Thomas Browne probably hadn't climbed up it himself (he was, after all, fifty-five – old for those days), his account of the view reads as if he had.

I must not omitt to saye something of the shaft or spire of this church,   138
commonly called the pinnacle, as being a handsome and well proportion'd fabrick, and one of the highest in England, higher then the noted
spires of Lichfeild, Chichester, and Grantham, butt lower then that of
Salisbury, for that spire being Raysed upon a very high tower becomes
higher from the ground, butt this spire considered by itself seemes at least
to equall that. It is a hundred and five yards and two foot from the top of
the pinnacle unto the pavement of the Quire under it.

The spire is very strongly built, though the inside bee of Brick. The
upper Aperture or windowe is the highest ascent inwardly, out of which
sometimes a long streamer hath been hanged upon the Guild or Maiors
daye. Butt at His majesties Restauration, when the top was to bee
mended, and a new guilded wethercock was to bee placed upon it, there
were stagings made at the upper windowe, and divers persons went up to
the top of the pinnacle. They first went up into the Bellfrey, and then by
eight Ladders on the inside of the spire till they came to the upper hole or
windowe; then went out unto the outside, where a staging was sett, and
so ascended unto the top stone on which the wethercock standeth. The
cock is three quarters of a yard high, and one yard and two inches long, as
is also the crosse barre and top stone of the spire, which is not flatt, butt
consisteth of a half globe and channell about it, and from thence are eight
leaves of stone spreading outward, under which beginne the eight Rowes
of crocketts, which go doune the spire at five foot distance. From the top
there is a prospect all about the countrey. Mourshold hill seems lowe &
flatt ground. The castle and high buildings do very much diminish. The
River lookes like a dich. The citty with the streets make a pleasant showe,
like a garden, with severall walks in it.

Thomas Browne, *c.*1680

The ancient colleges of Cambridge, as seen by a fastidious visitor.

What institution is more majestic than Trinity College? what can be more   139
touching to an American than the hospitality of such an institution? The
first quadrangle is of immense extent, and the buildings that surround it,
with their long, rich fronts of time-deepened gray, are the stateliest in the
world. In the centre of the court are two or three acres of close-shaven
lawn, in the midst of which rises a splendid gothic fountain, where the
serving-men fill up their buckets. There are towers and battlements and
statues, and besides these things there are cloisters and gardens and
bridges. There are charming rooms in a kind of stately gate-tower, and
the rooms, occupying the thickness of the building, have windows
looking out on one side over the magnificent quadrangle, with half a
mile or so of Decorated architecture, and on the other into deep-
bosomed trees. And in the rooms is the best company conceivable –
distinguished men who are remarkably good fellows. I spent a beautiful
Sunday morning walking about Cambridge, with one of these gentlemen, and attempting, as the French say, to *débrouiller* its charms. These
are a very complicated affair, and I do not pretend, in memory, to keep
the colleges apart. There are, however, half a dozen points that make

ineffaceable pictures. Six or eight of the colleges stand in a row, turning their backs to the river; and hereupon ensues the loveliest confusion of gothic windows and ancient trees, of grassy banks and mossy balustrades, of sun-chequered avenues and groves, of lawns and gardens and terraces, of single-arched bridges spanning the little stream, which is small and shallow, and looks as if it had been 'turned on' for ornamental purposes. The scantily-flowing Cam appears to exist simply as an occasion for these enchanting little bridges – the beautiful covered gallery of John's or the slightly-collapsing arch of Clare. In the way of college-courts and quiet scholastic porticoes, of gray-walled gardens and ivied nooks of study, in all the pictorial accidents of a great English university, Cambridge is delightfully and inexhaustibly rich. I looked at these one by one, and said to myself always that the last was the best. If I were called upon, however, to mention the prettiest corner of the world, I should heave a tender sigh and point the way to the garden of Trinity Hall. My companion, who was very competent to judge (but who spoke, indeed, with the partiality of a son of the house), declared, as he ushered me into it, that it was, to his mind, the most beautiful *small* garden in Europe. I freely accepted, and I promptly repeat, an affirmation so ingeniously conditioned. The little garden at Trinity Hall is narrow and crooked; it leans upon the river, from which a low parapet, all muffled in ivy, divides it; it has an ancient wall, adorned with a thousand matted creepers on one side, and on the other a group of extraordinary horse-chestnuts. These trees are of prodigious size; they occupy half the garden, and they are remarkable for the fact that their giant limbs strike down into the earth, take root again, and emulate, as they rise, the majesty of the parent tree. The manner in which this magnificent group of horse-chestnuts sprawls about over the grass, out into the middle of the lawn, is one of the most picturesque features of the garden of Trinity Hall. Of course the single object at Cambridge that makes the most abiding impression is the famous chapel of King's College – the most beautiful chapel in England. The effect it attempts to produce within belongs to the order of sublimity. The attempt succeeds, and the success is attained by means so light and elegant that at first it almost defeats itself. The sublime usually has more of a frown and straddle, and it is not until after you have looked about you for ten minutes that you perceive that the chapel is saved from being the prettiest church in England by the accident of its being one of the noblest. It is a cathedral without aisles or columns or transepts, but (as a compensation) with such a beautiful slimness of clustered tracery soaring along the walls, and spreading, bending and commingling in the roof, that its simplicity seems only a richness the more. I stood there for a quarter of an hour on a Sunday morning; there was no service, but in the choir behind the great screen which divides the chapel in half, the young choristers were rehearsing for the afternoon. The beautiful boy-voices rose together and touched the splendid vault; they hung there, expanding and resounding, and then, like a rocket that spends itself, they faded and melted toward the end of the building. The sound was angelic.

Henry James, 1883

King's College Chapel, founded by the saintly Henry VI. Wordsworth studied at St John's College.

    Tax not the royal Saint with vain expense,   140
    With ill-matched aims the Architect who planned –
    Albeit labouring for a scanty band
    Of white-robed Scholars only – this immense
    And glorious Work of fine intelligence!
    Give all thou canst: high Heaven rejects the lore
    Of nicely calculated less or more;
    So deemed the man who fashioned for the sense
    Those lofty pillars, spread that branching roof
    Self-poised, and scooped into ten thousand cells,
    Where light and shade repose, where music dwells
    Lingering – and wandering on as loth to die;
    Like thoughts whose very sweetness yieldeth proof
    That they were born for immortality.

William Wordsworth, 1822

In these lines of a masque performed in the Senate House, Thomas Gray, who lived in Cambridge for most of his life, evokes the spirit of Milton to apostrophize the University.

    Ye brown o'er-arching groves,   141
      That contemplation loves,
    Where willowy Camus lingers with delight!
      Oft at the blush of dawn
      I trod your level lawn,
    Oft woo'd the gleam of Cynthia silver-bright
    In cloisters dim, far from the haunts of Folly,
    With Freedom by my side, and soft-eyed Melancholy

Thomas Gray, 1769

Ipswich and the estuary of the Orwell, before the days of industrialization.

The Streets of *Ipswich*, like those of most other ancient Towns, which 142
have not been destroyed by Fire and rebuilt, do not run in Right lines;
and therefore do not strike a Stranger's Eye, as they would if they were
more regular; but they contain many good Houses, which generally are
better within, than their outward Appearance gives Reason to expect.
One favourable Circumstance is almost peculiar to this Place, which is,
that most of the better Houses, even in the Heart of the Town, have
convenient Gardens, adjoining to them, which make them more airy and
healthy, as well as more pleasant and delightful.

The many Walks and Rides which abound with a Variety of pleasing Views, together with the Goodness of the Roads in the *Environs* of Ipswich, do also contribute greatly towards making the Place agreeable. But however entertaining these Prospects on the Land may be, they are far exceeded by those that the *Orwell* affords; which, to speak cautiously, at least for the Extent of it, is *one of the most beautiful Salt Rivers in the World.* The Beauty of it arises chiefly from its being bounded with High-land on both Sides, almost the whole Way. These Hills on each Side are enriched and adorned with almost every Object that can make a Landscape agreeable; such as Churches, Mills, Gentlemen's Seats, Villages and other Buildings, Woods, noble Avenues, Parks whose Pales reach down to the Water's Edge, well stored with Deer and other Cattle, feeding in fine Lawns, *&c. &c.* all these and more are so happily disposed and diversified, as if Nature and Art had jointly contrived how they might most agreeably entertain and delight the Eye. Such are the Side-Views. As a Passenger sails from *Ipswich*, when he enters what is properly called *Orwell Haven*, the Scene terminates on the Right, with a View of *Harwich* and the high Coast of *Essex*; on the Left with *Landguard-Fort*, and the high Land of *Walton* and *Felixstow* Cliffs behind it; and with a Prospect of the main Ocean before him. As he returns to *Ipswich*, the Scene closes with a distinct View of that fair Town, displaying itself to some Advantage, and forming a Sort of Half-moon as the River winds.

John Kirby, 1735

Bury, the social centre of Suffolk, as recounted in the lively style of this prolific writer.

From this part of the Country I return'd North-West by *Lenham*, to visit St 143 *Edmund's Bury*, a Town of which other Writers have talk'd very largely, and perhaps a little too much: It is a Town fam'd for its pleasant Situation and wholsome Air, the *Montpelier* of *Suffolk*, and perhaps of *England*; this must be attributed to the Skill of the Monks of those Times, who chose so beautiful a Situation for the Seat of their Retirement; and who built here the greatest and in its time, the most flourishing Monastery in all these Parts of *England*, I mean the Monastery of St *Edmund* the Martyr: It was, if we believe Antiquity, a House of Pleasure in more antient Times; or to speak more properly, a Court of Some of the *Saxon* or *East-Angle* Kings; and, as Mr *Camden* says, was even then call'd *a Royal Village*; tho' it much better merits that Name now; it being the Town of all this Part of *England*, in proportion to its bigness, most thronged with Gentry, People of the best Fashion, and the most polite Conversation: This Beauty and healthiness of its Situation, was no doubt the Occasion which drew the Clergy to settle here, for they always chose the best Places in the Country to build in, either for richness of Soil, or for Health and Pleasure in the Situation of their religious Houses.

Daniel Defoe, 1724

Colchester under the Commonwealth, seen by a critical observer with Royalist sympathies.

The next day to *Colchester*, a faire Towne but now wretchedly demolished   144
by the late Siege; espe[c]ially the suburbs all burnt & then repairing: The
Towne is built on a rising, having faire meadows on one side, & a river,
with a strong antient Castle, said to have ben built by *K. Coilus* father of
Helena mother of *Constantine* the *Greate* of whom I find no memory, save
at the pinacle of one of their Woolstaple houses, where *Coilus* has a statue
of wood wretchedly carvd: The walles are exceeding strong, deeply
trenched & fill'd with Earth. It has 6 gates & some Watch toures; & some
handsome Churches; but what was shew'd us as a kind of miracle, at the
outside of the Castle, the Wall where (Sir *Charles Lucas & Sir Geo: Lisle*
those valiant persons who so bravely behav'd themselves in the late
siege, & were barbarously shot to death & murdered by *Ireton* in cold
blood & after rendission upon articles) the place was bare of grasse for a
large space, all the rest of it abounding with herbage: For the rest, this is a
raged, factious Towne, & now Swarming with Sectaries.

John Evelyn, 1656

Lynn, as approached from the Ouse; Belloc had arrived at this point after walking many miles along the shore line.

You can see the past effect of ownership and individuality in Lynn as   145
clearly as you can catch affection or menace in a human voice. The
outward expression is most manifest, and to pass in and out along the
lanes in front of the old houses inspires in one precisely those emotions
which are aroused by a human crowd.

All the roofs of Lynn and all its pavements are worthy (as though
they were living beings) of individual names.

Along the river shore, from the race of the ebb that had so nearly
drowned me many years before, I watched the walls that mark the edge
of the town against the Ouse, and especially that group towards which
the ferry-boat was struggling against the eddy and tumble of the tide.

They were walls of every age, not high, brick of a dozen
harmonious tones, with the accidents, corners, and breaches of perhaps
seven hundred years. Beyond, to the left, down the river, stood the masts
in the new docks that were built to preserve the trade of this difficult port.
Up-river, great new works of I know not what kind stood like a bastion
against the plain; and in between ran these oldest bits of Lynn,
somnolescent and refreshing – permanent.

The lanes up from the Ouse when I landed I found to be of a slow
and natural growth, with that slight bend to them that comes, I believe,
from the drying of fishing-nets. For it is said that courts of this kind grew
up in our sea-towns all round our eastern and the southern coast in such
a manner.

Hilaire Belloc, 1906

Thetford, with its intimations of former glory, as seen by a contemplative.

When erst in youth's gay prime and uncontrolled   146
O Thetford! round thy flow'ry fields I've strolled,
From Tutt-Hill's eminence and Croxton's height,
Have view'd thine ancient ruins with delight,
Thy sloping hills and wooded vallies gay,
Whose silv'ry Ouse meand'ring winds his way.
Though then, each lofty mound, each ruin'd tower,
Told but of war, and time's destructive power;
And thou, thy pristine grandeur long had'st lost,
Nor more of Kings, or mighty chiefs could boast;
Yet heartfelt joys beneath thy roots I found,
And peace, with all the social blessings crown'd.

George Bloomfield, 1821

Towns and cities, like all human institutions, have their natural lives; and, as a town, Dunwich is dead, overwhelmed by the gradual encroachment of the sea.

This town is a testimony of the decay of public things; things of the most   147
durable nature, and as the old poet expresses it:

By numerous examples we may see
That towns and cities die, as well as we.

The ruins of *Carthage*, of the great city of *Jerusalem*, or of ancient *Rome*, are not at all wonderful to me; the ruins of *Nineveh*, which are so entirely sunk as that it is doubtful where the city stood; the ruins of *Babylon* or the great Persepolis, and many capital cities, which time and the change of monarchies have overthrown; these, I say, are not at all wonderful, because being the capitals of great and flourishing kingdoms, where those kingdoms were overthrown, the capital cities necessarily fell with them; but for a private town, a sea-port and a town of commerce, to decay as it were of itself (for we never read of *Dunwich* being plundered or ruined by any disaster, at least not of late years); this I must confess seems owing to nothing but to the fate of things, by which we see that towns, kings, countries, families and persons have all their elevation, their medium, their declination and even their destruction in the womb of time and the course of nature. It is true this town is manifestly decayed by the invasion of the waters, and as other towns seem sufferers by the sea, or the tide withdrawing from their ports, such as *Orford* just now named, *Winchelsea* in *Kent*, and the like, so this town is, as it were, eaten up by the sea, as above, and the still encroaching ocean seems to threaten it with a fatal immersion in a few years more.

Daniel Defoe, 1724

Dead and buried is the former provincial capital of Imperial Rome, Venta Icenorum (south of Norwich, by Caistor St Edmund). Wyndham Ketton-Cremer was the owner of Felbrigg, and a distinguished biographer and local historian.

Nevertheless, three hundred years of continuous occupation have left   148
their memory, their intangible but most definite impress, upon these acres. All over the field, stirred to and fro for centuries by the plough, lie sherds and fragments of Roman Britain. Brick and tile, amphora and dish and wine-cup, kitchen-ware of coarse grey and black, elegant Samian vessels of polished sealing-wax red, their remnants are everywhere. The rim of a Samian bowl will shine from the depression where a partridge has been dusting. A great segment of a quern, worn down by ages of use, will lie among the gnarled thorn-roots of the surrounding hedge. There are oyster-shells innumerable, mostly shells of those big coarse oysters from the beds off Burnham and Brancaster, which have been eaten and enjoyed all through Norfolk history. And on a memorable day I picked up a cornelian intaglio, deeply cut with a Roman galley being rowed towards a lighthouse, a *pharos* with its streaming flame, once set in a ring worn by someone at Venta Icenorum nearly two thousand years ago.

The living soil has been replaced above the excavations, and the remains of temples and houses are far below the surface, 'ashes under Uricon'. May it always be so. Further diggings will no doubt be undertaken in years to come, and deeply interesting they will prove; but may the poor foundations never lie permanently exposed, with barbed-wire fencing, and little informative notice-boards, and fragments of mosaic pavement under dilapidated wooden sheds. For the whole expanse, so calm and so beautiful under the changing Norfolk skies, is symbolic of the continuity of English life. In spring the Roman sherds gleam amongst the rows of sprouting barley. In autumn the huge combine-harvester throbs above the lines of the ancient streets. There is always a cawing of rooks in the distance, and the calling of partridges, and larks singing overhead, as there must have been in the days of the Iceni; and somewhere a tractor, and usually an aeroplane, the characteristic sounds of our own age. Snipe drum above the stream in the meadows beyond; and the wind strains, day after day, across the grassy banks of the town which is only a great square field.

R. W. Ketton-Cremer, 1957

Villages can hold romance even in their names, as these in Norfolk. For the benefit of outsiders I should explain that Wymondham has traditionally been pronounced 'Wyndham', and Poringland 'Porland', Happisburgh 'Hazeborough' and Costessey 'Cossy'.

So Earlham was a liberal education, it is evident, at all hours of the day;   149
here am I receiving after tea, most unconsciously, a lesson in the moral and social geography of our packed little island. And I don't know that anything counted for more in it than the appealing romance of the Norfolk names, which stole into the mind and coiled about the fancy

with their clear and liquid syllables. Words like Hindringham, Walsingham, Burlingham, fell with a strain of rippling melody that echoed out of serene sky-spaces, shining reedy meres – if only it were possible to waylay these haunting intimations in plain prose. I never forget the little shock of delight with which I once heard our grand-mother casually mention a name in which this clean euphony is roused to positive excitement. Here it is – Wramplingham! – and to say all, I think it a name that should be set to music by Schubert. And then in another vein there is the erratic host of names that in speech have slipped the anchorage of their spelling – Wymondham, Happisburgh, Costessey, Poringland – names that we utter with a bland indifference (full of distinction, I felt) to the laws of the alphabet. If you pronounce them as they are spelt, I regard you with a glance of superiority, infinitely provoking. Merely to say 'Hazeborough', to say 'Cossey' – let these suffice – gives me a fine sense of community with an ancient province, the kingdom of the easterlings.

Percy Lubbock, 1922

Essex village names also have romance.

If you have not yet discovered Stambourne, let your ear attend to the   150
sounds of names more familiar to fame. Do you not know Toppesfield and Wethersfield, and Finchingfield and Bardfield? Are all these villages fresh fields to you? Are you so obscure as not to have heard of Sturmer and Helions Bumpstead? Must we give you up? We certainly shall if the august name of Steeple Bumpstead has never bumped against your memory. Hempstead we will not insist upon, though Dick Turpin was born there; for there seems to have been a Hempstead everywhere in days when hemp was the great vindicator of justice, and stood the magistrate in such excellent stead; when men would not be converted by the stocks, nor be sanctified by being whipped at the cart-tail. Harvey, the great Harvey, sleeps in pieces in the church of the aforenamed Hempstead; but it may be that your blood has circulated for years without your knowing who first discovered the fact. But then, you have a cousin living at Great Yeldham! Have you not? Surely, Yeldham Great Oak must have been one of the visions of your youth, and it must abide among the memories of your riper years. No? Not know Great Yeldham? Go to! Prisoner in some vast furnace of smoke, which is called a city, what knowest thou of the freshest, greenest, purest things which yet linger under the sun?

C. H. Spurgeon, 1892

The idyllic village scene, as set in a real village in high Suffolk. This passage is an early and effective counterblast to the cult of romanticism in nature.

The village of Polstead, with its surrounding scenery, is a sweet relief   151 from the sameness of the busy towns; a retired and delightful spot, breathing the true freshness of rusticity. The inhabitants are laborious, but there are no vestiges of want about them: if money be scarce among them, their necessities are but few; their industry produces competence, and perhaps, in possessing that, the inhabitants of Polstead may account themselves truly rich.

The scenery all around bears the general character of Suffolk scenery, and has few attractions for those who make *tours* in search of the bold and sublime. It has nothing of the gigantic features of primitive nature, such as we behold it in the northern parts of Scotland and Wales, or in the Alpine regions of Switzerland – none of that diversity, which ever and anon astonishes us by some unexpected spectacle. The traveller is not surprised and terrified by immense rocks, which appear to hang in ruins over his head; nor inundated by the sparkling mists which are scattered from lofty and resounding waterfalls: not suddenly stopped at the edge of a precipice, by the view of an abyss formed by an everlasting torrent below, on the depths of which he scarcely dares to look down; nor does he suddenly escape from such astounding scenes, to lose himself in the obscurity of a tufted wood, or the labyrinths of some verdant but uncultivated wilderness. There is nothing of all this; but there is what the lover of English scenery would delight in: – the hill and vale, picturesquely spread with fertile fields and luxuriant foliage – the rippling stream, by-road, and green lane – the farm-house and the cottage – the pointed spire, peering up from the thick bowers of beech and elm – of flowing horse-chestnut, larch, and sycamore; – while the tinkling bell of the flocks, the whistle of the passing peasant boy, and the song of the lark above, shall there be found to give life to the scene.

The village, when we saw it, contained about twenty houses which clustered together on the gentle slope of a hill, the top of which spread into a pleasant green, on which was situated a neat public house (the only one in the village); and here the neighbours occasionally met at fair or dance, – the old to chat of days gone by, the young for purposes more congenial to their years. At the bottom of the hill was a bright sheet of water, at one side of which passed the road; and rising from the other side, the pathway to the village church and church yard, – the walls and grave-stones of which latter mentioned, could be seen by the passenger through wide-spreading and majestic trees: waving over the water, were several willows; and the road, winding out from a thick grove at one side, passed down into a hollow covered with branches, and at the depth of which were to be seen two or three cottages, from which ascended their chimney-smoke to be lost in the clear air.

William Maginn, 1831

The nearly idyllic, as in an imaginary village in fenland.

It was a quaint, dull and dreamy place, old-fashioned, moving slowly and   152 lazily along in its dull prosaic round of duties. A canal, flanked with reed beds and bulrushes, among which water-hens built their nests and fish made their hiding-places, flowed through the centre of the village, whilst on its glassy surface, lighters laden with produce, coal or gravel, were punted along or drawn by horses from the towpath alongside. On either side, in the most irregular fashion stood the quaintest and oddest jumble of cottages, with thatched roofs, which kept their inmates snug and warm in winter and cool in summer, while oak beams and latticed windows betrayed their ancient origin. These old dwellings jutted out, shrunk back or even leaned against one another as if they were on friendly terms and were trying to hold one another up as long as possible. Intruding among these antiquated, but, nevertheless, picturesque cottages, overgrown with climbers and blooming plants, were some modern red-bricked and box-like houses built for use rather than for ornament, and with little regard for any other consideration than cheapness. Towering above the dwellings was the fine old church, with spire pointing the people upwards and lifting up their thoughts from the level expanse surrounding them to the higher ambitions of life. The edifice was the pride of the village, built centuries ago, when workmen vied with one another in beautifying the sacred buildings that were erected with so much skill under the direction of the monks of the neighbouring monasteries. Each period, with its distinctive features, told its own story and archaeologists compiled from its walls and arches, 'sermons in stones', which spoke of the vicissitudes of past generations, and their floods, fires or destructive periods. One could not help wondering if such spacious buildings could ever have been filled with worshippers, for in these Fen villages, many of these churches seem to be all but empty and on Sundays the clergyman's voice may often be heard echoing among the pillars to the small, scattered flock to whom his exhortations are addressed.

Frederic Gardiner, 1908

Beccles on a mad March day.

The March wind is hurrying the river to the sea; it is hurrying Suffolk 153 dust down the street and over the bridge into Norfolk. A cottage that was so derelict that nobody would bid for it, stands opposite Sir Alexander's Queen Anne mansion. It was the custom, before the nation's life had drained to London, for great families to move into little towns for winter quarters. That cottage was bought by the builder whose yard of ivy-covered buildings is like a bit of old Italy, backed by the river. He did it up, and then lots of people wanted it. It only needed an eye for its possibilities. Now it is neat as a new pin, with one over-peering dormer, which leans out as if enjoying the entertainment of 'Who goes by?' There is the musician, carrying his trumpet under his coat like an attack of indigestion, because it is raining. Then Mrs D——, plump in sunshine. A hairy great-granny – no, it is Mrs K.'s old dog, done up in a shawl, that she wheels in a bath chair.

Today, clouds are racing, puddles winking, scarves streaming, swinging signs groaning out their music in many painful keys. 'Fresh!'

people cry, bearing newly bought pot plants and wrestling with the wind for their tissue wrapping. The wind wins. The wind is the litter lout. Chimney cowls turn briskly, like turbines wasting power. Starlings chuckle and catcall, strung out along TV aerials. But the thrush, civilized bird, prefers the weeping elm that stands before the Quaker Meeting House. He sings there unbelievably loud. I stop, and miss the post (which is next door but two) listening to him.

Adrian Bell, 1964

Most villages were simply the centres of farming communities; they provided a full range of services, including carpentry.

Mendham street was like many another. There were groups of old 154 houses, some thatched, a blacksmith's shop in the middle. At the lower, western end a separate cluster of cottages stood on the south of the churchyard, where a pathway led across meadows to Withersdale and Metfield. The eastern, or top end of the street was a four cross-ways. Straight on led to the parishes of the Saints; the right to Metfield, Fressingfield and High Suffolk. The road to the left went by the carpenter's yard and shop and more cottages, the school and the vicarage, among shrubberies and trees, on rising ground to the right.

Just past the vicarage garden was the Glebe Farm, with its talkative occupant, Richmond Emmerson, known as Richmer. He was lame from soldiering. He had piercing eyes, a wide, clean-shaven mouth and grey side-whiskers, and he wore a black-and-white check scarf, a black, wideawake hat and sleeve waistcoat. I draw a picture of him because we always passed the Glebe Farm on our walks of long ago, and never without seeing Mr or Mrs Emmerson – a quiet, humble housewife, a second fiddle to the great Richmer.

The house was on the corner, where the road to our home turned sharp to the left – for me a corner full of history. At this spot my father had his memorable spill when the grey came past the house at full gallop with only the broken shafts at her sides.

The carpenter's shop and yard which I have mentioned is more than a landmark; it is a promontory, a mountain on my horizon. Its owner, Fairhead, had been in our lives, I might say, since we could first see or hear. If a rat died under the floors of the house and began to smell, Fairhead appeared, and like a terrier, marked the spot, took up the boards, and discovered it. He or his men were always doing repairs to the premises, either in the yards, house, mill or cottages. We loved seeing them about, their tool-bags spread on the floor, full of chisels, planes and foot-rules, screws and nails; and many petty thefts I made from those straw-plaited bags with handles when I wanted nails. Why I ever should have loved the sight of shavings and sawdust I can't imagine, but I did; and wherever the carpenters were at work there would I be.

Alfred Munnings, 1950

But in several of the larger villages towards the east coast there developed, in the
fifteenth century, a most remarkable system of cottage industry.

It had never been an easy industry to organize on a gild basis, because the   155
making of a piece of cloth entailed so many distinct processes. The
preliminary processes of spinning and carding were always by-
industries, performed by women and children in their cottages; but the
weavers, who bought the spun yarn, had their gild; and so had the
fullers, who fulled it; and the shearmen, who finished it; and the dyers,
who dyed it. All could not sell the finished piece of cloth, and in the group
of inter-dependent crafts, each with its gild, we sometimes find the
weavers employing the fullers and sometimes the fullers the weavers.
Moreover, since weaving is a much quicker process than spinning, the
weaver often wasted much time and found it hard to collect enough yarn
to keep his loom busy; and, as the market for cloth grew wider and was
no longer confined to the town of the weaver, the need was felt for some
middleman to specialize in the selling of the finished cloth. So by degrees
there grew up a class of men who bought wool in large quantities and
sold it to the weavers, and then by a natural transition began, not to sell
the wool outright, but to deliver it to the weavers to weave, to the fullers
to full, and to the shearmen to finish at a wage, receiving it back again
when the work was done. These men grew rich; they amassed capital;
they could set many folk at work. Soon they began to set to work all the
different workers who combined to make a piece of cloth; their servants
carried wool to the cottages for the women to card and spin; carried the
spun yarn in turn to dyers, weavers, fullers, shearers; and carried the
finished piece of cloth back to the industrial middleman – the clothier, as
he was called – who in his turn disposed of it to the mercantile
middleman, who was called a draper. The clothiers grew rapidly in
wealth and importance, and in certain parts of the country became the
backbone of the middle class. They pursued their activities in country
villages, rather than in the old corporate towns, for they wished to avoid
the restrictions of the gilds, and gradually the cloth industry migrated
almost entirely to the country. In the west of England and in East Anglia
(though not in Yorkshire) it was carried out by clothiers on this 'putting
out' system, right up to the moment when the Industrial Revolution
swept it out of the cottages into the factories and out of the south into the
north. Then the thriving villages emptied themselves, so that to-day we
must needs re-create again from scattered traces and old buildings, and
still older names, the once familiar figures of the East Anglian clothier
and his swarm of busy workmen.

Eileen Power, 1924

This cloth trade brought exceptional prosperity to towns and villages.

Another large benefitt wherewith this County is furnished is the   156
excellent commoditie of clothing, which of long time hath here
flourished, enriching the Country and bringing there vnto nott a little

praise and commendation. Now as the numbers of this trade are many, so are there clothes distributed into severall kinds, both for size, proportion culler and mixture all which being wrought and made up, are vented by the marchant into all parts of the world. Jt is observed that these artificers doe sett many poore persons a-worke which other wise knew nott how to live, especially of the women kind, whereof whole villages and townes, doe live and maintaine themselves by spinning, that know nott else what to doe to gett their living, in this trade it is reckoned that hee which maketh ordinaryly 20 broad cloathes every weeke, cannott sett so few a-worke as 500 persons, for by that time his wool is come home, and is sorted, saymed, what with breakers, dyers, wood setters, wringers, spinners, weavers, burlers, Sheermen, and carriers, besides his owne large family, the number will soon bee accomplished, some there bee that weekly sett more a-worke, butt of this number there are nott many, yett every for his rate, as his stock, creditt, knowledge, and diligence will serve, by reason whereof it is commonly observed that the country where these clothiers are seated, is better peopled and more inriched, then other parts where noe clothing is occupied.

Robert Reyce, 1618

Today the social and economic cohesion of the village has vanished irrevocably: that at any rate is the conclusion of this prominent social historian after his searching analysis of Foxton.

Yes, the opportunities for 'getting together' are there, and a lot of people   157
do get together for an hour or two from time to time to meet their fellow villagers and share an activity or interest. There is undoubtedly a 'social spirit' alive in the village, though perhaps less alive than it was in the days when everybody knew everybody else, and when one of the chief social pleasures lay in knowing and discussing everybody else's business, not necessarily in an uncharitable spirit. With the newcomers now far outnumbering the 'natives', this traditional feature of village life has gone, perhaps for ever, and it is only natural that the natives should feel a certain resentment at being deprived of what had seemed an established right. To offset this, however, there is the recognition that it is the newcomers who as often as not supply the driving-force in the village organisations. Not everybody is able, not everybody wants to take part in the activities of all or any of these organisations. Indeed the majority of people today seem just to want freedom to live their own lives in their own way, freedom to opt out if they choose to do so, freedom to join in if they feel like it, and the village is the ideal place for that. There is no longer any compulsion or restriction. True, our lives are subjected to more compulsions and restrictions than ever before – taxation, insurance, rates, regulations, stamps, forms, quotas, permits, etc., etc. – but they are all at national or regional level. I cannot think of one at village level.

For that reason alone I have doubts about the existence of a community spirit. It is an elusive and complicated thing. The more one thinks about it, the more elusive and complicated it seems, though I am fairly clear in my mind on two points: firstly that a community spirit cannot exist without real community of interest; secondly that it cannot manifest itself except under compulsion.

Rowland Parker, 1975

The churches are the marvels of East Anglia in general, and of Norfolk in particular.

Some are miracles of soaring lightness with wooden angels in their high   158
up roofs: some have painted screens, or Georgian box pews, or medieval carved bench ends or ancient stained glass. Each is different from its neighbour, even if it is less than a mile off or in the same churchyard. None is without a treasure of some sort in wood, stone, iron, tile or glass. Some are famous throughout Britain. Lovers of the Norfolk churches can never agree which is the best. I have heard it said that you are either a Salle man or a Cawston man. Others say that Walpole St Peter bears the palm.

Norfolk would not be Norfolk without a church tower on the horizon or round a corner up the lane. We cannot spare a single Norfolk church. When a church has been pulled down the country seems empty or is like a necklace with a jewel missing. Every Norfolk church that is left standing today, however dim, neglected and forgotten it looks, is loved by someone or it would have disappeared long ago.

Norfolk is a faithful county to have kept so many of its churches standing through the centuries. Like St Mary Magdalene, it has not suggested selling its precious gift to give to the poor, but has known the true value of witness to the faith. God save the Norfolk parish churches.

John Betjeman, 1972

Before the days of pylons, masts and other modern structures, church towers provided the main verticals in a horizontal landscape. John Kirby was a native of Wickham Market; his interesting assertion about the view presumably relates to the top of the steeple rather than of the tower.

WICKHAM-*Market*, seems now to be only called so to distinguish it from   159
Wickham-Brook and *Wickham-Skeith*; but it had a Market formerly, tho' it has been long disused. The Quarter-Sessions were formerly held there, where there was a Shire-Hall for that Purpose; but it was removed by Order of the Lord of the Manor, and a Farm-house therewith built at *Letheringham*, called the *Old Hall*. The Church and Spire-steeple are situated upon a Hill; and tho' the Steeple be not above Twenty-three Yards high: It affords the best Prospect of any in the County; and in a clear Day you may easily view from thence very near, if not altogether, Fifty Churches.

John Kirby, 1735

Some form of aesthetic appreciation is clearly desirable when visiting an old church, though few will attempt to indulge in fantasies of self-petrifaction when viewing, for instance, the west window at Snettisham (disguised by Leslie Hartley as 'Frontisham').

'Tucked away in this little-known corner of Norfolk,' the guide-book   160
said, 'is a treasure of the mediaeval mason's art that lovers of architecture come miles to see: the west window of Frontisham Parish Church. Inferior in mere size to the west window of York Minster and the east window of Carlisle Cathedral, the window at Frontisham easily surpasses them in beauty, vigour, and originality. It is unquestionably the finest example of flamboyant tracery in the kingdom; confronted with this masterpiece, criticism is silent.'

Eustace knew the passage by heart; he found it extremely moving and often said it over to himself. He did not share the guide-book's poor opinion of mere size: magnitude in any form appealed to him, and he wished that this kind of superiority, too, could have been claimed for Frontisham. But the book, which could not err, called the window the finest in the kingdom. That meant it was the best, the greatest, the grandest, the *ne plus ultra* of windows: the supreme window of the world. Eustace gazed at it in awe. It had entered for the architectural prize, and won; now it looked out upon the centuries, victorious, unchallenged, incomparable, a standard of absolute perfection to which all the homage due to merit naturally belonged.

It was not the window itself which fascinated him so much as the idea of its pre-eminence, just as it was not the guide-book's actual words (many of which he did not properly understand) that intoxicated him, so much as the tremendous, unqualified sense of eulogy they conveyed. He tried again, again not quite successfully, to see how the window differed from other church windows. But he could not see it through his own eyes, because he had so often visualised it through the eyes of the guide-book, nor could he describe it in his own words, because the author's eloquence came between him and his impressions. Feeling meant more to him than seeing, and the phrases of the panegyric, running like a tune in his mind, quickly started a train of feeling that impeded independent judgment.

Within the massive framework of the grey wall seven slender tapers of stone soared upwards. After that, it was as though the tapers had been lit and two people, standing one on either side, had blown the flames together. Curving, straining, interlocked, they flung themselves against the retaining arch in an ecstasy – or should we say an agony? – of petrifaction. But the builder had not been content with that. Higher still, in the gable above, was another window much smaller and with tracery much less involved, but similar in general effect. 'An echo,' the guide-book called it, 'an earthly echo of a symphony which was made in heaven'.

The word 'heaven', striking against his inner ear, released Eustace's visual eye from dwelling on the material structure of the mediaeval mason's masterpiece. The design with all its intricacy faded from his sight, to be replaced, in his mind's eye, by the window's abstract qualities, its beauty, its vigour, its originality, its pre-eminence, its perfection. With these, and not for the first time, he now began to feel at one. Disengaging himself from the tea-table he floated upwards. Out shot his left arm, caught by some force and twisted this way and that; he could feel his fingers, treble-jointed and unnaturally long, scraping against the masonry of the arch as they groped for the positions that had been assigned to them. Almost simultaneously his other limbs followed suit; even his hair, now long like Hilda's, rose from his head and, swaying like seaweed, strove up to reach the keystone. Splayed, spread-eagled, crucified (but for fear of blasphemy he must only think the shadow of that word) into a semblance of the writhing stonework, he seemed to be experiencing the ecstasy – or was it the agony? – of petrifaction.

Meanwhile the interstices, the spaces where he was not, began to fill with stained glass. Pictures of saints and angels, red, blue, and yellow, pressed against and into him, bruising him, cutting him, spilling their colours over him. The pain was exquisite, but there was rapture in it too. Another twitch, a final wriggle, and Eustace felt no more; he was immobilised, turned to stone. High and lifted up, he looked down from the church wall, perfect, pre-eminent, beyond criticism, not to be asked questions or to answer them, not to be added to or taken away from, but simply to be admired and worshipped by hundreds of visitors, many of them foreigners from Rome and elsewhere, coming miles to see him . . . Eustace, Eustace of Frontisham, Saint Eustace . . .

Eustace . . . the word seemed to be all round him.

'Eustace! Eustace!' His father's voice was raised in pretended indignation. 'Stop day-dreaming! We want some more tea! You've forgotten to ring the bell!'

L. P. Hartley, 1944

Appreciation of church architecture occurs more readily when attending a service. The roof of Dorothy Sayers' 'Fenchurch St Paul' was inspired by that of Upwell St Peter.

'Dearly beloved brethren – '   161

Wimsey scrambled to his feet and looked round.

At the first glance he felt himself sobered and awe-stricken by the noble proportions of the church, in whose vast spaces the congregation – though a good one for so small a parish in the dead of a winter's night – seemed almost lost. The wide nave and shadowy aisles, the lofty span of the chancel arch – crossed, though not obscured, by the delicate fan-tracery and crenellated moulding of the screen – the intimate and cloistered loveliness of the chancel, with its pointed arcading, graceful ribbed vault and five narrow east lancets, led his attention on and focused it first upon the remote glow of the sanctuary. Then his gaze, returning to the nave, followed the strong yet slender shafting that sprang fountain-like from floor to foliated column-head, spraying into the light, wide arches that carried the clerestory. And there, mounting to the steep pitch of the roof, his eyes were held entranced with wonder and delight. Incredibly aloof, flinging back the light in a dusky shimmer of bright hair and gilded outspread wings, soared the ranked angels, cherubim and seraphim, choir over choir, from corbel and hammer-beam floating face to face uplifted.

'My God!' muttered Wimsey, not without reverence. And he softly repeated to himself: 'He rode upon the cherubims and did fly; He came flying upon the wings of the wind.'

Dorothy L. Sayers, 1934

A purely practical approach is all that many people achieve, like the cleaner in this fictional village.

Not many miles from the Ancient Borough and noble University of 162 Cambridge stands the old Rectory of Cherryumpton in the tree-strangled and lilac-lit hamlet of the name. A yew-shaded drive and a little rectangular apple-garth within a wall of rubrical plinths fill the rectorial acre. The better harvested acre of God adjoins one side of the wall, while the acres of the Trywilliam family lie behind wind-chopped elms on the other. The Rectory is only a bungled-looking bungalow, the brick and tiled patchwork of two centuries, compared to the Georgian Manor House and the restored Norman Church, whose cream-plastered tower shows in winter-time behind the grille of a million naked twigs and rides through the summer over their green billowy tops like a crenellated cardboard box at sea.

The straggly street of Cherryumpton never seemed equal or proportional to the solemn and stately Church, which resembled a high-hatted, much-arched Archdeacon wedded to some forlorn and rural little bride. All the week they might seem severally occupied, the large male Church untroubled and aloof, contemplative of next Sunday and of a thousand Sundays to come, while the wifelike hamlet was fussed and flurried about many things many times every day. On Sundays alone she sat quiet, or, at the voice of her booming husband, tripped into his bosom in adoring submission to his pompous will. And the next week was the next.

Nothing ever happened to the Church between Sundays save the irruption of the old female sexton Mrs Judbud, who dusted on Saturdays, pew-opened on Sundays, and wiped up on Mondays.

There was a curious contrast between the line of soaring pillars, the chamfered mouldings and floriated stone traceries, and the mean pews, cheap hassocks, Carpenter's Gothic pulpit, and low unlighted trestle of an altar. The Church was like the finely proportioned crumbling white skeleton of a giant tied up with a few shabby ribands. Dead white and gaping were the window eyes. The necklike chancel was separated from the ribbed nave by the six painted stumps of an old rood screen, which a saw had neatly reformed from garish idolatry in the sixteenth century. The chancel was glazed with white diamond panes except for the middle light of the East fenestry, which was like a crazy quilt of many-coloured fragments, an *omnium gatherum* of mediaeval reds and blues, cobalts and chlorines, old golds and dingy yellows like the cells in a painter's mind. Antiquarians sometimes sorted the pudding: here a decapitated seraph or an angel with the angles hacked off, or the benedictional hand of Thomas à Becket, a cutting of yellow hair from Judas, with a half ALLELUIA and a chip of ANGELUS stained in broad black Gothic letter. Through the splayed windows in the tower and the neat perpendicular lights of the nave, through quarries of dusty crystal streamed rays as pure and colourless as the doctrines taught on Sundays. In spite of Puritan and iconoclast, the old Parish Church kept a few time-worn Catholic heirlooms like a Prima Donna who has known better days and treasures some unpawned jewel in the twilight of exile, for the country churches of England contain a choice collection of the ritual growth of ages — screens and chalices, carved roofs and aumbrys, painted tombs and wrought imagery; but so singly and infrequently that each relic has fallen into the position of a parish curiosity. The Church of England, the *Ecclesia Anglicana*, is indeed like unto a Bride once kept by the King of Heaven, that has since been cast into the almshouse of the State.

The pride of Cherryumpton was the brass tomb of a superb Crusader, who had survived the gun-smelting Parliamentarians as well as the chisels of Gothic restorers. With grimmest grin and legs crossed he flatly defied the weekly washing administered by Mrs Judbud as well as the tracing-papers of those enthusiasts who spend their holidays taking black and yellow rubbings from mediaeval Church brasses. By charging half a crown per rub, successive rectors made the Crusader pay half Mrs Judbud's salary. Sir Roger de Cherryumpton had survived fame and defame, and across the centuries he inspired a legendary chivalry and wonder, almost a godlike sentiment. Local saint or god he would have been, had not all gods been killed in England and gone with the good ballads and the Great Bustards. But the pious soul of Mrs Judbud venerated him, and there was tenderness in the way she polished and dried the cuts and crevices in the brass. She might have been scrubbing the Almighty's buttons.

Shane Leslie, 1926

The pub has for long been the centre of village social life, as this at Weston Colville. James Withers was the local poet.

Just down the road beside the bowling green   163
The weather-beaten sign-post still is seen;
No artist's labour could the host afford,
But three hot horse-shoes branded on the board,
Here once a-year at what was called the fair,
Though horse was never bought nor cow sold there,
Here met the village youths on pleasure bent,
And the long-hoarded halfpence freely spent:
The stalls were doors placed on a barrel's head,
With cakes, and sweets, and penny whistles spread.
In the old parlour was the rustic ball,

Shone on by candles stuck against the wall;
And on the green was seen the crowded ring,
Where wrestlers tugged, each tried his man to fling;
And youth feels proud when age his skill approves,
Pleased by sore legs to win a pair of gloves.
In the old kitchen by the chimney wide,
With foaming ale in good stone mugs supplied,
The old folks talked of times when they were young,
And the same songs, year after year, were sung:
'Lord Bateman', 'Spanking Jack', and 'Black-eyed-Sue',
'Will Watch', and 'Crazy Jane', and 'Bonnets o'Blue'.
'Twas here the jolly hostess sat and smiled,
Whilst on the ample grate the logs were piled:
Here was the roasting jack with wheels and weights,
And on the dresser shone the pewter plates.

James Withers, 1856

Larger than the pubs, the coaching inns were important enterprises; Scole was strategically situated halfway between Ipswich and Norwich. Francis Blomefield produced the most exhaustive of the early histories of Norfolk.

Here are two very good inns for the entertainment of travellers; the *White*   164
Hart is much noted in these parts, being called, by way of distinction, *Scole Inn*; the house is a large brick building, adorned with imagery and carved work in several places, as big as the life. It was built in 1655, by *John Peck*, Esq. whose arms, impaling his wife's, are over the porch door. The sign is very large, beautified all over with a great number of images of large stature carved in wood, and was the work of one *Fairchild*; the arms about it are those of the chief towns and gentlemen in the county, *viz.* *Norwich*, *Yarmouth*, Duke of *Norfolk*, Earl of *Yarmouth*, *Bacon* of *Garboldisham*, *Hobart*, *Cornwaleis* impaling *Bukton*, *Teye*, *Thurston*, *Castleton*, and many others. *Peck*'s arms are *arg.* on a chevron, ingrailed *gul.* three croslets pattee of the field; his wife's are *arg.* a fess between two crescents in chief, a lion rampant in base *gul.* which coat I think is born by the name of *Jetheston*. Here was lately a very large round bed, big enough to hold fifteen or twenty couple, in imitation (I suppose) of the remarkable great bed at *Ware*. The house was in all things accommodated, at first, for large business; but the road not supporting it, it is in much decay at present, though there is a good bowling-green and a pretty large garden, with land sufficient for passengers horses. The business of these two inns is much supported by the annual cock-matches that are here fought.

Francis Blomefield, 1736

Of the coaching inns within the cities, the Great White Horse at Ipswich was one of the largest: so large that Mr Pickwick lost his way in it, and entered someone else's room by mistake.

The more stairs Mr Pickwick went down, the more stairs there seemed to   165
be to descend, and again and again, when Mr Pickwick got into some
narrow passage, and began to congratulate himself on having gained the
ground-floor, did another flight of stairs appear before his astonished
eyes. At last he reached a stone hall, which he remembered to have seen
when he entered the house. Passage after passage did he explore; room
after room did he peep into; at length, just as he was on the point of
giving up the search in despair, he opened the door of the identical room
in which he had spent the evening, and beheld his missing property on
the table.

   Mr Pickwick seized the watch in triumph, and proceeded to retrace his steps to his bed-chamber. If his progress downwards had been
attended with difficulties and uncertainty, his journey back, was
infinitely more perplexing. Rows of doors, garnished with boots of every
shape, make, and size, branched off in every possible direction. A dozen
times did he softly turn the handle of some bed-room door, which
resembled his own, when a gruff cry from within of 'Who the devil's
that?' or 'What do you want here?' caused him to steal away on tiptoe,
with a perfectly marvellous celerity. He was reduced to the verge of
despair, when an open door attracted his attention. He peeped in – right
at last. There were the two beds, whose situation he perfectly remembered, and the fire still burning. His candle, not a long one when he first
received it, had flickered away in the drafts of air through which he had
passed, and sunk into the socket, just as he closed the door after him. 'No
matter,' said Mr Pickwick, 'I can undress myself just as well, by the light
of the fire.'

   Charles Dickens, 1837

Houses and Homes

Framlingham Castle was the principal stronghold of the Howard family (and their predecessors, the Mowbrays). It was from here that Mary Tudor raised her standard and achieved her succession to the throne.

Framlingham Castle was founded in the Saxon heptarchy by king Redwald, and remained a royal demesne till Henry I granted it to Earl Bigod, to whom the present structure is attributed. Subsequently it was given by Edward I to his second son, Thomas of Brotherton, and from him it descended to the Howards, the dukes of which race made it their principal residence. The site of the castle is a high mound, from which springs the source of the river Orr. This stream supplied the three moats, which are in the summer season gaily enamelled with golden irises. On the edge of the mound is reared a magnificent circle of walls and towers, enclosing an area of more than an acre. These walls remain to this day nearly entire; they are forty feet in height, and more than eight feet in thickness, and are studded with thirteen square towers. Within the area surrounded by these bulwarks once stood the baronial residence occupied by queen Mary; the fragments existing are small, yet the traces of the state apartments are, as it were, curiously mapped on the mighty walls which once sustained them. After crossing a walled causeway over the double moat, and passing through the gate-tower, the spectator enters the spacious area. To the right, nearly opposite, are seen several chimneys, whose summits are hollow pillars of wreathed brickwork, very elaborately wrought. The chimney of the state bedchamber, on the second floor, still remains; on one side of it is a recess about the size of a dressing room, with an arched window looking towards the east: this is declared by tradition to have been Mary's chamber, but it is evidently the oriel, or private oratory pertaining to her state chamber, which, of course, was the room to which the chimney belonged.

Agnes Strickland, 1842

Childerley Hall, where Charles I was held for some days by the Parliamentarian army in 1647.

I found myself in a place of incomparable beauty. It was a long terrace,   167
rather wild and neglected; below there were the traces of a great, derelict
garden, with thick clumps of box, the whole surrounded by a large
earthwork, covered with elms. To the left lay another pool; to the right,
at the end of the terrace, stood a small red-brick chapel, with a big
Perpendicular window. The house was to the left of us, in the centre of
the terrace, of old red brick, with tall chimneys and mullioned windows.
My friend the farmer chatted pleasantly about the house, but was
evidently prouder of his rose-trees and his chrysanthemums. The day
grew darker as we wandered, and a pleasant plodding and clinking of
horses coming home made itself heard in the yard. Then he asked me to
enter the house. What was my surprise when he led me into a large hall,
with painted panels and a painted ceiling, occupying all the centre of the
house. He told me a little of the history of the place, of a visit paid by
Charles the First, and other simple traditions, showing me all the time a
quiet, serious kindness, which reminded one of the entertainment given
to the wayfarers of the *Pilgrim's Progress.*

Once more we went out on the little terrace and looked round; the
night began to fall, and lights began to twinkle in the house, while the fire
glowed and darted in the hall.

But what I cannot, I am afraid, impart to you is the strange
tranquillity that came softly down into my mind; everything took its part
in this atmosphere of peace. The overgrown terrace, the mellow
brickwork, the bare trees, the tall house, the gentle kindliness of my host.
And then I seemed so far away from the world; there was nothing in sight
but the fallows and the woods, rounded with mist; it seemed at once the
only place in the world, and yet out of it. The old house stood patiently
waiting, serving its quiet ends, growing in beauty every year, seemingly
so unconscious of its grace and charm, and yet, as it were, glad to be
loved.

Arthur Christopher Benson, 1904

Of Jacobean houses, none can surpass Blickling.

The first sight of Blickling Hall is one of the greatest surprises that can   168
possibly befall the traveller in search of the picturesque. Every one, in
these days of broadcast photographs, is in some sort familiar with the
look of the Hall, and most people can tell you it looks like another, and a
better, Hatfield House; but no one is prepared on coming downhill past
the church into the village, to find the main front of this finest of
Jacobean mansions, this dream of architectural beauty, actually looking
upon the road, unobstructedly, from behind its velvet lawns. No
theatrical manager, no scene-painter, cunning in all the artful accessories of the stage, could devise anything more dramatic, and you –
Columbus of the roads, who steer into unwonted byways in search of the

beautiful – cannot repress the involuntary tribute of an admiratory O! at sight of it. There it stands, like some proud conscious beauty, isolated. No meaner building shoulders it, and for all the stir you see or sound you hear, it might be some enchanted palace, not waked to life and love.

Charles Harper, 1904

Before the days of the National Trust, it needed a carriage, fine clothes and a thick skin to gain access to Blickling.

In the morning, about ten we left Aylsham, and proceeded to Lord 169 Buckinghamshire's, which was not more than two miles distant. We were afraid of being too soon, but on sending in our names, were admitted. We found they had breakfasted, and my lord's horses stood at the door, though the servant told us he was gone out. We saw no other traces of her ladyship than two or three work bags, and a tambour. I believe we drove her from room to room, but that we could not help. We saw only the old part of the house, over which a very dirty housemaid, with a·duster in her hand, conducted us. The new wing is not finished, but, after all, I think there is nothing worth seeing in the house, except the library. No pictures, and the furniture all very bad, and, what is tolerable, not all adapted to the house; at least in my opinion, for I should never look for chinese papers, washing beds, window curtains and chairs, in an old gothic mansion. From the house we drove round the park, which certainly is fine, and the water good, if it was not so near the house. We went into a belvedere, which is built on rather a rising ground and commands a good prospect: Woolerton in particular looks well from it. There is a tea room intended, but it is not yet finished. My lord overtook us in our approach to it, made a thousand courtier-like speeches, but they were so little worth attending to, that they went in at one ear and out at 'tother. One thing, however, I could not help remarking: he said he was mortified beyond expression that he happened to be out when we came, and you know I have mentioned his horses being at the door when we went in. He might have spared his apologies to me, for I was much better pleased to survey his house by ourselves.

Letitia Beauchamp-Proctor, 1772

The park at Blickling; the metaphorical cloud detected by James Grigor relates to the execution of Anne Boleyn, whose family had once owned Blickling.

The park and pleasure-grounds on this estate are of noble dimensions, 170 comprising together about 1000 acres, richly diversified with old plantations, and containing an extensive lake, which is considered to be one of the finest in the kingdom. In some parts, this lake is beautifully encompassed with masses of beech and chestnut, which partly over-shadow it; in others, it is surrounded by open lawns, sloping to the water's edge; and in some instances, with clumps of young plantations, composed of chestnut, oak, and ash, which carry the sylvan scene to the recesses of the woods behind. The scenery of this spot on a summer's evening, abounding in all that nature and art can accomplish; its beautiful expanse of water; its aged trees, declining to the dust from which they sprung, and the rising of a new generation in their stead; its cattle upon their rightful hills; its fowls, aerial and aquatic, so happy in their existence; its lawn of living green, which environs and graces all, conspire to fill up a landscape of exceeding loveliness; and which, but for its association with a sad page in our history, which hangs around it like a cloud, would form perhaps one of the happiest pictures of English pleasure-ground scenery within our land.

James Grigor, 1841

Upkeep of a great house can be very trying, especially for impractical intellectuals. Horace Walpole was at this time a trustee for his nephew, the third Earl of Orford.

You know, Madam, I do not want a sufficient stock of family pride, yet   171 perhaps do not know, though I think it far from a beautiful place, how very fond I am of Houghton, as the object of my father's fondness. Judge then what I felt at finding it half a ruin, though the pictures, the glorious pictures, and furniture are in general admirably well preserved. All the rest is destruction and desolation! The two great staircases exposed to all weathers; every room in the wings rotting with wet; the ceiling of the gallery in danger; the chancel of the church unroofed; the water-house, built by Lord Pembroke, tumbling down; the garden a common; the park half covered with nettles and weeds; the walls and pales in ruin; perpetuities of livings at the very gates sold; the interest at Lynn gone; mortgages swallowing the estate, and a debt of above forty thousand pounds heaped on those of my father and brother. A crew of banditti were harboured in the house, stables, town and every adjacent tenement; and I have but too great reason to say that the outpensioners have committed as great spoil – much even since my nephew's misfortune. The high treasurer who paid this waste, and shared it, is a steward that can neither read nor write – This worthy prime minister I am forced to keep from particular circumstances – I mean if I continue in office myself – but though I have already done something, and have reduced an annual charge of near twelve hundred a year, the consequences of which I believe were as much more, I mean the waste made and occasioned by bad servants, dogs and horses, still I very much doubt whether I must not resign, from causes not proper for a letter.

In the shock and vexation of such a scene was I forced to act as if my mind was not only perfectly at ease, but as if I, who never understood one useful thing in my days, was master of every country business, and qualified to be a surveyor-general. Though you would have pitied my sensations, you would have smiled, Madam, I am sure, at my occupations, which lasted without interruption from nine every morning till twelve at night, except that, a few times, I stole from the steward and lawyers I carried with me, to peep at a room full of painters, who you and Lord Ossory will like to hear, are making drawings from the whole collection, which Boydell is going to engrave. Well, the morning was spent in visiting the kennels, in giving away pointers, greyhounds and foreign beasts, in writing down genealogies of horses – with all my heraldry I never thought to be the Anstis of Newmarket – in selling bullocks, sheep, Shetland horses, and all kind of stock – in hearing petitions and remonstrances of old servants, whom I pitied though three were drunk by the time I had breakfasted; in listening to advice on raising leases; in ordering repairs, sending two teams to Lynn for tiles; in limiting expense of coals, candles, soap, brushes, etc., and in forty other such details. About one or two arrived farmers to haggle on leases, and though I did not understand one word in a score that they uttered, I was forced to keep them to dinner, and literally had three, four, and five to dine with me six days of the eight that I stayed there – nor was I quit so, for their business literally lasted most days till eight or nine at night. They are not laconic, nor I intelligent; and the stupidity and knavery of the steward did their utmost to perplex me, and confound the map of the estate, every name in which he miscalled, as if he was interpreting to an Arabian ambassador. The three last hours of the night were employed in reducing and recording the transactions of the day, in looking over accounts, and methodizing debts, demands, and in drawing plans for future conduct – Oh! I am weary even with the recollection – is not your Ladyship with the recapitulation?

   Horace Walpole, 1773

Frederick Hervey, Earl of Bristol and Bishop of Derry, had firm opinions about Ickworth, his new building project in Suffolk, as he told his daughter in a letter from Naples.

You beg me on your knees that Ickworth house may be built of white   172
stone brick. You know, my dear, what Ranger says to his cousin, and upon my knees I beg you too. What, child, build my house of a *brick* that looks like sick, pale, *jaundiced* red brick that would be red if it could, and to which I am certain our posterity will give a little rouge as essential to its health and beauty? White brick always looks as if the bricklayers had not burnt it sufficiently, had been niggardly of the fuel; it looks all dough and no crust. I am ever looking out for its crust, so, my dear, I shall follow dear impeccable Palladio's rule, and as nothing ought to be without a covering in our raw damp climate, I shall cover the house, pillars, and pilasters with Palladio's *stucco*, which has now lasted 270 years.

   Frederick Augustus Hervey, 1796

Ickworth was built as a great house, rather than as a family home.

Above £40,000 was expended, and it would require much more than   173

forty more to finish it on the original plan, after which it would be
nearly uninhabitable. Lady Bristol used to call it a stupendous monu-
ment of folly; but the most extraordinary circumstance in relation to it
was, that he [the Earl] began it while he disliked the spot, from the
wetness of the soil, and would often tell me that he should never have
been such a fool as to build in so wet a situation. It was then generally
imagined that as he must inherit Rushbrooke he would wait till that
period, and if he built at all, would do it there. It was begun and carried
on till the time of his death without his ever having seen it; and he
often declared in letters that he would never set his foot in England till
it was finished and furnished with all the *vertu* that he had collected in
Italy. He never did set his foot in England again, for the shell of this
fantastic building, and that of its still more extraordinary possessor,
were finished at the same time, and my Lord left the whole, as if by
design, a burthen to his son and successor, with whom he had been on
the worst of terms, and from whom he gave away by will the very
furniture of the old habitable house at Ickworth.

   Arthur Young, 1820

*A foreigner was impressed by the cleanliness of Suffolk houses, except for the
cooking and eating habits, which were filthy.*

What always gives the most delight is the dominant impression of   174
cleanliness: the houses are washed very often, inside and out, which is
done, as a rule, on Saturdays. People go to great lengths to preserve all
this spruceness, with mats and carpets down everywhere, and strips of
moquette on the stairs: nowhere a speck of dust. All this amazed me
when I first saw it, and I did what I could to see whether this cleanliness is
natural to the English, and thus inherent in all they do, or whether it is
just for show, merely superficial, and I came to see clearly that it is a
matter of show: everything that is likely to be seen has this precious
quality, but they manage to overlook what you are not supposed to see.
To give an example, I will refer only to the kitchen, which when people
have any instinct for cleanliness should naturally be spotless. The worst
thing you could do would be to go into the kitchen before dinner: you
can't imagine the squalor. This is usually the work of women; they are
black as coal, their arms bare to the elbow or revoltingly filthy and, to
save time, they actually handle the pieces of meat. You may go into the
kitchen of the greatest nobleman and you will find perhaps ten women at
work, but I wager you will not see two napkins or dish-cloths; and if you
were to find one in use, you will not want to wipe your hands on it, for it
is used for everything.
   One thing that everyone observes is the way all the beer is drunk
out of the same glass, even when there are twenty at table. When you ask
for a drink, they top up the old dregs in the bottom of the glass, and you
have to drink or let it pass. This custom, dirty and sometimes disgusting,
is so time-honoured that it has become a matter of politeness, at a ball for
instance, to drink either punch or another drink after the lady has drunk,

from the same glass, to show that you are not averse to what she leaves. One can happily do it sometimes, but there are many ladies to whom I should not care to make this gesture of politeness.

François La Rochefoucauld, 1784 (translation, Norman Scarfe)

But the same observer found even the kitchen clean at Heveningham Hall, where everything delighted him – that is, once the ice had been broken with its owner, who had commissioned the new house seven years earlier.

We arrived at Sir Gerard Wanneck's house at nine in the morning and presented a letter from Mr Symonds. He received us very coldly and, keeping his hat on, asked us in. No notice need be taken of that kind of thing in England, the intention is good, the forms alone are lacking. We withdrew to put on our own hats, then we entered.

175

Sir Gerard's sister was at breakfast, we took tea with her, and the conversation became less frigid every moment. Sir Gerard talked a little, and we saw how well-disposed he was towards us and how his first greeting had given us quite the wrong idea of him. After breakfast we went over the house, which is superb and which I shall describe to you in some detail.

There was at one time a small, much older house, which was extremely run down, though its site was agreeable. Ten or twelve years ago, Sir Gerard had all the internal walls knocked down and made his hall (or vestibule) out of the shell: everything else has been added; and in truth, in the middle of the handsome modern building, one would not doubt that the old one is there. This hall is 72 feet by 24, with columns and great altitude. It is extremely noble, magnificent, all clad in the finest possible stucco, statues were lacking when I was there, but their provision will not be overlooked.

To the right of this superb room is the breakfast room, oblong, the finest proportions, large and hung with beautiful pictures; it is covered in a light blue paper, simple but elegant: the mantelpiece is of very well-carved white marble.

From this room we went into another, small, papered in blue and with prints pasted straight on it like pictures: a gay effect. It's a little room, but a pretty oval in shape. Here Sir Gerard dines when he's on his own. From here, we went through two other small rooms, then, turning back on our tracks, we crossed the hall and entered the dining-room.

I have never seen anything comparable with the perfect balance of the proportions of this room combined with the elegance of its decoration: its dimensions are thirty-two (feet) by twenty-four; three large windows distribute a powerful daylight. I should still think it impossible to contemplate a more beautiful room if we had not immediately entered the library, which wiped it at once from my sight. This room is the masterpiece of taste. Doubling [he means 'paired with the dining-room, at the back of the house'] is a saloon, not yet finished.

The bedrooms are large and convenient. They are designed generally with only the bedroom; in accordance with custom here, some of them have a little sitting-room. The private staircases are numerous and all the conveniences are to be found in this house. I even went to see the kitchen, which is very fine, cleanliness supreme, and running water on all sides. The one inconvenience of this house is that the vestibule is so tall that it cuts the house completely in two, so that one wing has no communication with the other.

The exterior matches the interior in magnificence. It is built in the classical taste; twenty-three window-bays form the front, the ground floor is without ornament, but the windows are round-arched: the first floor is adorned with columns, very grand and all of the same order: the bricks are white and painted deep grey, which looks pretty odd at close quarters but very well at a distance. The roof is flat, in the Italian way.

François La Rochefoucauld, 1784 (translation, Norman Scarfe)

Holkham was the ideal of a great house and the centre of a model estate, under the enlightened ownership of Thomas Coke ('Coke of Norfolk').

I have had another opportunity of visiting Holkham; I have again been gratified in seeing one of the first *places* in the kingdom, whose scenery, combining the different picturesque beauties of rich, varied, and highly decorated ground, of magnificent wood, expanded water, and extended prospect, including occasional views of the sea, cannot but delight every lover of nature, and more than meet the high raised expectations of the admiring stranger. But it has a character even surpassing the highest natural beauty; it has a moral character which leaves a more lasting and a more satisfactory impression, on the benevolent mind, than woods and waters, green fields, and the most highly decorated grounds. It exhibits man under his best features, and in his happiest state; it is the field of human industry, and it shews its rich reward; – talent and invention, – science and experiment, – the principles of mechanics, – the discoveries of chemistry, and the investigations of natural history, are all here applied to the promotion of the first and most important of human arts. The labors of agriculture are facilitated, its processes are improved, its valuable products greatly increased, and its various benefits widely extended. Society at large, – the proprietor of the soil, – the farmer who occupies and cultivates it, and the laborer and artisan who work upon it, all share in these benefits, – all partake of the great good which bounteous nature, from the bosom of the earth, returns to the skill and industry of man.

Edward Rigby, 1819

Holkham was from the start much visited by the gentry, who at times were obliged to wait for guided tours.

When we came to the house the servant told us we could not see it for an hour at least as there was a party going round, and it was but just ten o'clock. We wished to have filled up the time with a review of the park and buildings, but there was no one disengaged to attend us. Therefore we were obliged to be shut up with Jupiter Ammon and a whole tribe of people, till the housekeeper was ready to attend us. Nothing could be more disagreeable than this situation. We all stared at one another, and not a creature opened their mouths. Some of the Masters amused themselves with trying to throw their hats upon the head of the bust, while the Misses scrutinised one another's dress. Sir William, indeed, and an old terror, did chat a little, and by this means we found out they were the whole family of the Swailes, going the Norfolk tour; and a young one made itself known to Miss G, being acquainted with her brother. At length the long wished-for time arrived. The good woman appeared, and we rushed on her like a swarm of bees. We went the usual round, all but the wing my lord and lady used to inhabit themselves: this was new doing up. I dragged them all into the attics, for which I believed none of them thanked me, especially one poor woman very big with child. I wanted to look at the sea, but it was so hazy, we could not distinguish it from a cloud. The tower library has been put in order; two librarians from London have been at work there ten weeks, and it is just finished. When we came down the party vanished, but we were conducted a second time to Mr Jupiter, where we poured libations of chocolate on his alter; that is, we had some set out in great form in the Leicester style, and a most elegant little Birmingham vehicle to hold the rusks was placed on the tables. I made Mr Fetch-and-Carry tell me where it was bought, and am determined to have one. I enquired, you may be sure, after her ladyship, and left all proper compliments. I thought I had missed none of the beauties inside or out of Holkham, but I found several I had not remarked before, among others, in the landscape room, over the chimney is a Claude, which has a tree in it that you may fancy you see wave with the wind.

Letitia Beauchamp-Proctor, 1772

The large-scale planting of the park at Felbrigg, the home of the Windham family, was begun in the eighteenth century by William Windham III. Most of the tree plantations were utilitarian rather than ornamental, but the impression created was one of natural charm.

Of the park we have to speak in high terms. Like the true English park of the better caste, it forms a magnificent piece of human skill and industry, yet exhibiting no mark of either, and, to the uninitiated, reposing in the same natural outline it had at the beginning. It looks like Nature's own production; and all fine parks present the same picture. Its trees appear to have sprung up naturally; some in thickets, others in groups of two or three, whilst solitary individuals seem to have risen fortuitously, yet in harmony with a design which connects and beautifies the whole. It is one of those spots characteristic of English scenery, such as is to be met with in no other country, – full of calm and solitary charms, and forming at once a place of rest and retirement. Does any one, in dreaming of sunnier

climes, fancy that such a charming picture is to be realised elsewhere?
Then he is mistaken: for where shall we go to find it? In Italy? No: the sun
may look gloriously upon that country, and the soil may teem almost
with perpetual verdure and luxuriance; but so far as matters of taste and
design in park and pleasure-ground scenery are concerned, it is,
generally speaking, benighted.

James Grigor, 1841

*When well run, great houses were to a large extent self-sufficient. James Howell
was tutor to the family of Lord Savage, of Melford Hall.*

Though considering my former condition of life I may now be called a   179
countryman, yet you cannot call me a rustic, as long as I live in so civil
and noble a family, as long as I lodge in so virtuous and regular a house as
any I believe in the land, both for aeconomical government and the
choice company; for I never saw such a dainty race of children in all my
life together: I never saw yet such an orderly and punctual attendance of
servants, nor a great house so neatly kept: here one shall see no dog nor
cat nor cage to cause any nastiness within the body of the house. The
kitchen and gutters and other offices of noise and drudgery are at the fag
end; there's a back gate for the beggars and the meaner sort of swains to
come in at. The stables butt on the park, which for chearful rising ground,
for groves and browsing ground for the deer, for runlets of water, may
compare with any for its highness in the whole land. It is opposite to the
front of a great house, whence from the gallery one may see much of the
game when they are hunting. Now for the gardening and choice of
flowers, for fruits of all sorts, there are few the like in England. Here you
have your Bon Christian pears and Bergamot in perfection; your
Muscatel grapes in such plenty that there are some bottles of wine sent
every year to the king; and one to Mr Daniel, a worthy gentleman hard
by, who hath been long abroad, makes a good store of his vintage. Truly
this house of Long Melford, tho' it be not so great, yet it is so well
compacted and contrived with such dainty conveniencies every way,
that if you saw the landskip of it you would be mightily taken with it, and
it would serve for a choice pattern to build and contrive a house by.

James Howell, 1619

*Earlham was the home of the large and closely united Gurney family. A small
grandson, Percy Lubbock, experienced an overwhelming love of place when
staying there.*

But first there is a chatter and a crowd about the front-door, where a   180
carriage waits for the departure of the visitors. We all collect for a friendly
farewell, and there is kissing and waving, stamping and jingling, and the
carriage bowls away under the blackness of the chestnut-grove. The
children go scampering after it – but indeed the shadows, once you are

round the corner and out of sight of the house, are lonely and solemn by now; I prefer to slip away into the open, over the short roll of the park that descends towards the church and the village. There the light comes raking across from the west, warm with the faint rose-flush of an afterglow; very still and warm and grass-scented is the air in the open, away from the trees. If you wander off in that direction you come upon the other drive, the one that marches straight from the steps of the front-door, under the towering limes, to the white gate by the church; it passes through the short tunnel of the limes, and then over the open park to the gate and the road. I find myself veering down towards that gate – though really it is impossible to suppose that I could travel so far at this hour of the dusk; but in fancy, at any rate, I reach the further end of the straight drive, for you get a glimpse of the house from there which besets my thought.

Suppose you were passing along the highway at that point, coming from Norwich and knowing nothing of Earlham, and you happened to pause at the gate and glance up the straight cart-road (I ought not to call it a drive) – here would be your first sight of the house, so thickly the trees are massed about it to the east; and knowing nothing of Earlham, you divine little or nothing of what it really is. Your eye follows the line of the cart-road, across the open park, till it disappears in the shadow of the lime-avenue, and between the trees you catch this single glimpse of the house – the front-door only, with its low pediment, and a window or two beside and above it. It is a sight that tells you nothing of the place; you might think it rather formal and forbidding. The house on this side, you remember, had been plastered over and painted – by one of Joseph John's puritanical wives, so we understood, who was all for keeping a house (like herself) as plain and drab as possible. So she had plastered the old brickwork of the house-front and painted it a pinkish, buffish white; and the glimpse that you had from the road gave you nothing but the impression of an ordinary respectable mansion, a 'hall' like any other, withdrawn in gentlemanly discretion among the trees of its park. With a considerable effort of imagination I picture the sight as it would be seen by a stranger. If I were the stranger I should not look twice at the house, I should pass on down the road to the bridge and the river.

But to us that peep of a plain bare house among the trees had peculiar intimations of poetry. Its aspect of solemn gentility was always connected, you see, with the thought of arriving at Earlham. We approached it on this side, and with that prim-mouthed look, so untrue to itself, our Earlham received its children. Did the house seem stiff and ungenial in its manner of welcome? We knew better – knew what a different expression it showed as soon as you were fairly in its arms. There was charm in the thought that it turned a dumb mask to the world, revealing nothing to the casual stranger on the highway; and the friendly freedom and sweetness of its intimacy were enhanced by the contrast. So to me as I stand at the gate of the church-drive, like any chance passer-by, this appeal of the prospect is renewed, the waft of sensation returns – and I could revolve the thought, caressingly, of all that is screened from unknowing eyes. It is an ordinary-looking mansion, oh yes, and a few yards down the road you come to the bridge, and to Borrow's fishing-pool, and to a stretch of water-meadows that are very pretty with their buttercups and loosestrife – pass on and admire them, for you may. But if you knew, if you knew the heart of beauty and life and romance that lies up there among the trees, quietly waiting, you would stay by the gate and tenderly fondle the thought. Half way up to the house, in the open of the park, stood a genteel wellingtonia, and to a stranger that too, I suppose, would wear a formal look – but if you knew!

Percy Lubbock, 1922

Lady Bedingfeld, the wife of the owner of Oxburgh, analyses her feelings for the house in a dialogue between her head and her heart (under the pseudonym of Camilla). The house had been leased out for reasons of economy, and the Roman Catholic Bedingfelds had retreated to Ghent.

Head Well Camilla, I have been looking over Your Letter List, which by the by You have turned into a Sort of Journal, and I find You have been going over the same ground as You did three Years ago, when You brought Your Family to settle at Ghent. How long have You been staying in England?

Camilla Since last May; the greater part has been Spent at Oxburgh, a place I am so fond of that to be there is in itself Happiness!

H. That is to Say, Oxburgh being the ancient Seat of the Bedingfelds and the future property of Yr Descendants, you take a pleasure and interest in what might otherwise appear Melancholy and Dull.

C. Perhaps – but I do not like the Idea that Oxburgh can be dull to anybody having active Spirits for *out of Doors*, or intellectual resources to occupy them within –

H. Active Spirits and Intellectual resources are certainly great Embellishers of every prospect; but You forget, when You speak of residence at Oxburgh, that you packed up all the Books, and Sir R. allowed no Shooting in the Autumn, and you had no Instrument but the organ, without Music. Your daughters were with Your family, Your Husband measuring timber all day; what were You about?

C. Oh, I had Continued Occupation. First, as I packed up the Library, the pleasant amusement of looking into every Book, noting down the title, date and Edition, reading a little in one, and a little in another, so that I passed My days in most agreeable Mixed Company. When I had packed up 1700 Vols I took the Outline of more than 80 pictures, reducing them by a Scale. Then I numbered every Article of the Furniture, added new, mended the Old. And I hope I need not Mention My Visits to the Cottages, and My lingering Steps, in the grown up Walks!

H. You had not been at Oxburgh for 10 Years.

C. No, not to stay, and was actually a week before I could believe I was there. Yet every Object, Every Corner, was so well remembered, that I soon felt as if I had never been away. Yet also what changes in the Inhabitants of our Village; Slim young Girls become Pale hard working Mothers! – the Auburn Locks thinned and darkened, and many a grey head laid low! Boys, whose little weak hands could scarcely hold the

White gate open when I drove thro' it at My departure, were now the Robust young men that honored my return with the loudest Peal Village Bells could produce.

Charlotte Bedingfeld, 1820

But not everyone likes to live in a stately home, even if they own it. The fictional owner of 'Arcady Hall' (which is loosely based on Oxburgh) preferred travelling by train.

As he spoke there was a sudden loud hissing sound, and a white cloud   182 drifted past the window.

'Is Chloe in the cab?' Lord Flamborough asked.

'Yes, dear,' his wife replied.

Lord Flamborough picked up a guard's peaked cap that was resting on the window ledge and put it on his head. Then he took a large gold watch from his waistcoat pocket.

'One seventeen,' he said. He put the watch away, took a whistle from another pocket, and blew two sharp blasts on it. There was an answering toot from the locomotive.

'Care to flag her out?' asked Lord Flamborough.

I was not sure what he meant until I realized that Lady Flamborough was handing me a green flag.

'We haven't got a guard's van,' said Lord Flamborough. 'You have to use the door behind me. Wait till you hear the "away" whistle.'

Hesitantly I got up, took the green flag, walked down the car and stepped out on to the platform.

Leaning from the cab of the engine was a fair-haired woman, dressed in brown overalls. From within the dining car came a long shrill whistle. I gave a tentative wave of the flag and the woman's head disappeared. With a burst of smoke from the funnel and a clanking of coupling rods the train began to move.

I jumped back into the coach and shut the door after me. As I returned to my seat and handed the green flag to Lady Flamborough her husband was studying his watch again.

'One nineteen precisely,' he announced.

'Will you have soup?' said a low, soft voice at my shoulder. I turned to see Lady Matilda holding a silver soup tureen on a tray.

'Thank you,' I said.

She gave me a long searching glance, just as she had done in the ruined chapel, then helped me to a portion of steaming mulligatawny.

'Don't slop it, Tilly,' said her mother.

'Go into the saloon, Tilly,' said her father, 'and put "Bughouse Blues" on the phonograph.'

I looked out of the window. In imperturbable calm the sober Suffolk landscape was gliding by.

Fifty-eight minutes later, by the Earl of Flamborough's gold watch, the train drew up at the Halt for Arcady Hall. During that time we had eaten an excellent four-course lunch, served by Lady Matilda, and the train had travelled to Flaxfield Junction and back again.

At Flaxfield Junction, as though to mark the distinction between British Railways and the Earl of Flamborough's Folly, the Branch Line terminated abruptly in a high corrugated iron fence which had been thrown across the rails some fifty yards from the station platform. A group of local children had gathered at this unimpressive terminus to watch the train steam in, and Lord Flamborough leaned out of the dining-car window to make a distribution of some sticky sweets which he called Arcady Rock. The train eventually made its departure from Flaxfield Junction to the accompaniment of shrill cheers from the spectators. Evidently its visit was a daily occurrence which afforded much innocent pleasure.

The line from Flaxfield to Arcady passed along the edge of the park surrounding Arcady Hall, but for most of its course the Hall was hidden by high hedges or woods. There was only one opening through which the whole building could be seen from the train, its gatehouse rising from the placid landscape like some castle of the imagination sketched in the background of a Flemish primitive by Dirk Bouts or Memling.

In this opening was the Halt, which comprised a short wooden platform and a very small but elegant brick-built shelter, with Gothic windows, a Regency verandah, and castellations round the roof.

'Here you are, my dear fellow,' said Lord Flamborough. 'It's only a couple of hundred yards from here up to the Hall.'

'Aren't you coming too, sir?'

'Not me. The Hall is entirely in the Professor's keeping. I live in the train.'

'You sleep here, too?' I asked.

'Of course. The front coach is a sleeper. And very comfortable, too. Now off you go, or I shan't be back at the terminus on time. There's Quirky on the platform, waiting to welcome you.'

As I stepped out and shut the carriage door behind me I heard the blast of Lord Flamborough's whistle, and the green flag appeared through the window. The female engine-driver, whom I took to be the Flamboroughs' eldest daughter, waved to me and set the train in motion.

John Hadfield, 1959

The houses of the cloth-merchants (like this one at Coggeshall) were more compact but scarcely less elaborate than those of the landed gentry.

Paycocke's house is full of relics of the cloth industry. The merchant mark   183 of the Paycockes, an ermine tail, looking like a two-stemmed clover leaf, is to be found on the carved beams of the chimney, on the breast-summers of the fire-places, and set in the midst of the strip of carving along the front of the house. Thomas marked his bales of cloth thus, and what other armorial bearings did he need? The whole house is essentially middle class – the house of a man who was *nouveau riche* in an age when to be *nouveau riche* was not yet to be vulgar. His prosperity has blossomed out into exquisitely ornate decoration. A band of carving runs along the front of the house, and from the curved stem of it branch out a hundred charming devices – leaves, tendrils, strange flowers, human heads, Tudor roses, a crowned king and queen lying hand in hand, a baby diving with a kick of fat legs into the bowl of an arum lily, and in the midst the merchant's mark upon a shield and the initials of the master of the house. In the hall is a beautiful ceiling of carved oakwork, exceedingly elaborate and bearing at intervals the merchant's mark again. Upstairs in the big bed-chamber is a ceiling of beams worked in bold roll mouldings; and there is an exquisite little parlour, lined with linen fold panels, with a breastsummer carved with strange animals. This elaboration is characteristic. It is all of a piece with Coggeshall Church, and with all those other spacious East Anglian churches, Lavenham, Long Melford, Thaxted, Saffron Walden, Lynn, Snettisham, lofty and spacious, which the clothiers built out of their newly won wealth. The very architecture is characteristic, *nouveau riche* again, like those who paid for it, the elaborate ornament and sumptuous detail of the Perpendicular taking the place of the simple majesty of the Early English style. It is just the sort of architecture that a merchant with a fortune would pay for. The middle class liked some show for its money; but again it was the ostentation without the vulgarity of wealth. Looking upon his beautiful house, or worshipping beside his family tombs, with the merchant's mark on the brasses, in St Katherine's aisle, Thomas Paycocke must often have blessed the noble industry which supported him.

Eileen Power, 1924

Before the days of cheap coal, even the houses of rectors could be fearfully cold in winter; and the churches too – so cold that this rector skipped service on Christmas Day.

DEC. 25, XMAS DAY, SUNDAY. We breakfasted, dined, &c. again at home. This Day the coldest we have had yet and Frost more severe. It froze all the Day long and within Doors, the last Night intensely cold. Mr Corbould read Prayers & administered the H. Sacrament this Morning at Weston Church. He called on us as he went and also on his return from Church. He said the cold at Church was so great as to make him tremble again. We did not go, the Weather being so severe. This being Christmas Day, the following People had their Dinner at my House, Widow Case, old Thos Atterton, Christ. Dunnell, Edwd Howes, Robt Downing and my Clerk, Thos Thurston. Dinner to day, Surloin of Beef rosted, plumb Puddings and mince Pies. My Appetite this very cold Weather very bad. The Cold pierces me thro' almost on going to bed, cannot get to sleep for a long time. We however do not have our beds warmed. Gave the People that dined here to day before they went, to each of them 1 Shilling o. 6. o. After they had dined they had some strong Beer.

James Woodforde, 1796

184

Home life in the nineteenth century, as recalled by the son of the Dissenting Minister at Wangford, was extremely simple.

Our home life was simple enough. We went early to bed and were up   185
with the lark. I was arrayed in a pinafore and wore a frill – which I
abhorred – and took but little pleasure in my personal appearance – a
very great mistake, happily avoided by the present generation. We
children had each a little bed of garden ground which we cultivated to
the best of our power. Ours was really a case of plain living and high
thinking. Of an evening the room was dimly lighted by means of a dip
candle which constantly required snuffing. To write with we had the
ordinary goose-quill. The room, rarely used, in which we received
company was called the parlour. Goloshes had not then come into use,
and women wore in muddy weather pattens or clogs. The simple
necessaries of life were very dear, and tea and coffee and sugar were sold
at what would now be deemed an exorbitant price. Postage was
prohibitory, and when any one went to town he was laden with letters.
As little light as possible was admitted into the house in order to save the
window-tax. The farmer was generally arrayed in a blue coat and yellow
brass buttons. The gentleman had a frilled shirt and wore Hessian boots. I
never saw a magazine of the fashions; nowadays they are to be met with
everywhere. Yet we were never dull, and in the circle in which I moved
we never heard of the need of change. People were content to live and
die in the village without going half-a-dozen miles away, with the
exception of the farmers, who might drive to the nearest market town,
transact their business, dine at the ordinary, and then, after a smoke and
a glass of brandy and water and a chat with their fellow-farmers, return
home. Of the rush and roar of modern life, with its restlessness and
eagerness for something new and sensational, we had not the remotest
idea.

   James Ewing Ritchie, 1898

The medieval peasants lived in mere hovels.

As for the houses themselves, they were squalid enough for the most   186
part. The manor house was often built of stone, when stone was to be
had, or where, as in Norfolk, no stone was to be had, then of flint, as in so
many of our church towers. Usually, however, the manor house was
built in great part of timber. The poorer houses were dirty hovels, run up
'anyhow', sometimes covered with turf, sometimes with thatch. None of
them had chimneys. Six hundred years ago houses with chimneys were
at least as rare as houses heated by hot-water pipes are now. Moreover,
there were no brick houses. It is a curious fact that the art of making
bricks seems to have been lost in England for some hundreds of years.
The labourer's dwelling had no windows; the hole in the roof which let
out the smoke rendered windows unnecessary, and, even in the houses
of the well-to-do, glass windows were rare. In many cases oiled linen
cloth served to admit a feeble semblance of light, and to keep out the rain.

The labourer's fire was in the middle of his house; he and his wife and
children huddled round it, sometimes grovelling in the ashes; and going
to bed meant flinging themselves down upon the straw which served
them as mattress and feather bed, exactly as it does to the present day in
the gipsy's tent in our byways. The labourer's only light by night was the
smouldering fire. Why should he burn a rushlight when there wa
nothing to look at? and reading was an accomplishment which fev
labouring men were masters of.

Augustus Jessopp, 1866

*But in later times people became houseproud, and some kept their cotta
scrupulously clean. Camilla Gurdon lived at Grundisburgh.*

But the glory of the cottage (which is a poor dilapidated place) does
consist in such things as these. In the scrupulously clean living-ro
there is mahogany and horse-hair furniture, brought to such a stat
shining polish that it strikes the beholder with awe and admiratiuu.
Amos Copping was a lad of seventeen when he married his first wife,
Alice, who was a servant at the rectory. Work was slack, and Amos
enlisted in a regiment that was ordered out to the Crimea. He behaved
himself so well that after the war he was, to quote his old mother, who
told me the story 'promoted to ride a-hoss-back, and to go to Cork'.
Meanwhile Alice had returned to service, and during the time that
husband and wife were parted she had earned money to buy a little
furniture. She must have denied herself many things, for when he joined
her she had saved every penny of her wages, and bit by bit the precious
household goods were bought. He left the army when his time was up,
and they settled in the cottage in the Gull. Alice was as 'houseproud' as
only eastern county women can be; exquisitely clean, slaving for her
furniture, bestowing a world of loving care upon the poor ugly things,
putting her life, as it were, into the polishing and furbishing of the little
rooms. No children came to disturb the spotless neatness of the chairs,
shrouded in elegant crochet antimacassars of her own making; no dirty
little boots clambered impiously on the sacred sofa; no little sticky claws
clutched at the china dogs sitting in state on the mantelshelf; no cunning
little arms slipped themselves round her neck, drawing her heart away
from the furniture.

Camilla Gurdon, 1897

Cottages by the sea were often full of nautical mementoes.

A small cottage, always within hearing of the sea. In summer a friendly   188
sparkling sea, murmuring a lullaby on the tiny pebbles at the waters
edge. In winter, a crashing roaring surf pounding the shingle. By day a
slate-grey seething cauldron; by night a howling void, a very Nifelheim.
It was a very friendly, fascinating cottage, redolent of sooty kettles

and tarry ropes. Yellow oilskin smocks, glistening with an accumulation of sprat and herring scales, hung in the alcove at the foot of the stairs. Huge leather sea-boots lay in an inextricable jumble beneath the table. One had to kick them from under one's feet at meal times.

Beneath the stairs was a large shadowy recess; which, in years gone by, had held poached game and demi-johns of smuggled gin.

Upon the cottage walls were pictures, in crude yet effective oils, and ancient yellow chromo-plates; pictures of sailing ships carrying impossible suits of canvas, schooners, cutters and fishing smacks. Each ship told a tale of speed and seaworthiness; while some recalled sagas of incredible hardship and privation, of daring and superb seamanship.

There were also ships in bottles, and ships in glass cases – models of the *Sunk, Cross Sand* and *Shipwash* lightships. Occupying the place of honour in the parlour was a large model of the *Gypsy*, a relic of the days when the fishermen of Aldeburgh sailed north to the Faroes, and thence to Iceland 'long-lining' for Cod.

George Goldsmith Carter, 1945

The dwelling which, above all others, exemplifies cottage-cosiness was on the beach itself, at Yarmouth; Dickens had seen just such a structure there when he was a boy.

Ham carrying me on his back and a small box of ours under his arm, and Peggotty carrying another small box of ours, we turned down lanes bestrewn with bits of chips and little hillocks of sand, and went past gas-works, rope-walks, boat-builders' yards, shipwrights' yards, ship-breakers' yards, caulkers' yards, riggers' lofts, smiths' forges, and a great litter of such places, until we came out upon the dull waste I had already seen at a distance; when Ham said, 189

'Yon's our house, Mas'r Davy!'

I looked in all directions, as far as I could stare over the wilderness, and away at the sea, and away at the river, but no house could *I* make out. There was a black barge, or some other kind of superannuated boat, not far off, high and dry on the ground, with an iron funnel sticking out of it for a chimney and smoking very cosily; but nothing else in the way of a habitation that was visible to *me*.

'That's not it?' said I. 'That ship-looking thing?'

'That's it, Mas'r Davy,' returned Ham.

If it had been Aladdin's palace, roc's egg and all, I suppose I could not have been more charmed with the romantic idea of living in it. There was a delightful door cut in the side, and it was roofed in, and there were little windows in it; but the wonderful charm of it was, that it was a real boat which had no doubt been upon the water hundreds of times, and which had never been intended to be lived in, on dry land. That was the captivation of it to me. If it had ever been meant to be lived in, I might have thought it small, or inconvenient, or lonely; but never having been designed for any such use, it became a perfect abode.

It was beautifully clean inside, and as tidy as possible. There was a table, and a Dutch clock, and a chest of drawers, and on the chest of drawers there was a tea-tray with a painting on it of a lady with a parasol, taking a walk with a military-looking child who was trundling a hoop. The tray was kept from tumbling down, by a Bible: and the tray, if it had tumbled down, would have smashed a quantity of cups and saucers and a teapot, that were grouped around the book. On the walls there were some common colored pictures, framed and glazed, of scripture subjects; such as I have never seen since in the hands of pedlars, without seeing the whole interior of Peggotty's brother's house again, at one view. Abraham in red going to sacrifice Isaac in blue, and Daniel in yellow cast into a den of green lions, were the most prominent of these. Over the little mantel-shelf, was a picture of the Sarah Jane lugger, built at Sunderland, with a real little wooden stern stuck on to it; a work of art, combining composition with carpentry, which I considered to be one of the most enviable possessions that the world could afford. There were some hooks in the beams of the ceiling, the use of which I did not divine then; and some lockers and boxes and conveniences of that sort, which served for seats and eked out the chairs.

All this, I saw in the first glance after I crossed the threshold – childlike, according to my theory – and then Peggotty opened a little door and showed me my bedroom. It was the completest and most desirable bedroom ever seen – in the stern of the vessel; with a little window, where the rudder used to go through; a little looking-glass, just the right height for me, nailed against the wall, and framed with oyster-shells; a little bed, which there was just room enough to get into, and a nosegay of seaweed in a blue mug on the table. The walls were whitewashed as white as milk, and the patchwork counterpane made my eyes quite ache with its brightness. One thing I particularly noticed in this delightful house, was the smell of fish; which was so searching, that when I took out my pocket-handkerchief to wipe my nose, I found it smelt exactly as if it had wrapped up a lobster. On my imparting this discovery in confidence to Peggotty, she informed me that her brother dealt in lobsters, crabs, and crawfish; and I afterwards found that a heap of these creatures, in a state of wonderful conglomeration with one another, and never leaving off pinching whatever they laid hold of, were usually to be found in a little wooden outhouse where the pots and kettles were kept.

Charles Dickens, 1849

Farming

Thomas Tusser reflects on the annual cycle and life's cycle. He farmed at Cattawade and there began his treatise on farming, written entirely in verse. Unfortunately, despite all his practical precepts, he was an unsuccessful farmer, and twice had to sell out.

Of God to thy doings, a time there is sent,
Which endeth with time that in doing is spent:
For time is itself, but a time for a time,
Forgotten full soon, as the tune of a chime.

In Spring-time we rear, we do sow, and we plant;
In Summer get victuals, lest after we want.
In Harvest, we carry in corn, and the fruit,
In Winter to spend, as we need of each suit.

The year I compare, as I find for a truth,
The Spring unto Childhood, the Summer to Youth.
The Harvest to Manhood, the Winter to Age,
All quickly forgot, as a play on a stage.

Time past is forgotten, ere men be aware:
Time present is thought on, with wonderful care:
Time coming is feared, and therefore we save
Yet oft ere it come, we be gone to the grave.

Thomas Tusser, 1557

In the same locality, two centuries later, the farmers were prospering greatly.

Arthur Young and three French visitors were on a fact-finding tour of Suffolk.

Soon after, we met a burly farmer mounted on a good horse and out   191
looking at his crops. He had the air of a wealthy man, and though he was
dressed like a farmer, something in his manner revealed a man of
affluence!

Mr Young stopped him and asked several questions, most of
which I remember though something may have slipped my memory,
but this was the gist: nearly all the farmers round here own their farms,
which they could do only after acquiring some wealth; the farms are
not large, worth, as a rule, not more than three or four hundred pounds
sterling; they get their muck from London and a sort of chalk they mix
with it from Kent; they arrange for the muck to come from London on
the barges that take there the local produce and that otherwise might
return empty, so the cost is low (it argues intelligence and imaginative
calculation to enrich the soil with fertiliser that has been transported a
hundred miles and make a profit on it). He added that the lands never
lie fallow but are cropped in the four-year rotation: first, turnips;
second, barley sown with clover; third, the same clover by itself; fourth,
wheat.

What I found absolutely astonishing is the way in which not only
the farmer but everyone Mr Young questioned on the way replied to his
questions with – everyone – more intelligence than peasants are
supposed to have.

I forgot to say that a mile or so back we passed this man's farm: a
large house is surrounded and set off by a small, beautifully tended,
flower-bed and there are trees he has planted solely to please himself.

François La Rochefoucauld, 1784 (translation, Norman Scarfe)

*The nineteenth century brought harder times for the farmers, though worries
could be forgotten at the dinner after the January rent audit. Though better
known for his adventure novels, Henry Rider Haggard farmed near
Ditchingham and served on various agricultural commissions.*

When the tenants have been interviewed, or most of them, dinner is   192
announced, about three o'clock generally, and everybody adjourns to a
long, old-fashioned room. Here the landlord takes the head of the table,
and the agent the foot, while the tenants range themselves in solemn
lines on either side, in order of seniority and social precedence. Then
grace is said and the meal begins; and an excellent meal it is, by the
way, though perhaps it would not recommend itself to the guests at a
London dinner party. Here is the menu, which never varies from year
to year:

Clear Ox-tail Soup.
Fried Soles.
Boiled Cod.
Roast Beef.
Boiled Mutton.

Chicken and Tongue.
Roast Turkey.
(For this festival is always celebrated early in January.)
Plum Pudding. Mince Pies.
Cheese.
Beer, Port, and Sherry.

Such is the feast, most admirably cooked in the good old English fashion with the old English accessories, and it is one to which hungry men who have eaten nothing since the morning certainly do justice.

After the meal is finished glasses are filled and the landlord proposes 'The Queen', which is loyally drunk, but in silence, as though to her Majesty's memory. Then comes a solemn pause, till the largest tenant present at the feast – as regards his holding, not his person – his eyes fixed sternly upon vacancy, rises and proposes the health of the landlord in a few brief but kindly sentences.

Another pause and the landlord rises to reply. How well he knows that speech! It begins invariably with a solemn wail or lament over the shocking bad times, which, as a general rule, he is obliged to confess are even worse than they were at the last gathering. Then, while his audience shake their heads and sigh, he rises to a more cheerful note and talks of the inherent pluck and nobility of the character of Englishmen, which, as he firmly believes, will, if persisted in, enable them in the end to put up the price of corn – how, he prefers not to specify. He also discourses hopefully of signs of better fortune upon the horizon of the year, if he can find any, and points out (which is perfectly true) that the interests of the landlord, the tenant, and the labourer, and indeed of all who live by the land, are one interest, whatever agitators and mischief-makers may say to the contrary. Then he gives some account of the farming of whatever country he may last have visited, America, or Iceland, or Egypt, or the Hebrides, or Mexico. This is generally the most popular part of the speech, as there is a slight novelty about it, the rest being somewhat of a formula. Finally he ends with the best peroration that occurs to him and resumes his seat amidst the jingling of glasses, to rise again presently and propose the health of the agent, to whose many virtues he delicately alludes.

Next the agent replies, paying him back full measure and running over in the coin of compliment, and exhorting the tenants to make up their minds that the bad times are done with, and to pay their rent like men and Britons. Finally he ends by proposing their healths, calling on two of them to respond. This does not take long, for the average farmer is no great speaker, and when the last of them sits down with a sigh of relief the oratorical programme is exhausted.

Then the songs begin – the pipes, long clay churchwardens, have been lit already. These songs are generally three in number, and always the same. One, a very long one, is of a local character, for it describes the glories of Bungay, the chorus at the end of each verse being, 'For old Bungay is a wonderful town.' Another is a melancholy ditty descriptive of the ills of life and the dangers and disasters that beset each profession; even the lawyer, who, so says the song, is invariably rich and happy in every other way, must beware of the spite of Fate, since, while he is comfortably fleecing his clients, his clerk 'is a-kissing of his wife'. The third song is of a patriotic nature, and has for a refrain something about 'twisting the lion's tail'. Perhaps it was written in America.

H. Rider Haggard, 1899

The landlord–tenant relationship was surely never better maintained than by Thomas Coke of Holkham in the early nineteenth century. He gave an annual dinner in the Holkham Statue Gallery at the time of the summer sheep-shearings.

In spite of a few *contretemps* of this description, however, the speeches   193
which accompanied these toasts were both interesting and amusing. Men of such varied rank and outlook, of such different professions and experience, could not fail to have something to relate which presented new ideas to the majority; though often the anecdotes with which they enlivened the company were not more appreciated than the efforts of those speakers who were unconsciously humorous. Not the least popular part of the proceedings was the speeches made in broken English by the foreigners, or, as has before been mentioned, the oracular utterances of Lord Erskine. The farmers, too, whom Coke encouraged to express their opinions freely, were often, wholly unsuspected by themselves, a source of diversion to an audience who, we are informed, were 'in high good humour' after their ample meal.

The shortest speech on record at the Clippings is said to be the following. A certain farmer was observed to be making efforts to rise to his feet, but each time was hustled back by his companions, who, probably on the principle that a prophet is without honour in his own country, recommended him to hold his tongue. 'Sit down, will 'ee!' they reiterated firmly, when suddenly Coke noticed the little commotion, and interfered. 'I see,' he said, 'that good fellow has something to say to us; pray let him speak!' The man, thus encouraged, rose triumphantly to his feet and hammered upon the table. Profound silence at once reigned through the room, and he delivered himself as follows: 'Maister Coke, and gentlemen, what ah wish to say is – if more landlords would döe as Maister Coke *he* döe, there'd be less döe as they döe döe!' and amid thunders of applause, he reseated himself.

A. M. W. Stirling, 1908

The uncertainties of the weather have always bred pessimism among farmers.

Hark how that blaow, jes what I thought   194
    That barley field'll all be sp'iled.
A Saddy's moon is good for nought –
    That fare to make me wholly riled.

You want it wet, tha's olluz fine,
　　You want it cowd, that's olluz mild,
You want it dry, there's nought but räin,
　　That fare to make me wholly riled.

There's olluz summat; if 'taint that
　　Its tother – fare to drive yer wild.
Don' matter tuppence what yer at,
　　Things olluz make yer wholly riled.

Anon., nineteenth century

A certain unimaginative cunning often characterizes successful farmers. However, few have been blessed with five bovine sons to command, as was this dreadful patriarch – fortunately fictional.

Benjamin Geaiter drained his teacup, pushed back his chair, and having lighted his pipe, looked down the kitchen table at his sons as they in their turn drained their cups and lit their pipes. They were all men now, or nearly so, for Harry, the youngest, was eighteen and almost as tall as the others. They were all of middle height and stockily built, but none of them quite so deep-chested or strong in the arm as their father, though they all bore the stamp of his heavy, expressionless features and ruddy complexion except Harry who was pale and thin-faced like his mother. But Benjamin was not thinking of his sons. It was the sixth anniversary of Mrs Geaiter's death, but he was not thinking of that. His thoughts were busy with the sheep, calculating whether there would be enough feed to last them till the turnips came on. Maria Cragg, hollow-cheeked and more wizened than ever, sat at the foot of the table pouring out another cup of tea for Harry who had a great appetite for tea and always drank one more cup than the rest. Maria no longer talked to Mrs Pearman of giving notice: indeed she had long ceased to talk to Mrs Pearman at all and counted the years since she last went down into the village instead; she was only to leave the farm once more. All except Harry had finished and were quietly smoking. It was time to wash up and she was about to begin gathering the dirty cups and saucers together when the kitchen door rattled. She looked up. 195

'Who is it?' she said, as she rose to go to the door.

'Fare to me it's a gentleman,' said Ben, who was facing the window. 'I wonder what he want here.'

'Shall I ask him into the parlour?' said Maria, looking at Benjamin.

'No,' growled Benjamin. 'Ask him his business first.'

Maria shuffled to the door and opening it as narrowly as possible, peered through the crack at the stranger. At once a hearty voice, with a slight foreign twang in it, came ringing through the crack into the kitchen.

'Can I see Mr Geaiter?'

Everyone stared at the door.

'Let him in,' said Benjamin in a surly tone.

Maria opened the door and the stranger, a tall, strongly built man, well-shaven and neatly dressed in town clothes, strode into the room. No one moved from the table.

'I hope you won't think me rude,' he said, stepping forward and addressing himself to Benjamin in the same cheerful voice, 'but the fact is I once had this farm myself twenty years ago, and jolly glad I was to get out of it, though I was bankrupt when I went. I happened to be passing this way to-day and when I saw how well the fields looked, I said to myself, "It's a real man who's got this farm now. I should like to ask him how he does it." So here I am.'

'Oh,' said Benjamin. 'I see.'

'My name's Wilburn,' said the stranger. 'I hope I'm not intruding.'

'We don't mind,' growled Benjamin, still staring at the man as if he were some exotic animal.

As no one offered him a chair, he sat down of his own accord in Maria's empty place at the foot of the table.

'Well, Mr Geaiter,' he said genially, 'how do you do it?'

'Do what?' said Benjamin obtusely.

'Why, make a do of Crakenhill,' he replied. 'When I was here, it was the dirtiest, sourest, hardest, damnedest bit of land I ever came across.'

'So it was when I came,' said Benjamin.

Ben nodded in sympathy.

'But I never saw such a piece of wheat on it,' Wilburn went on, 'as you've got down there by the road. How do you do it?'

Benjamin had never been asked such a question before: he could farm a piece of land well enough, but to theorise on farming was not in his line. He looked steadily at Wilburn and pulling up his shirt sleeve, scratched his great brown arm.

'Ah,' said the stranger, 'now I see.'

'See what?' said Benjamin in surprise.

'Those arms of yours,' said the stranger. 'Now I know how it's done.'

Benjamin was not used to compliments and only stared harder at him: perhaps the man wanted to get something out of him: he distrusted him.

'Let me see,' continued the stranger, 'a hundred acres, isn't it?'

'Two,' Benjamin corrected.

'What, do you rent another hundred?' said Wilburn.

'No, bought it last year,' said Benjamin.

Wilburn whistled.

'Well,' he said, 'I don't know how you do it. When I came here, I had quite a bit of cash behind me and I swore I'd bring the place round or bust: but I bust. Do you remember that field down by the gull, all sodden and under water sometimes in the winter, full of the foulest rubbish, dodder and twitch and bellbind and paigle?'

The company became a little less hostile; they knew that field too.

'Yes,' said Benjamin, 'that took us a tidy time to clean. We drained it first. It cost a lot, but it have paid for itself since.'

'Maybe,' said Wilburn, 'but it broke my heart. But if you have draining to do, you need a lot of labour.'

'I've got my five sons,' replied Benjamin.

He had never said such a thing before, and he experienced a rudimentary feeling of pride as he uttered the words. Maria went on clearing the tea things away: but no one offered the stranger a cup of tea.

'Yes,' said Ben, speaking for the first time, 'me and Hiram and Bob here, we go to plough.'

'Suffolk punches?' queried the stranger.

'Ay,' answered Ben. 'We like 'em best on this heavy land: they keep their fetlocks clean. And Ern and young Harry look after the stock and milk the cows.'

'Now that is the way to farm,' said Wilburn. 'If only I had had five sons like that when I was here. Your sons work twice as well for you as a hired man because they know they're working for themselves.'

H. W. Freeman, 1928

Exploitation of labourers provoked criticism from Norfolk's future national hero, Horatio Nelson, in a letter to the Duke of Clarence, the future William IV. Nelson was at the time a naval captain on half pay, living in his native village, Burnham Thorpe.

That the poor labourer should have been seduced by promises and hopes   196
of better times, your Royal Highness will not wonder at, when I assure you, that they are really in want of everything to make life comfortable. [Nelson originally wrote, 'Hunger is a sharp thorn, and they are not only in want of food sufficient, but of clothes and firing.'] Part of their wants, perhaps, were unavoidable, from the dearness of every article of life; but much has arose from the neglect of the Country Gentlemen, in not making their farmers raise their wages, in some small proportion, as the prices of necessaries increased. The enclosed paper will give your Royal Highness an idea of their situation. It is most favourable; but I have been careful that no Country Gentleman should have it in his power to say, I had pointed out the wants of the poor greater than they really are. Their wages have been raised within these three weeks, pretty generally, one shilling a week: had it been done some time past, they would not have been discontented, for a want of loyalty is not amongst their faults; and many of their superiors, in many instances, might have imitated their conduct with advantage.

Horatio Nelson, 1792

Exploitation was still in evidence over a century later.

The second week that I was at this new farm I had to drive a herd of cattle   197
to Ipswich. I was thirteen and had lived only ten miles away all my life, but I had never been to this big town before. The farmer went ahead in his trap and waited for me at Ipswich market. He sold the cows and

bought some more, and told me to drive them back to the farm. Most of my work was like this, walking cattle along the roads backwards and forwards to the market – about twenty-five miles a day. The farmer was a dealer. I stayed with him a year and four months and was paid 4s. 6d. a week. And then I got into a hell of a row. I'd driven a flock of sheep from Ipswich and the next morning they found that one had died. The farmer was in a terrible stew. He ran down the field and met my mother on her way to chapel and told her all about it. I had driven the sheep too hard, he said. 'And you drive boys too hard!' said my mother – she had no fear at all. Well, the truth of the matter is that she said a lot of things she'd only thought until then, and so I left the farm. It must seem that there was war between farmers and their men in those days. I think there was, particularly in Suffolk. These employers were famous for their mean-ness. They took all they could from the men and boys who worked their land. They bought their life's strength for as little as they could. They wore us out without a thought because, with the big families, there was a continuous supply of labour. Fourteen young men left the village in 1909–11 to join the army. There wasn't a recruiting drive, they just escaped. And some people just changed their sky, as they say, and I was one of them.

Leonard Thompson, 1969

Here is the labourer breaking turnips for the cattle in winter. Robert Bloomfield lived at Honington and Sapiston before he went to London, when he was fifteen years old, in conditions of extreme poverty. His poem about the farming year brought him instant success.

Beneath dread WINTER's level sheets of snow   198
The sweet nutritious *Turnip* deigns to grow.
Till now imperious want and wide-spread dearth
Bid Labour claim her treasures from the earth.
On GILES, and such as GILES, the labour falls,
To strew the frequent load where hunger calls.
On driving gales sharp hail indignant flies,
And sleet, more irksome still, assails his eyes;
Snow clogs his feet; or if no snow is seen,
The field with all its juicy store to screen,
Deep goes the frost, till every root is found
A rolling mass of ice upon the ground.
No tender ewe can break her nightly fast,
Nor heifer strong begin the cold repast,
Till GILES with pond'rous *beetle* foremost go,
And scatt'ring splinters fly at every blow;
When pressing round him, eager for the prize,
From their mixt breath warm exhalations rise.

Robert Bloomfield, 1800

The cultivation of the turnip effected an agricultural revolution.

But the great piece of husbandry in which Norfolk excels, is in the   199
management of turnips, from which it derives an inestimable advantage.
This important crop is the great source of abundance to the country, and
has been gradually rising to perfection in its cultivation, for upwards of
seventy years. Not only this county, but many other parts of England,
are indebted to the Townshend family, for the original introduction of
this root into this country. Before that time, turnips were only cultivated
in gardens and small spots, and hoed by gardeners; but in the reign of
George I the then Lord Viscount Townshend, grandfather of the present
noble Marquis, attended the King to Hanover, in the quality of Secretary
of State, and observing the advantage of this valuable root, as there
cultivated at that time, and the fertility it produced, brought the seed and
practice into England, and recommended it strongly to his own tenants,
who occupied a similar soil to that of Hanover. The experiment
succeeded, and by degrees, it gradually spread over this county, and, in
the course of time, to other parts of England, though their cultivation is
by no means so general as it continues here. A good acre of turnips in
Norfolk will produce between thirty and forty cart loads, as heavy as
three horses can draw; and an acre will fat a Scotch bullock, from forty to
fifty stone, or eight sheep. – But the advantage of this crop does not end
here, for it generally leaves the land so clean, and in such fine condition,
that it almost insures a good crop of barley and a kind plant of clover; and
the clover is a most excellent preparative for wheat, so that in the
subsequent advantages, the value of the turnip can hardly be estimated.

   Nathaniel Kent, 1796

Here is an amateur cutting mangolds at Benfield St George. Adrian Bell's
voluntary apprenticeship to an old-fashioned farmer gave him the soundest of
footings for his extensive writings about Suffolk.

I arrived in the mangold field and took out my knife. The men greeted me   200
with grins, saying, 'So you have come to give us a hand, sir? That's good;
we shan't be long now.' They evidently anticipated entertainment; nor
were they disappointed.
    The carts went up the rows. Three men went with a cart, one
behind to deal with the two rows that the wheels spanned, and one on
either side. The method employed was this: you grasped the leaves of the
mangold with the left hand with much the same motion as a cow's
tongue makes encompassing a bite of grass. You pulled the mangold out
of the ground, swung it upwards, and at the right moment slipped your
knife-blade through the leaves where they joined the root. Then, if you
had judged correctly, the mangold flew into the cart and you were left
with the leaves in your hand. You dropped them, and stooped to pull
another. The whole process took the labourer one second.
    The men showed me by example how to do it. I took up my
position at the side of the tumbril. But my first mangold flew right over
the tumbril and hit the man on the other side.

'You are too strong, sir,' he smiled.

The next mangold hit the wheel, and the next the shaft. For five minutes I bombarded the tumbril in vain. It shook and rattled. I could not judge the right moment at which to sever the leaves from the root. Sometimes the globe fell at my feet, sometimes even it hit the horse, who did not seem to mind, but stood unmoved. I grovelled about picking up my misses and putting them in the tumbril. My hands were muddy. The men were highly amused. I felt hot and impotent, as though the whole thing were a practical joke at my expense.

At last I got one in, and there was a cry of, 'Well done, sir; now another.' By a stroke of luck the next one went in also. I began to smile. I discovered that the whole thing was a matter of rhythm, and by lunchtime I was getting four out of six into the tumbril.

As I was very slow, the man at the back gave me a hand with my two rows besides pulling his own. This hurt my pride, and by the time we knocked off at one I managed to keep up with the tumbril unaided by working twice as hard as they.

At lunch Mr Colville asked me how I was getting on.

'Mind you don't cut your hand,' he warned me. 'That is what everybody does the first time they pull mangolds.' He showed me a scar on his finger. But I smiled, for I was beginning to feel expert, and said I should be particularly careful.

However, the afternoon was not far advanced before the knife slipped and my finger bled. It was, luckily, only a scratch; I bound my handkerchief round it and continued. I was beginning to enjoy the work. The rhythm was restful after my early struggles. It was pleasant to feel the mangold's weight vanish at the jerk of the knife, and see the globe, rosier for the sinking sun, go bounding into the cart. The big ones thundered in, the small ones pattered.

Near the gateway of the field the clamp was set, and thither the loads were taken. A man was stationed there, building up the clamp, and every now and then there would be a deep rumble as he tipped a load down and the mangolds rolled out. Then he arranged them and covered them with straw, so that the clamp was as steep and smooth as a cottage roof.

Sometimes, between loads, the men would slice a mangold, exposing the juicy saffron flesh, and eat it. They found it refreshing. I tasted a slice; it was sweet and cold and crisp. The mangolds in this field were of a kind called 'Golden Tankard', one of the men told me.

There was a glow upon us all. The sun grew large and red, became the king of mangolds there on the horizon. The air turned frosty, the coarse leaves crackled in our hands, and, trampled, gave up their odour. Twilight came on, and horse and tumbril moving clampwards became a silhouette of toil.

We stretched. That was all for to-day. Matches were struck, illumining faces, and pipes glowed. A minute's contemplation of the sky.

'Rain? No, bor, it won't rain.' A word to me. 'You done wonderful well, sir, considerin'.' And the group toiled homeward over the fields.

Adrian Bell, 1930

And here is a Norfolk girl determined to do a man's job on the land.

'Liza Green wos smart an' strappin',   201
   With the roses on har cheek;
When she met our Perish Council,
   'Liza worn't afeard to speak.
Squire set thare, whu owns the willage,
   An' our Paarson (in the chaar);
But that mawther up and told 'em
   What she wanted, then and there!

Bor, yow oughterer sin' our paarson,
   How he kinder smiled – ses he,
'Du yow really want this 'lotment
   For *yerself?*' 'I *du,*' ses she.
'But we carn't let *ladies* hev' em,'
   Paarson say – and she say, 'Oh!
Du it say so in yar bye-laws?'
   Paarson he say, 'Hem! well, no!'

So she say, 'I'm young and strong, sir.
   I can dig, an' rake, an' ho;
If yow'll let me hev' a 'lotment,
   Yow'll sune see my 'taters grow!'
Well, they set some time an' argered,
   But the paarson got his way.
''Liza,' ses he, 'yow can hev' one.'
   'Thank ye, sir,' our 'Liza say.

So she got her bit of gardin;
   'Tworn't tu small, nor yit tu big,
An' young Billy Cross, he built a
   Sty, so she could keep a pig!
How that gardin grew – 'twos mazin!
   Crops o' parsnips, 'taters, beans,
Onions, paas – there worn't no 'lotment
   Round for miles, like 'Liza Green's!

Edwin Hewitt, 1928

The farms were supported by skilled workmen; James Cornish recalls the scenes of his youth at Debenham, where his father was vicar.

The two wheelwrights, Harry Howes and Charles Howes, were our close   202
friends when we were boys, especially Harry Howes, whose workshop
was close by. The timber he needed was put to season on the green in
front of his house. He and his apprentice would saw out planks from the
logs in the adjacent saw-pit, and we would watch quite entranced the
whole process. A great log roughly squared out by the axe would be

placed above the pit and the width of the planks marked by rubbing chalk on a line and drawing it taut from end to end and then 'snapping the line' by lifting and suddenly releasing it. The accuracy with which the work was done was really wonderful. The upright, square figure of Harry Howes, the top sawyer, guided the saw along each line with a steady upward pull and downward thrust, while his assistant below swung his weight on the pull and relaxed for the upward draw. They would continue by the hour with never any deviation from the lines of chalk.

The building of a great farm wagon was an event, and the whole of the work, from the cutting out of the wood to the painting of the finished wagon, was carried through by the wheelwright himself, with the single exception of the ironwork. What delighted us most of all was to watch the completion of the wheels when the tyres were fitted. Then Harry Howes and his brother, Charles Howes, would each take a wheel to the blacksmith's shop, and we were pleased to see that Harry Howes, our favourite of the two brothers, excelled in the art of running a wheel along the road. The great wheel was immensely heavy, but he would balance it and run it along the road at a sharp trot, pushing his right hand along the rim and steadying it with his left, while his taller brother often let his wheel lose pace, with the result that it tumbled over and had to be hauled up and restarted. On reaching the blacksmith's shop the wheel was placed on a great circular plate and the tyre brought hot from the furnace and slipped over the rim of the wheel. Buckets of cold water were sluiced over it and a cloud of steam rolled away. Next came our supreme joy, the 'smiting'. The wheel was raised upright and slowly turned while two men with heavy sledge-hammers pounded the warm iron, and here Charles Howes came into his own. Tall, spare and muscular, he was a grand man with the sledge, and always worked one of the hammers while the smith followed him with the second.

James George Cornish, 1938

Suffolk was renowned for its rock-like cheese, made from thrice-skimmed milk.

Unrivall'd stands thy country CHEESE, O Giles!   203
Whose very name alone engenders smiles;
    Whose fame abroad by every tongue is Spoke,
The well-known butt of many a flinty joke,
That pass like current coin the nation through;
And, ah! experience proves the satire true.
Provision's grave, thou ever craving mart,
Dependant, huge Metropolis! where Art
Her poring thousands stows in breathless rooms,
Midst pois'nous smokes and steams, and rattling looms;
Where Grandeur revels in unbounded stores;
Restraint, a slighted stranger at their doors!
Thou, like a whirlpool, drain'st the countries round,
Till London market, London price, resound
Through every town, round every passing load,

And dairy produce throngs the eastern road:
Delicious veal, and butter, every hour,
From Essex lowlands, and the banks of Stour;
And further far, where numerous herds repose,
   From Orwell's brink, from Waveny, or Ouse.
Hence Suffolk dairy-wives run mad for cream,
And leave their milk with nothing but its name;
Its name derision and reproach pursue,
And strangers tell of 'three times skim'd sky-blue'.
To cheese converted, what can be its boast?
What, but the common virtues of a post!
If drought o'ertake it faster than the knife,
Most fair it bids for stubborn length of life,
And, like the oaken shelf whereon 'tis laid,
Mocks the weak efforts of the bending blade;
Or in the hog-trough rests in perfect spite,
Too big to swallow, and too hard to bite.

Robert Bloomfield, 1800

This cheese came into its own on long sea voyages.

Their Cheese, tho' not so generally esteemed at Home, yet is prized much   204
in other Countries, being carried to the great Advantage of the
Inhabitants into *Germany*, *France* and *Spain*, where *Pantaleon Medicus* tells
us, they are compared to the Cheese of *Placentia* in Colour and Taste; but
supposing (as some think) that Author extols it for want of Judgment, it
hath another undeniable Quality, which makes it as useful as the best
Cheese of *England*, which is, That it bears the Sea better than any, and so
is in general Vogue among Sailors, especially in long Voyages. We have
heard, that tho' it be a lean, hard Sort of Cheese, yet the Sea so mellows it,
that it becomes very good and palatable, and thereby is so desirable, that
it hath been sold for Twelve Pence *per* Pound.

Thomas Cox, 1724

Farming naturally also comprised the husbandry of sheep.

The sheep come next under consideration; and here it is necessary to   205
premise, that great part of this country is known to have been, within the
space of a century, a wild, bleak, unproductive country, comparatively
with what it now is; full half of it was rabbit-warrens and sheep-walks;
the sheep were as natural to the soil as the rabbits, being hardy in their
nature, and of an agile construction, so as to move over a great deal of
space with little labour. When great tracts of this land were brought into a
better state of cultivation, the Norfolk sheep gave great aid to the new
improvement, as they fetched their sustenance from a considerable
distance, and answered penning as well as any sheep whatever. Folding

became in high estimation, and, aided by marling, brought the improvement of the country rapidly forward. Soon after, the turnip system followed, which enabled the farmer to improve his stock considerably by better keeping; so that, at this time, they are become respectable and profitable in their return, and in as high estimation, at Smithfield, as any sheep whatever, for no better mutton can be put upon a table; and though they produce but little wool, it is of good quality.

Nathaniel Kent, 1796

The harvest is the climax of the farming year, and no other county was so predominantly arable as Suffolk.

The Harvest! the Harvest! how fair on each plain   206
It waves in its golden luxuriance of grain!
The wealth of a nation is spread on the ground,
And the year with its joyful abundance is crowned:
The barley is whitening on upland and lea,
And the oat-locks are drooping all graceful to see;
Like the long yellow hair of a beautiful maid,
When it flows on the breezes, unloosed from the braid.

The Harvest! the Harvest! how brightly the sun
Looks down on the prospect! its toils are begun,
And the wheat-sheaves so thick in the valleys are piled,
That the land in its glorious profusion has smiled;
The reaper has shouted the furrows among,
In the midst of his labour he breaks into song;
And the light-hearted gleaners, forgetful of care,
Laugh loud, and exult as they gather their share.

Agnes Strickland, 1850

But no longer does it involve the total labour of the entire community, as in the Middle Ages. John Cullum, an early and admirable local historian, here reconstructs the scene at his native Hawstead.

What a scene of bustling industry was this! for, exclusive of the baker, 207 cook, and brewer, who, we may presume, were fully engaged in their own offices, here were 553 persons employed in the first year; in the second, 520; and in a third, of which I have not given the particulars, 538: yet the annual number of acres of all sorts of corn did not much exceed 200. From this prodigious number of hands, the whole business (except some smaller parcels put out by the job) must have been soon finished. There were probably two principal days; for two large parties were hired, every year, for one day each. And these days were perhaps at some distance from each other, as all the different sorts of corn were scarcely ripe at the same time. Yet I know not, if the object was to finish the general harvest in 2 or 3 days, whether all the crops might not be sown so as to be all fit to be cut at once. The farmers at present sow their different grains with a view to a harvest of about 5 weeks continuance.

These ancient harvest days must have exhibited one of the most cheerful spectacles in the world. One can hardly imagine a more animated scene than that of between two and three hundred harvest people all busily employed at once, and enlivened with the expectation of a festivity, which perhaps they experienced but this one season in the year. All the inhabitants of the village of both sexes, and of all ages that could work, must have been assembled on the occasion; a muster, that in the present state of things would be impossible. The success of thus compressing so much business into so short a time must have depended on the weather. But dispatch seems to have been the plan of agriculture at this time, at least in this village. We have seen before, that 60 persons were hired for one day to weed the corn.

These throngs of harvest people were superintended by a person who was called the head-reaper (*supermessor*, elsewhere emphatically *messor*, and *praepositus*), who was annually elected, and presented to the lord by the inhabitants; and it should seem that in this village at least, he was always one of the customary tenants. The year he was in office, he was exempt from all or half of his usual rents and services, according to his tenure; was to have his victuals and drink at the lord's table, if the lord hept house (*si dominus hospitium tenuerit*), if he did not, he was to have a livery of corn, as other domestics had; and his horse was to be kept in the manor stable. He was next in dignity to the steward and bailiff.

John Cullum, 1784

There was a nobility in the rhythmical action of the reapers.

I am at heart a simple man and there are things which I find it hard to   208
express, but as I see it, in all contemplation of the past and assessment of values there is an evocation and an answering of the spiritual part of us to dim tradition which no mechanized profit or economic exigency can wholly remove or still. To regret the past for the mere sake of the past is foolishness maybe, but to regret the good in the past is surely a kind of goodness in itself.

I remember a morning when I was no more than nine years old. There was an errand my father wished me to do at a hamlet beyond Shopleigh, and he and I were up before dawn and while I had my breakfast he put Grey Jack in the sulky and then I set off. After some miles my way led by a field known as the Hundred Acres and as I came to it by a slight rise I let the pony walk. It was a superb morning of early August and as I came to the height of land and looked across the great field I saw a something I shall never forget. In the near distance at least a score of men were mowing barley, the lord at their head. There was the faint swish as the scythes met the standing corn and the steady, ceaseless rhythm of arms and bodies and scythes in unison. Each man was spaced regularly behind the man ahead and the young sun would catch the gleaming scythes as they swung, and in the labour of those score of men was an incredible beauty and an energy as of some relentless purpose.

Since then I have seen most of the great orchestras of the world. I have seen the bows of the strings move in unison and yet I have been only momentarily stirred. For the unison and the rhythm have always recalled to me a something beyond the magic of music and the superbity of man's skill and the discipline of a baton. What I think of is a small boy in a pony-cart and the dew on the barley and the swing of those scythes in that Hundred Acre field.

Michael Home, 1944

The stacks of corn were gathered for threshing.

    Yow, Jack, bring them 'ere hosses here –   209
        Get this 'ere waggin out;
    I think the weather mean to clear,
        So jest yow look about!
    Come, put old Jolly to, right quick –
        Now then, hook Di'mond on,
    (There chuck yow down that plaguy stick!)
        An' goo an' call old John.

    John bo' the 'Cart shod close' we'll try
        (Get yow upon the stack);
    I'm sure the whate's by this time dry –
        Bring them 'ere forks here, Jack.
    Blarm that 'ere chap! where is he *now*?
        Jest look yow here, my man,
    If yow don't want to have a row,
        Be steady, if yow can.

    Ope that 'ere gate. Wish! Jolly – Wo!
        Cop that 'ere rope up, Sam;
    Now I'll get down an pitch, bo; so
        Jump yow up where I am.
    Load wide enough, mate – that's the style –
        Now hold ye! Di'mond! – Wo-o!
    Jack! – that 'ere boy do me that rile –
        Jest mind yow where yow goo!

    There goo a rabbit! Boxer, hi! –
        She's sure to get to grownd,
    Hold ye! Now then bo', jest yow try
        To turn them nicely round.
    Don't knock them shoves down! Blarm the boy! –
        You'll be in that 'ere haw!
    That feller do me so annoy;
        But *he* don't care a straw!

How goo the time? I kind o' think
  Our fourses should be here.
Chaps, don't *yow* fare to want some drink? –
  There's Sue with the old beer.
The rain have cleared right slap away,
  An' if it hold out bright,
Let's work right hard, lads (what d'ye say?)
  An' clear this feld to night!

John Lushington, nineteenth century

After which the gleaners had their day.

Why, listen yow – be quiet, bo'! – the bell is tolling eight! –   210
Why don't yow mind what yow're about? – We're allers kind
  o'late!
Now, Mary, get that mawther dress'd – oh dear! how slow yow
  fare –
There come a lot o' gleaners now – Maw', don't stand gawkin' there!

Now, Jane, goo get that 'ere coach, an' put them pillars in –
Oh! won't I give it yow, my dear, if I do once begin!
Get that 'ere bottle, too – ah, yow may well stand there an' sneer;
What *will* yowr father say, d'ye think, if we don't taak his beer?

Come, Willie! – Jane, where *is* he gone? Goo yow an' fetch that
  child;
If yow don't move them legs of yow'rn, yow'll maak me kind o'
  riled!
There, lock the door, an' lay the key behind that 'ere old plate;
An' Jemmy, yow run on afore, and ope the whatefeld gate.

Well, here we be at last – oh, dear! how fast my heart do beat!
Now, Jane, set yow by this 'ere coach, an' don't yow leave yowr
  seat
Till that 'ere precious child's asleep; then bring yow that 'ere sack,
An' see if yow can't try, to-day, to kind o' bend yowr back!

Yow'll all wish, when the winter come, and yow ha'ent got no
  bread,
That for all drawlin' about so, yow'd harder wrought instead;
For all yowr father 'arn most goo old Skin'em's rent to pay,
An' Mister Last, the shoemaker; so work yow hard, I pray!

Dear me! there goo the bell agin – 'tis seven, I declare;
An' we don't 'pear to have got none: – the gleanin' now don't fare
To be worth nothin'; but I think – as far as I can tell –
We'll try a comb, some how, to scratch, if we be 'live an' well.

John Lushington, nineteenth century

These operations called for the consumption of immense quantities of beer.

As has already been stated the home-brewing was an important event,   211
demanding the utmost care and vigilance; for there would be a great loss
to the household if the brew went wrong. Moreover, beer at that time
was recognized as an essential part of the farm-worker's diet; and during
times of extra work on the farm allowances of hops and malt were made
by the farmer to his men. Robert Savage, for instance, got a *lambing
'lowance* of two bushels of malt and two pounds of hops so that Prissy
often made two brews during the lambing season.

One lady from a nearby village remembers how, as a child, she
hurried down with her brothers and sisters on the morning after the
brewing to see whether the crown of yeast had spread all over the top of
the beer. The children knew that if they saw the welcome froth of yeast
the brew had been successful; and they were glad. The children's interest
in the brew was chiefly theoretical – if they were good they might be
given a glass of mild beer as a special treat with their Sunday dinner – but
they rejoiced to the greater glory of the household. The largest amount of
beer was naturally consumed by the father; and the good man in most
households worked hard enough to deserve it.

The old community had many terms connected with beer which
are worth passing note: *dew beer* was the beer bought with the shilling
earnest money given by the farmer to each worker when the harvest
contract was signed. With the dew beer the workers *wetted the sickle*, by
filling a ceremonial cup to the success of the harvest. *Trailing beer* was
bought out of the fines paid to the Lord of the Harvest by anyone who
had trampled down the standing corn or hay, thus making it more
difficult for it to be cut. The farmer's wife at one of the Blaxhall farms
once had to pay trailing beer money to the Lord of the Harvest because
she had allowed her hens to stray into a field of uncut corn. *Key beer* was
the strongest beer of all, so-called because for reasons of policy it was kept
under lock and key.

But home-brewed beer had other uses in addition to its legitimate
one. Thick beer was often used to help cure hams; also many women
here believed that beer was the ideal hair-wash; it was supposed to make
the hair shine. Another use for it was the staining of furniture. This was
before the invention, or at least the widespread marketing, of furniture
polish.

George Ewart Evans, 1956

*Manual labour was supported by the labour of the horse. Robert Hughman kept
a school at Yoxford.*

Now let me give my pencil all its force   212
To paint the powers condens'd within thy Horse.
Survey his honest front! the Highland Bull
Scarce boasts the honour of a thicker skull:
His neck, arch'd like a bow at fullest strain,
Shakes the thick glories of his shaggy mane;

Full and erect his firm-distended chest,
His body short, and like a sphere comprest,
With sturdy limbs well fit to carry all the rest:
Hind-quarter'd like an ox – his tail divides
The just proportions of his brawny sides,
And sweeps the dusty turnpike as he strides.
Sound in his lungs, and on his legs secure,
He, like the hound, though slow, is always sure.
SUFFOLK! one bumper to thy Horse, I say,
For he at every Show has borne the prize away.

Robert Hughman, c.1840

No other breeds were as muscular as the Suffolk Punches.

Having mentioned horses, I must take this opportunity of doing justice to   213
a most useful breed of that noble animal, not indeed peculiar to this
parish, but, I believe, to the county. This breed is well known by the
name of *Suffolk Punches*. They are generally about 15 hands high, of a
remarkably short and compact make; their legs bony; and their
shoulders loaded with flesh. Their colour is often of a light sorrel, which
is as much remarked in some distant parts of the kingdom, as their form.
They are not made to indulge the rapid impatience of this posting
generation; but, for draught, they are perhaps as unrivalled, as for their
gentle and tractable temper; and to exhibit proofs of their great power,
drawing matches are sometimes made; and the proprietors are as anxious
for the success of their respective horses, as those can be, whose racers
aspire to the plates at Newmarket. An acre of our strong wheat land,
ploughed by a pair of them, in one day, and that not an unusual task, is
an achievement that bespeaks their worth, and which is scarcely credited
in many other counties. Though natives of a province, varied with only
the slightest inequalities of surface, yet when carried into mountainous
regions, they seem born for that service. With wonder and gratitude have
I seen them, with the most spirited exertions, unsolicited by the whip,
and indignant, as it were, at the obstacles that opposed them, drawing
my carriage up the rocky and precipitous roads of Denbigh and
Caernarvon shires. But truth obliges me to add, though not to the credit
of my compatriots, that these creatures, formed so well by nature, are
almost always disfigured by art. Because their long tails might, in dirty
seasons, be something inconvenient, they are therefore cut off frequently to within four inches of the rump, so that they scarcely afford
hold for a crupper; and as absurdity never knows where to stop, even the
poor remaining stump has frequently half its hair clipped off. In a
provincial paper, a few years ago, one of these mutilated animals was
expressively enough described, as having a shorn mane, and *a very short
bung'd dock*.

John Cullum, 1784

Catlin's Duke 296 was a champion, born in 1846. Herman Biddell produced a formidable work on the pedigree of the breed, though he attributes this particular description to a 'Mr M. Biddell'.

Take him all in all he was the most perfect horse that I can call to mind. From a foal to his decrepit old age he was a great favourite with all who could forget or forgive the alloy in his composition. He first came out as a two-years-old when he at once made his mark, although he then looked to some, rather too 'punchy', but from that time he grew in length and certainly became the most popular horse of his day; and if his work be measured by his produce he exceeds all Suffolk horses in the number of winners at shows left by him, both colts and fillies. His procreative powers were extraordinary, and I had it on the authority of his leader, Charles Row, a man of undoubted integrity, that one season he booked eleven score mares to him, and it is well known that no horse left a greater per centage of mares in foal. In colour he was a good chesnut, 16½h. – fairly wide; his forelegs slightly crooked, very bent in at his knees, which caused him to 'dish' his feet out a bit in his action, which lost him the prize at Norwich. His head was a little too wide (showing the alloy); the width of his back caused by the great development of the muscles was remarkable. I remember seeing him at Woodbridge, and hearing the late Mr Webber exclaim that the hollow there formed would 'hold a basin of soup'. 'A basin,' exclaimed Mr Flatt, 'why it would hold a pail full.' His temper and constitution were all that could be wished; the former all his produce inherited, temperate in work, and a child could manage them; while no common day's work tired them, they always left off work with a good appetite for any kind of food. A few years before his death he had an attack of fever in his feet, otherwise he died in a good old age – perfectly sound – having I suppose left more recorded descendants than any other horse.

214

   M. Biddell, 1880

The horses responded to their traditional names and words of command.

This continuity of tradition manifests itself in various ways. It is apparent in the names of the farm animals. Certain names for horses are common all over both counties, and are to be found on almost every farm, while others betray local and personal influences. From an average of a considerable number of farms, I think it will be found that the most popular names are Beauty, Captain, Brag and Prince, while other traditional names are Gipsy, Billy, Darling, Dipper and Depper, Kitty, Tinker, Boxer, Briton, Daisy, Peggy, Proctor, Snip, Farmer, Punch, Diamond, Smart, Duke, Short, Flower, Bunny, Tom or Tommy, Blossom, Smiler, Nelson and Scot. Then there is the group of personal names – Dolly, Gilbert, Jack, Sammy, Judy, Fred, George, Fanny, and May; those which may be taken as complimentary to appearance or breeding, such as Bonnie, Spruce, Jolly, Spanker, Smiler, Jove, Sprite, Duchess and Damsel; and those with some ancient relation to the animal

215

which it is difficult now to understand. This includes Toppler, Gyp, Tinker, Sharper, Snip, Trimmer and Traveller. With the ordinary farm horses the naming is usually left to the teammen, and this accounts for the persistence of certain traditional terms over a wide area. The cows on an average farm are named in somewhat similar fashion, but here the range is wider in one sense, and more limited in another, for feminine Christian names are usually applied, and Rose, Daisy, Polly, Molly, Jenny, with a few variations such as Blossom, Cherry and Brighteyes are those most generally in use.

Unchanging tradition is further evidenced by the words of direction to farm horses, and the various calls to stock. With the increasing employment of mechanical methods for agricultural operations, it is by no means improbable that the next generation of farm labourers will find no use for the conventional cries of command to plough-horses. In a sixteenth century song the waggoner is described as 'with nailed shooes and whipstaffe in his hand, who with a hey and a ree the beasts command'. 'Hey' corresponds with 'heit', and tells the horse to bear hither, or to the left. In East Anglia this command is either 'cup-hey', 'cub-baa', 'cub-bay', 'coopy-hay', 'cuppy-whoa', 'cuppy-whee', 'cuppy-hoult', or 'hait-wo' (French *hay ho*), and is applied to horses in a team. The 'ree' of the mediaeval waggoner meant right, as in 'riddle-me-ree'. To turn a horse to the right the forms are 'wooch', 'woosh', 'wish', and 'whoash', from the French gauche, yet used with the reverse meaning, as 'Wooch wo', go to the right. The ordinary calls 'Weh!' 'Woh!' for stopping the horse, and 'gee-ho', are traceable to Norman-French, and are known in France, while in Italy 'Gee-ho' is 'Gio'. Cowley, in his 'Guardian', has a line: 'Ere Phoebus cry Gee-hoe unto his team'. 'Gee-up' is the East Anglian form, and probably the child's 'Gee-gee' has a like origin. 'Coop, coop', or 'cup, cup', are the usual calls to horses in a pasture.

W. G. Clarke, 1921

But the eventual redundancy of the farm horse was implied in the original use of mechanical power in farming practices.

Mr GOOCH, of Quiddenham, in Norfolk, having a water-mill which was   21€
sometimes unemployed for want of water, erected a steam-engine contiguous, at the expense of about 500l. The stove which heats the boiler, is so contrived as to burn coal to coke for his malt-house. One man attends both the engine and the cinder oven. It was, in the drought of 1800, of singular use to the whole country, for wind and water having both failed in a great measure, corn was brought from ten miles distance, to be ground by this engine: he has two pair of stones to the water-wheel, and two pair to the engine. The power, that of twelve horses.

The first steam-engine erected in Norfolk for merely agricultural purposes, and, for what I know, in England, is one now erecting at Haydon, by Colonel BULLER. He has contracted for the sum of 600l. It is to do the work of ten horses; to work a threshing-mill that shall thresh and dress six lasts a day: it is to grind corn also, and cut straw; to grind nine bushels of wheat with one bushel of good Newcastle coals, of 84lb. weight, and this with all the other works going on at the same time: the Colonel to find timber. Last year his hay and straw cutting cost above 70l. therefore little doubt can be entertained of the plan answering.

Arthur Young, 1804

Sport and Competition

When the Prince of Wales purchased the Sandringham Estate in 1861, primarily for its excellent partridge and pheasant shooting, he found a critical and obstinate adversary in his farming tenant, Louisa Cresswell. She eventually obliged the Estate to settle her complaints, and landlord and tenant thereafter maintained a jovial, though somewhat uneasy, relationship.

For the benefit of the uninitiated, I will describe a Royal battue in the open. The fields were cleared for action early in the morning, and I had to stop the work and keep the men at home, field machinery, &c., at a standstill. One year I lost part of the turnip crop in that way, for having engaged a gang of thirty hands from a distance to 'pull, top and tail, heap and mould up' by the acre, they were ordered off the fields for three days in succession; a frost set in, and the roots remained out in it, exposed to the weather and game.

I was not legally compelled to allow this, but, in the country, legality goes for very little, and, had I made any resistance, I might have been accused of all sorts of things – of complaining of the game, and then preventing it from being killed down – of spoiling sport, and so forth, and been in a worse position than before. I should have made a stand over the turnip crop, only I was in another part of the farm when the people were turned out, and when those gangs have dispersed and gone to work in different directions, you cannot get them together again.

A complete silence having been secured for miles round, the day was ushered in by a procession of boys with blue and pink flags, like a Sunday School treat, a band of gamekeepers in green and gold, with the head man on horseback, an army of beaters in smocks and hats bound with Royal red, a caravan for the reception of the game, and a tailing off of loafers to see the fun, for HRH is very good-natured in allowing people to look on at his amusements, provided they do not interfere with them, and, if it could be conveniently managed, would perhaps have no objection to everybody's life being 'skittles and beer' like his own.

At about 11 o'clock the Royal party arrive in a string of wag-gonettes, and range themselves in a long line under the fences or behind the shelters put up for that purpose, each sportsman having loaders in attendance with an extra gun or guns to hand backwards and forwards, to load and reload. The boys and beaters are stationed in a semi-circle some distance off, and it is their place to beat up the birds and drive them to the fences, the waving flags frightening them from flying back. On they come in ever increasing numbers, until they burst in a cloud over the fence where the guns are concealed. This is the exciting moment, a terrific fusilade ensues, birds dropping down in all directions, wheeling about in confusion between the flags and the guns, the survivors gathering themselves together and escaping into the fields beyond. The shooters then retire to another line of fencing, making themselves comfortable with campstools and cigars until the birds are driven up as before, and so on through the day, only leaving off for luncheon in a tent brought down from Sandringham, or in very cold weather it is carried into the nearest house.

It requires good, steady marksmanship for this style of shooting (for involving neither danger nor fatigue it can hardly be called 'sport'), and the birds have one chance of escape; indeed, after a few engage-ments, the old ones become quite strategical and know the flags are their friends and fly back through them, or veer round to the right or left out of range. This is altogether superior to the pheasant battue, when the birds are brought up in hen-coops and turned out tame into the woods to be shot down in thousands. Any fine autumn evening at Sandringham you may see them perched on the park wall and not greatly disconcerted at your approach.

The hares are dispatched upon a still lower scale of slaughter, and they might as well have fired into a flock of sheep in a fold, an amusement which I am thankful to say did not suggest itself to them, or I tremble to think of what the uncompensated consequence might have been.

A wild open country was the proper place for these military manoeuvres instead of highly cultivated farms; for on the partridge-driving days, if the Royal party did not do any individual harm, the village boys made it a Carnival, enjoyed trampling down all before them, breaking fences and gates, and doing as much mischief as they could, unconsciously carrying out the latest philanthropic craze, of the greatest happiness of the greatest number, the sacrifice of the few to the many, the elevation of the masses and other benevolences with which I had no sympathy. Personal loss and inconvenience is a curious antidote to sentimental views upon the rights of property. When riding round after the invaders had retired, seeing the general air of devastation left in their wake, the empty cartridges strewed about, and listening to the mournful chirruping of the poor little birds for their lost relatives, I felt it to be a 'dree' accompaniment to my solitude.

Louisa Cresswell, 1887

*The sport reached its zenith just before the First World War. At Elveden on 5
November 1912, 3248 head were shot, a source of pride to the head keeper.*

I have been told that the first day (5th November) is a record in this   218
country for a mixed bag of pheasants and partridges shot in one day, also
that the Hon. H. Stonor, one of the Guns, told a friend of his that it was
the finest day's shooting he had ever had, killing over 1,000 head of
winged game himself. This I can well believe, as he was a magnificent
shot, and at the top of his form in those days.

That year we had reared some twenty thousand pheasants on the
Estate, and about half of these were placed on the beats shot over in the
three days. Both wild pheasants and partridges had also done exceptionally well. So, providing weather conditions were kind, it was reasonable
to expect a large bag when the King came to shoot. In fact, prospects were
so good that it was decided beforehand to make a special effort and see
what could be done.

The morning of the 5th opened with a nasty drizzle of rain, putting
the start of the day back half an hour, which was not encouraging. There
were more than eighty beaters out and including the gamekeepers over
one hundred men were in the line or picking-up. At first the beaters were
divided up into three or four gangs, each gang having a number of
keepers with it.

We drove all the country in from Rakeheath and Chamberlain's
Buildings on to the Sugarloaf beat. Eriswell Hall and Village beats were
also brought in, altogether the biggest sweep-in we ever did on the Estate
and covering many hundred acres.

Fortunately this turned out to be one of the days the birds would do
anything you wanted them to, and they came forward in hundreds.
Careful timing in such a large sweep was necessary, as partridges driven
off their own lands would only remain away a certain time before trying
to work back; also if pushed too much they might start flying over a stand
before the Guns were in position. If a few started doing this they might
easily lead others on and spoil the stand. So the beaters driving in had to
be halted at certain points and at the right time.

We started the day with the One Hundred Acres Covert, the Guns
standing with their backs to the High Lodge road, the birds being driven
towards Sugarloaf as usual. We had a fine shoot here and a great number
of partridges were killed and many pheasants as well. Then we had
Sugarloaf Broom over; this is situated at the north-east corner of
Sugarloaf Wood, in the edge of which the Guns stood. This proved to be
another good stand, and it also helped to fill up Sugarloaf and King's
Hazard. After this the Guns and beaters walked Sugarloaf Wood up in
line into King's Hazard, when the Guns quickly took up their stands with
their backs to Sugarloaf, and the great King's Hazard drive commenced.
This covert is about half a mile long, a quarter mile wide, and runs from
the Brandon Road downhill towards Sugarloaf. The beaters driving in
from the Eriswell side had been halted on the Brandon Road, with very
wide flanks similar to a horseshoe.

As soon as the beaters started into King's Hazard the birds began to
rise, flying right above the centre of the covert in flocks, in fact I saw more

birds on the wing that day than any other day in my life. The French partridges as usual went over the Guns first, followed by coveys of English partridges and pheasants, in a continual stream. I wouldn't care to judge how many birds were on the wing together, but they went on and on over the Guns the whole of the drive without a pause. It was certainly a wonderful sight and one which I shall always remember, nor shall I ever see the like again.

It is quite usual for this stand to take some forty-five minutes continual shooting, it has been timed on a number of occasions, and for five hundred head of winged game to be killed there; but though I have no record of this particular day, the shooting must have lasted considerably longer than that and probably nearly double that amount of birds were killed.

At these big stands two or even three cartridge bags, each containing 100 cartridges, might not be enough for each gun; and so the loaders collected their cartridge magazines from the cartridge cart and placed them by their side before the drive began.

The King's Hazard stand brought us to lunch. The bulk of the shooting had been done in the morning, and things had gone very well indeed. After lunch we finished the day by taking the same drives a second time.

T. W. Turner, 1954

Gluttony and snobbery were never far away from the mass slaughter of the grand shoots. Kenneth Clark's father's estate was at Sudbourne.

After breakfast the guns left for the district where the beats were to take place, in the Delaunay-Bellevilles. My father trotted after them in the governess-cart with Tommy, and occasionally Lord Dewar. I ought perhaps to explain that the birds were driven over the guns by an army of beaters who, at Sudbourne, wore specially designed smocks with red lapels. They crashed through the wintry woods, shouting 'Hi, hi, hi', and beating the trees with their sticks. They were accompanied by keepers, who wore bowler hats and carried guns to deal with any defaulters. Each district had about five beats and the six or seven guns were so aligned that the birds flew out of a wood high over their heads. Naturally the guns in the middle had the best chance, and in order to secure their positions they used to draw lots – little silver spillikins. If, by ill luck, some famous shot found himself at the end of the line, with some duffer in the centre, the day's troubles would begin. At lunch time they were joined by the ladies in enormous hats with veils, and the whole party would then repair to thatched pavilions in the woods which had been specially constructed, one in each district, to contain a lunch party of fourteen. Striped awnings were stretched round the walls and from brass-bound hay-boxes there appeared a magnificent meal. How they ate! Local oysters and liver pâté, steak and kidney pudding, cold turkey and ham, treacle tart, double Cottenham cheese and always, to fill in the corners (as was often said with satisfaction), a slice of plum cake. The guns also

219

drank as much as they dared (which was a good deal), but they sometimes had to forgo that second glass of Kümmel, because on the afternoon beats the ladies would be at their sides and they would be more than ever anxious to show their skill. No one, of course, could have been invited who was not a good shot; but this was a highly competitive sport, and throughout England shots were graded, like seeded lawn-tennis players, with Lord Ripon and the Prince of Wales (George V) at the summit. It sometimes happened that a famous performer had an off day. Then his chagrin knew no bounds. The lady at his side would withdraw and he would return silently to the house, not to be seen again till dinner. Indeed, if things had gone really badly, he would refuse to come down to dinner and a tray would be taken up to his room.

Kenneth Clark, 1974

Arrogance often surfaced where shooting rights were involved. Larry Banville was gamekeeper to Thomas Buxton of Sheringham.

Wednesday 5 of September 1827   220
This was also a fine shooting day. I was out with Master H. Buxton, a keen sportsman although only a child. In the course of the day I saw a party of gentlemen sporting on a part of my manor which I left Master Buxton and I went to them and addressed them as follows, 'Gentlemen I come to say that you are over the bounds of your manor.' By that Mr Baring said to me 'You are [an] Irish blackguard,' and things that he thought of and that he would tell Mr Buxton of it and that if he was a gentleman of the County he would give me such a beating that I ne'er got in my life and that I was fit for nothing only to be put aboard of a King's ship where I would be flogged well. I told this gentleman that no-one had any right to beat me. One of the young Windhams said if I would be saucy to Mr Baring he would kick my arse, so I looked hard at him and said 'You kick my arse? What a fine thing for gentlemen to come to shoot a man's game and then their keeper to take it away and then tell him that they [will] kick [him].' But they all knew better, but Mr Baring said if he had his keeper with him that was in Dorsetshire he would make him kick me all round the field. Which my answer was that he would find [it] a rum job to do it as the field was so large. I believe there were near 100 acres without a few, but all is over. My master was afraid that I said anything to offend the gentleman. He is to shoot with my master tomorrow if all do be well, so then my doom will be at a end.
        10 o'clock, troubled mind.

Thursday 6 of September 1827
This was a fine morning. My master started off to Felbrigg Hall and Mr Baring went with him to shoot Sheringham. At night after dinner my master called for me and he told me that Mr Baring was very sorry for it and he had not been in such a passion for 20 years and that he was sorry for it and hoped that I would not think any more of it, which he acted like a gentleman there which I am happy to hear. My master let me out of the

room this night without drinking for the first time since I first knew his honour, but that is all right at present.

Larry Banville, 1827

Newmarket is the original centre of English horse-racing, which dates from the early seventeenth century. Charles II's patronage of the Newmarket races gave the sport widespread popularity.

Cambridgeshire is one of the so-called ugly counties; which means that it 221 is observably flat. It is for this reason that Newmarket is, in its own peculiar fashion, so thriving a locality. The country is like a board of green cloth; the turf presents itself as a friendly provision of nature. Nature offers her gentle bosom as a gaming-table; card-tables, billiard-tables are but a humble imitation of Newmarket Heath. It was odd to think that amid this gentle, pastoral scenery, there is more betting than anywhere else in the world. The large, neat English meadows roll away to a humid-looking sky, the young partridges jump about in the hedges, and nature does not look in the least as if she were offering you odds. The gentlemen do, though – the gentlemen whom you meet on the roads and in the railway carriage; they have that indefinable look – it pervades a man from the cut of his whisker to the shape of his boot-toe – which denotes a familiarity with the turf. It is brought home to you that to an immense number of people in England the events in the *Racing Calendar* constitute the most important portion of contemporary history. The very air about Newmarket appears to contain a vague echo of stable-talk, and you perceive that this is the landscape depicted in those large coloured prints of the 'sporting' genus which you have admired in inn-parlours.

Henry James, 1883

Thomas Holcroft was a thirteen-year-old stable boy at Newmarket in 1758.

The morning's exercise often extends to four hours, and the evening's to 222 much about the same time. Being once in the stable, each lad begins his labour. He leads the horse into his stall, ties him up, rubs down his legs with straw, takes off his saddle and body clothes; curries him carefully, then with both curry-comb and brush, never leaves him till he has thoroughly cleaned his skin, so that neither spot nor wet, nor any appearance of neglect may be seen about him. The horse is then reclothed, and suffered to repose for some time, which is first employed in gratifying his hunger, and recovering from his weariness. All this is performed, and the stables are once more shut up, about nine o'clock.

Accustomed to this life, the boys are very little overcome by fatigue, except that early in the morning they may be drowsy. I have sometimes fallen slightly asleep at the beginning of the first brushing gallop. But if they are not weary, they are hungry, and they make themselves ample amends for all they have done. Nothing perhaps can exceed the enjoyment of a stable-boy's breakfast: what then may not be said of mine, who had so long been used to suffer hunger, and so seldom found the means of satisfying it? Our breakfast consisted of new milk, or milk porridge, then the cold meat of the preceding day, most exquisite Gloucester cheese, fine white bread, and concluded with plentiful draughts of table-beer. All this did not overload the stomach, or in the least deprive me of my youthful activity, except that like others I might sometimes take a nap for an hour, after so small a portion of sleep.

For my own part, so total and striking was the change which had taken place in my situation, that I could not but feel it very sensibly. I was more conscious of it than most boys would have been, and therefore not a little satisfied. The former part of my life had most of it been spent in turmoil, and often in singular wretchedness. I had been exposed to every want, every weariness, and every occasion of despondency, except that such poor sufferers become reconciled to, and almost insensible of suffering, and boyhood and beggary are fortunately not prone to despond. Happy had been the meal where I had enough; rich to me was the rag that kept me warm; and heavenly the pillow, no matter what, or how hard, on which I could lay my head to sleep. Now I was warmly clothed, nay, gorgeously, for I was proud of my new livery, and never suspected that there was disgrace in it; I fed voluptuously, not a prince on earth perhaps with half the appetite, and never-failing relish; and instead of being obliged to drag through the dirt after the most sluggish, obstinate, and despised among our animals, I was mounted on the noblest that the earth contains, had him under my care, and was borne by him over hill and dale, far outstripping the wings of the wind. Was not this a change, such as might excite reflection even in the mind of a boy!

Thomas Holcroft, 1816

Riding in fenland in June.

Cow parsley wither high, voluptuous,   223
vegetable diamonds, if not mineral emeralds,
waves a green sea passage pliantly before the vibrant hooves,
catching a melted icicle of star momently
now in the strict bright stirrup or
now in the chestnut leather of the soap-flexed saddle.
Lady's lace that would embrace the muscled animal.
You stalk him green. He tosses you; denies.
But your seductive power lies impalpable,
thick-hot in the laden air, smell heavy as gall
and tanged, engendering all summer in the nostril:
makes him leap.
The improbable consummation is complete: Grass and flesh,
mingling an airy potency with blood and sweat,
daughter forth this June, this skirted girl beget.

Mervyn Coke, 1977

Setting dogs on rats and weasels.

In a frosty sunset   224
  So fiery red with cold
The footballers' onset
  Rings out glad and bold;
Then boys from daily tether
  With famous dogs at heel
In starlight meet together
  And to farther hedges steal;
Where the rats are pattering
  In and out the stacks,
Owls with hatred chattering
  Swoop at the terriers' backs
And, frost forgot, the chase grows hot
  Till a rat's a foolish prize,
But the cornered weasel stands his ground,
Shrieks at the dogs and boys set round,
Shrieks as he knows they stand all round,
  And hard as winter dies.

Edmund Blunden, 1930

*William Kemp was a comic actor and a dancer. He morris-danced from London to
Norwich for a heavy bet. It took him nine days of dancing to cover the 120 miles,
and for one mile outside Sudbury he was joined by a lusty girl.*

In this towne of Sudbury there came a lusty, tall fellow, a butcher by his   225
profession, that would in a Morrice keepe mee company to Bury: I being
glad of his friendly offer, gaue him thankes, and forward wee did set; but
ere euer wee had measur'd halfe a mile of our way, he gaue me ouer in
the plain field, protesting, that if he might get a 100 pound, he would not
hold out with me; for indeed my pace in dauncing is not ordinary.

As he and I were parting, a lusty Country lasse being among the
people, cal'd him faint hearted lout, saying, 'If I had begun to daunce, I
would haue held out one myle though it had cost my life.' At which
wordes many laughed. 'Nay,' saith she, 'if the Dauncer will lend me a
leash of his belles, Ile venter to treade one mile with him my selfe.' I lookt
vpon her, saw mirth in her eies, heard boldnes in her words, and beheld
her ready to tucke vp her russet petticoate; I fitted her with bels, which
[s]he merrily taking, garnisht her thicke short legs, and with a smooth
brow bad the Tabrer begin. The Drum strucke; forward marcht I with my
merry Maydemarian, who shooke her fat sides, and footed it merrily to
Melfoord, being a long myle. There parting with her, I gaue her (besides
her skinfull of drinke) an English crowne to buy more drinke; for, good
wench, she was in a pittious heate: my kindnes she requited with
dropping some dozen of short courtsies, and bidding God blesse the
Dauncer. I bad her adieu; and to giue her her due, she had a good eare,
daunst truely, and wee parted friendly. But ere I part with her, a good

fellow, my friend, hauin writ an odde Rime of her, I will make bolde to set it downe.

> A Country Lasse, browne as a berry,
> Blith of blee, in heart as merry,
> Cheekes well fed, and sides well larded,
> Euery bone with fat flesh guarded,
> Meeting merry Kemp by chaunce,
> Was Marrian in his Morrice daunce.
> Her stump legs with bels were garnisht,
> Her browne browes with sweating varnish[t];
> Her browne hips, when she was lag
> To win her ground, went swig a swag;
> Which to see all that came after
> Were repleate with mirthfull laughter.
> Yet she thumpt it on her way
> With a sportly hey de gay:
> At a mile her daunce she ended,
> Kindly paide and well commended.

William Kemp, 1599

Skating on the fens became popular in the last century.

During the closing years of the last century and the beginning of this, anyone with warm blood in their veins, at the least chance of bearing ice would take down their skates, polish the blades and be off to Littleport skating ground. Births would be postponed, deaths delayed, and the pilgrimage would begin. Tom Mott would suddenly become, as the owner of the Moors, the most important man in Littleport. To keep the ice in good trim for skaters, he employed one Tom Gotobed, who in summer put up bottles of 'hoss mixture' for sale by his employer. But in November he would start up a steam-driven pump and slowly the Moors would flood with water from the river. It stayed there all winter, frost or no, and was let off in March, quite often because it stank from stagnation, offending even the then none too particular sense of hygiene. But in such a year as 1895 the ice would bring as motley a crowd as one could see. Dons and undergraduates from Cambridge, canons from Ely, Cockneys and even bookmakers and pickpockets from London would take to skates or take from skaters, but giving the speedy Fenmen a wide berth if they knew what was good for them. Such Fen Tigers as Swearing Jack Cooper, Roany Smith, the Porters from Methwold Fen represented by Muckey, Traps, Ratty and Barley, whilst the Oslers from that parish had nicknames that were not used in polite society. Old Chafer Legge, the last of the real old type of Fenmen would be there in otterskin cap, moleskin waistcoat and Crabitt trousers, having skated from Southery Fen with his sons, Noah, Jack, Boosen and Harry, and his daughter Susan. A clannish family, willing to skate or fight against anyone for a wager. The Smarts and others from Welney would be there, on edge to uphold their pride.

226

Pathos skated side by side with humour in those days. Young children there to watch stood shivering in the icy blast with faces pinched and white for lack of wholesome food, unable to sport the ha'penny for a hot potato on sale. There were races for nearly all, for men young or old, for young spinsters and those whose husbands egged or almost drove them to the starting line. In one race, Chafer Legge's daughter Susan was well on the way to the winning line, ahead of those against. Chafer was skating outside the course, shouting his encouragement to run though and make sure of the stone of beef, when things began to go wrong. From beneath her wind blown skirts a white garment appeared, dropping lower and lower with each stroke she took. Susan was baffled and perplexed, since modesty as well as the speed she would lose discouraged her from hitching the garment up. 'Kick it orf gal!' shouted her father, gruffly. 'Kick it orf – but keep a gooin – you never wore none till you went in service!'

W. H. Barrett, 1958

The rowing eights of the Cambridge colleges at practice. This author knew what he was talking about, having rowed number six in the King's College boat.

Rowing day after day, Edward recognised the divinities of the tow-path, 227 passing like gods of the underworld in the mists and fogs. The scarlet-clad crews of St John's were accompanied year in and year out by a stiff, stout, stubborn gentleman with a Trial cap on his head and a demi-cart-horse beneath him. And the Jesus College crews were owned, leased, chosen, moulded and made, licked and lugged into shape by 'Beeve'. Great and absolute and unchallenged, the famous Coaches dominated the rowers on the Cam.

King's was not a rowing College in the great sense instanced by Jesus College or Trinity Hall or the Elysian society of Old Etonians known as 'Third Trinity'. Edward overheard the May-boat men talking during the endless shivering waits on the boat-house balcony.

'There's a Hall boat. Pretty rough!'

'Hall are professional bargees refined to style!'

'Look at that Jesus boat creeping down the river!'

'Bloody Jesuits! that's what they are. Any means to reach the end. Head of the river at all cost. To practise their May boat they will keep men from rowing for the Varsity.'

'Where's the Beeve?'

'I can hear if I can't see him.' And at that moment a sound like a wounded bull broke the fog and an enormous anthropoid man leisurely balanced on a strengthened bicycle was seen upbraiding a distant crew.

'SPRING AND DRAW,' said the voice, and echoed itself, 'SPRING AND DD-RR-AW!' And a crew of men in black and red ribboned vests sprang and drew. They slipped into the fog, but that remorseless voice followed, bellowing; followed after, 'Finish long! Finish long! Wait till the cows come home.' The Jesus Eight eased behind the bend, but out of the distance came a clearly enunciated comparison of their efforts to old women bed-bound. The Jesus Eight pulled themselves together and passed rhythmically onward with the sound that true Coaches envy and know. 'Tap her along! TAP HER ALONG! *Tap her along!*' and the mighty voice died away. The harmonious ring of the Jesus Eight was drowned in the scurry and sprawl and splash of crews from less disciplined Colleges. All that afternoon the green grease of the Cam was cupped and eyed and eddied by octaves of perspiring oarsmen.

Shane Leslie, 1926

From their earliest days the bumping races brought all sorts to the river, including Edward Fitzgerald of Trinity, briefly interrupting his conversational flow.

Shortly after this, the rest of us agreed it was time to be gone. We walk'd   228
along the fields by the Church, (purposely to ask about the sick Lady by the way,) cross'd the Ferry, and mingled with the crowd upon the opposite shore; Townsmen and Gownsmen, with the tassell'd Fellow-commoner sprinkled here and there – Reading men and Sporting men – Fellows, and even Masters of Colleges, not indifferent to the prowess of their respective Crews – all these, conversing on all sorts of topics, from the slang in *Bell's Life* to the last new German Revelation, and moving in ever-changing groups down the shore of the river, at whose farther bend was a little knot of Ladies gathered up on a green knoll faced and illuminated by the beams of the setting sun. Beyond which point was at length heard some indistinct shouting, which gradually increased, until 'They are off – they are coming!' suspended other conversation among ourselves; and suddenly the head of the first boat turn'd the corner; and then another close upon it; and then a third; the crews pulling with all their might compacted into perfect rhythm; and the crowd on shore turning round to follow along with them, waving hats and caps, and cheering, 'Bravo, St John's!' 'Go it, Trinity!' – the high crest and blowing forelock of Phidippus's mare, and he himself shouting encouragement to his crew, conspicuous over all – until, the boats reaching us, we also were caught up in the returning tide of spectators, and hurried back toward the goal; where we arrived just in time to see the Ensign of Trinity lowered from its pride of place, and the Eagle of St John's soaring there instead. Then, waiting a little while to hear how the winner had won, and the loser lost, and watching Phidippus engaged in eager conversation with his defeated brethren, I took Euphranor and Lexilogus under either arm, (Lycion having got into better company elsewhere,) and walk'd home with them across the meadow leading to the town, whither the dusky troops of Gownsmen with all their confused voices seem'd as it were evaporating in the twilight, while a Nightingale began to be heard among the flowering Chestnuts of Jesus.

Edward Fitzgerald, 1851

Bicycling comes to Norwich.

Messrs Jolly and Son, coachbuilders, Norwich, advertised that they had   229
'arranged to supply from a noted French maker the celebrated bicycle
velocipede, so much in vogue in Paris'. The price of the machine was
from 8 gs upwards. On the 30th there was an editorial announcement to
the effect that 'an attempt is being made to introduce this latest novelty in
locomotive machinery, now so fashionable in Paris, to the Norwich
public, by Mr C. Thorn, who has two at his establishment, for the
inspection of the curious'. The 'first velocipede journey of any considerable distance from Norwich' was performed on March 30th by Mr B. W.
Jolly, who travelled from Norwich to Yarmouth, including a stoppage of
fifteen minutes at Acle, in 2 hours 30 minutes. 'The progress of the
traveller was considerably retarded by the roughness of the roads and a
powerful gale.' A short time previously Mr G. W. Bellamy, of
Saxlingham, on a velocipede built by Messrs Jolly and Son, but under
much more favourable conditions as to roads and weather, accomplished
the distance of 56 miles in 6 hours 25 minutes, exclusive of a short delay
midway on the journey. A Norwich Velocipede Club was established in
the month of April, and on the 29th an exhibition of the machines was
held at the Corn Hall, under the management of Mr Thorn. On the same
occasion was exhibited 'one of the old-fashioned dandy horses, the
original of the velocipede tribe', but, it was added, 'the new velocipede is
more easily managed'. The first velocipede races took place at the athletic
sports of the Norwich Gymnastic Society, held on Newmarket Road
Cricket Ground, on May 24th. A 'slow race', ridden by Messrs Jolly,
Griffiths, and Goldsmith, was won by the last-named. A 'plank race', in
which the bicycles were ridden upon a seventy yards' length of plank,
was won by a competitor named Ewing. A one mile 'fast race' was ridden
in heats, the first of which was won by Kent, of Beccles, and the second
by Bellamy. Kent was the winner of the final heat, in 4 minutes 49
seconds. 'He came over on his bicycle from Beccles in the morning, and
returned the same way after the sports.' By the end of the year there was
a marked increase in the number of local cyclists. Accidents to inexperi-
enced riders were frequently recorded, and many complaints were made
by drivers of the alarm occasioned to horses by the appearance of these
new-fangled machines.

Norfolk Chronicle, 1869

*Camp was a primitive version of Rugby football. In this description a side's
'goals' are what we would now term the opponent's goals. The players were
stripped to the waist, and barefoot.*

CAMP   A game formerly much in use among schoolboys, and occasion-   230
ally played by men in those parts of Suffolk on the sea-coast – more
especially in the line of Hollesley Bay between the Rivers Orwell and
Alde – sometimes school against school, or parish against parish. It was
thus played –

Goals were pitched at the distance of 150 or 200 yards from each other – these were generally formed of the thrown off clothes of the competitors. Each party has two goals, ten or fifteen yards apart. The parties, ten or fifteen on a side, stand in line, facing their own goals and each other, at about 10 yards distance, midway between the goals, and nearest that of their adversaries. An indifferent spectator, agreed on by the parties, throws up a ball, of the size of a common cricket ball, midway between the confronted players, and makes his escape. It is the object of the players to seize and convey the ball between their own goals. The rush is therefore very great; as is sometimes the shock of the first onset, to catch the falling ball: – he who first can catch or seize it speeds therefore home pursued by his opponents (thro' whom he has to make his way) aided by the jostlings and various assistances of his own *sidesmen*. If caught and held, or in imminent danger of being caught, he *throws* the ball – but must in no case *give* it – to a less beleaguered friend, who, if it be not arrested in its course or he jostled away by the eager and watchful adversaries, catches it; and he hastens homeward, in like manner pursued, annoyed, and aided – winning the notch (or snotch) if he contrive to *carry* – not *throw* – it between his goals. But this in a well matched game, is no easy achievement, and often requires much time, many doublings, detours, and exertions. I should have noticed that if the holder of the ball be caught with the ball in his possession, he loses a *snotch*, if, therefore, he be hard pressed, he *throws* it to a convenient friend, more free and in breath than himself. At the loss (or gain) of a *snotch*, a recommence takes place, arranging which gives the parties time to take breath. Seven or nine notches are the game – and these it will sometimes take two or three hours to win.

It is a most noble and manly sport; in the whole little, if at all, inferior to cricket, or hunting, or horse-racing. The eagerness and emulation excited and displayed in and by the competitors and townsmen, are surprising. Indeed it is very animating to see twenty or thirty youths, stripped to the skin, and displaying the various energies that this game admits of; rushing with uplifted eye, breast to breast, to catch the descending ball, and all, at once, running full *ding* to gain a point, and when nearly gained, half falling over the stumbling object of pursuit (for the game is always played where the grass is short and slippery) and after much scuffing to see the ball again in the air, thrown to a wily distant sidesman – and seized and carried in the contrary direction – backwards and forwards perhaps half a score times, amid the shouting and roaring of half the population of the contiguous villages.

Sometimes a large foot-ball was used – and the game was then called 'kicking camp' – and if played with the shoes on, 'savage camp'.

Edward Moor, 1823

Ipswich won the Cup Final in 1978.

The coach finally set off back to Ipswich shortly after midday and it   231
provided yet another lasting memory for the players. They were picked

up by a police escort between Brentwood and Chelmsford with people already gathering by the roadside to catch a glimpse of the returning heroes.

After a slight detour to replenish depleted supplies of alcoholic refreshment they were at last on the final leg home and the welcoming crowds built up with every mile.

The coach eventually pulled into the Portman Road ground at 2.30 p.m. and after a short break the players boarded the open top bus for their triumphant tour of the town centre.

Nothing had ever been seen in Ipswich to compare with the scenes that Sunday afternoon. Every pavement was jam packed full of people while thousands risked life and limb to scale every conceivable vantage point – some even climbing along the jib of a giant construction crane overlooking the Cornhill – to catch a glimpse of the players.

A conservative estimate is that somewhere in the region of 100,000 people poured into the town centre that day.

It was slow-going through the packed streets, while on the Cornhill – where some of the crowd had been waiting since early morning – the atmosphere was quite unbelievable. The Suffolk Fire Service Band entertained from the Town Hall stage while thousands of fans filling every inch of space on the ground, hanging precariously from the sides of buildings, perched in every window overlooking the town square, and standing on the roof tops, sang the hours away.

Finally, just after 4 p.m. the Town bus drew into the square and the crowd erupted. Blue and white flags filled the air and the cheering must have been heard for several miles.

Ken Rice, 1978

Low Life

George Borrow's first encounter with the gypsies was at their encampment at Norman Cross, outside Peterborough; his fascination with them was complete, and he went on to live with them and learn their language.

One day it happened that, being on my rambles, I entered a green lane which I had never seen before; at first it was rather narrow, but as I advanced it became considerably wider; in the middle was a drift-way with deep ruts, but right and left was a space carpeted with a sward of trefoil and clover; there was no lack of trees, chiefly ancient oaks, which, flinging out their arms from either side, nearly formed a canopy, and afforded a pleasing shelter from the rays of the sun, which was burning fiercely above. Suddenly a group of objects attracted my attention. Beneath one of the largest of the trees, upon the grass, was a kind of low tent or booth, from the top of which a thin smoke was curling; beside it stood a couple of light carts, whilst two or three lean horses or ponies were cropping the herbage which was growing nigh. Wondering to whom this odd tent could belong, I advanced till I was close before it, when I found that it consisted of two tilts, like those of waggons, placed upon the ground and fronting each other, connected behind by a sail or large piece of canvas which was but partially drawn across the top; upon the ground, in the intervening space, was a fire, over which, supported by a kind of iron crowbar, hung a caldron; my advance had been so noiseless as not to alarm the inmates, who consisted of a man and woman, who sat apart, one on each side of the fire; they were both busily employed – the man was carding plaited straw, whilst the woman seemed to be rubbing something with a white powder, some of which lay on a plate beside her; suddenly the man looked up, and, perceiving me, uttered a strange kind of cry, and the next moment both the woman and himself were on their feet and rushing out upon me.

I retreated a few steps, yet without turning to flee. I was not, however, without apprehension, which, indeed, the appearance of these two people was well calculated to inspire: the woman was a stout figure, seemingly between thirty and forty; she wore no cap, and her long hair fell on either side of her head like horse-tails half way down her waist; her skin was dark and swarthy, like that of a toad, and the expression of her countenance was particularly evil; her arms were bare, and her bosom was but half concealed by a slight bodice, below which she wore a coarse petticoat, her only other article of dress. The man was somewhat younger, but of a figure equally wild; his frame was long and lathy, but his arms were remarkably short, his neck was rather bent, he squinted slightly, and his mouth was much awry; his complexion was dark, but, unlike that of the woman, was more ruddy than livid; there was a deep scar on his cheek, something like the impression of a half-penny. The dress was quite in keeping with the figure: in his hat, which was slightly peaked, was stuck a peacock's feather; over a waistcoat of hide, untanned and with the hair upon it, he wore a rough jerkin of russet hue; smallclothes of leather, which had probably once belonged to a soldier, but with which pipeclay did not seem to have come in contact for many a year, protected his lower man as far as the knee; his legs were cased in long stockings of blue worsted, and on his shoes he wore immense old-fashioned buckles.

Such were the two beings who now came rushing upon me; the man was rather in advance, brandishing a ladle in his hand.

'So I have caught you at last,' said he; 'I'll teach ye, you young highwayman, to come skulking about my properties!'

George Borrow, 1851

Besides the gypsies there were others not afraid to live rough, like this oddball at Scarning. Augustus Jessopp, the rector of Scarning, was, like George Borrow, concerned about the down-and-outs of society, and did his best to help them.

I ventured to touch further upon matters of domestic economy. Ben was   233 perfectly open; he had nothing to hide; he made no secrets. I had heard that he was a really good labourer, who could do anything he put his hand to. Did he happen to have dealings with a savings' bank? Was it impertinent to ask what he did with all the money he earned? '*All* on it? Oh! Ah!' He exhibited great appreciation of that joke, chuckled, and writhed, and shook his filthy old garments. Every wrinkle seemed to be saying to me, 'I never see sich a man!' Hoarding he regarded as a most ludicrous form of insanity. Work was a disagreeable necessity some-times. Sometimes it might come in as a relief to the monotony of life; occasionally, too, it might provide him with a pair of boots, which, however, as well as all other garments that he must needs wear, no rational man would purchase except second-hand. I gathered that he had never in his life possessed a *new* coat. He was perfectly contented with his lot. If there was anything that he had to blame his Maker for, it was that he couldn't sing! Music had been denied him. More's the pity.

When he was tired of working (and he was just as likely to leave a job half finished and disappear for ten days, after having secured an advance of pay), he repaired to the nearest public-house that would take him in – for it was not every public-house which he was allowed to frequent, or where he was permitted to sit down – and while the mood was on him there he would stay, occasionally eating his bread, and invariably and continuously consuming his beer. When the public-house closed what did he do then? That question he seemed disposed to fence with, and I at once refrained from pressing it. He saw I did not mean to impose upon his candour, and, with a certain generosity, he returned to the point of his own accord. There was just a little mystery about the way in which he spent his nights. That too was 'accordin''.

During the bitter winter of 1880–81 some of the roads were blocked by the snow, and Ben was at work with a gang of men making cuttings through the dangerous drifts. The miserable weather lasted for weeks, and some of the labourers were wet through all day long. It is almost incredible, but it is none the less true, that during all that winter Ben never slept in a house, but buried himself in the straw of a barn where he had leave to lay himself down. I asked him, with a shudder, whether he was not afraid of the rats? He laughed aloud with triumphant glee. 'I make no more count of them rats than if they was fleas!' He could not have expressed his indifference more contemptuously. Nay, the rats rather amused him, except that he objected to their tails – *they tickled his face sometimes!* Didn't he suffer from the cold? He didn't know what folks meant by being cold. Had he never been ill? Yes, he'd been 'bad' once aboard ship; he would not try that again! Never had rheumatism? What call had folks to get rheumatics? He 'didn't hold wi' rheumatics'.

During the last year or two I am told the county police have been molesting Ben, and stopped his sleeping in barns with or without leave. It appears there's some law against it. The consequence has been he has every now and then been driven to the Union for a night's lodging. I hear it is telling upon him, and he is not the man he was. When he can escape the argus eyes of the constabulary he still rolls himself up anywhere, in summer or autumn under a hedge, at other times in any hovel that he can skulk into; now and then in a warm pigsty. That *is* delicious! The astonishing constitution of the man seems to have been proof against all exposure, want, infection, drink, or irregularity of every kind. It is to be supposed that he will die some day, but if ordinary causes could have killed him, he would have been dead half a century ago.

Augustus Jessopp, 1882

The purveyors of moral tracts were also active, as here on the river Cam.

At this moment, a man with one arm habited as a Sailor was seen 234
approaching on the opposite side of the river; he carried in his hand a bundle of Tracts, the perusal of which afforded him mental pleasure and the sale a scanty livelihood: as he drew near he perceived the smoke eddying from the Waterman's pipe, and he hailed him with 'mate, will

you give an old sailor a quid of tobacco.' 'Aye' replied the Waterman 'if you'll give me one of your little books,' – the bargain was soon made and the goods bartered. 'Ah! heavens endow the Tract with success!' ejaculated the honest Tar, for *Will Spread* soon pushed off the house-boat to the bank and made her fast, and handed over a quid of tobacco from his leathern pouch, asked the old Sailor to look out a book for him, saying 'I know not a letter, but I have a little boy of mine who can read, for he goes to a Sunday School at Cambridge there!' The old Sailor selected from his bundle 'The Swearer's Prayer' for him, being aware of the shocking propensity that Watermen in general indulge themselves in, by using horrid oaths with almost every word they utter; *Will* took the Tract, and earnestly looking at it, enquired what it was all about, 'why,' answered the veteran, 'it says every one that sweareth shall be cut off', and it is about a man who was struck dead for swearing. 'Ah!' cried *Will* 'my boy will read all about it to me when I gets to Cambridge, but it was a shocking thing to die swearing.'

Wonba Smythe, 1825

Always there have been some who are simply incapable of looking after themselves, like this woman in Norwich Cathedral Close.

Over there, in the Cathedral Close . . .   235

Beautiful, the Close, a retreat of peace, a place of quiet, of elegant Queen Anne houses, walled gardens, fragrant flowers, ripening fruit, gentle bells chiming the quarters, unhurried clergy about the work of the Lord, cloistered and sequestered . . .

Anyway, over there on that bench, there's this woman: no telling how old she is, could be anything from forty to sixty, perhaps more, hardly less. Dirty as they come, can smell her yards away. A man's trilby, dank hair the colour of tarred rope, an army greatcoat minus buttons, a skirt of sacking, gum-boots in surprisingly good condition. Both hands tucked well up into her sleeves, yet trying to reach deeper . . . searching for what remembered comfort? What lost assurance of the flesh? Face a map of isolation beyond the frontiers of loneliness or suffering. Eyes everywhere, seeing nothing except the creatures of her private landscape. Talking to herself, muttering, whispering . . . listening. Flanked by her parcels and carrier-bags, three, four, five and a bundle, mostly old paper.

Twenty minutes, half an hour . . .

People veer away to pass – not much, but enough. Nobody seems to look, though everybody knows she's there. Can't miss her . . .

She accepts a fist of loose change without a word, the hand filthy, blotched, grasping.

Ten minutes, fifteen, twenty . . .

She gets up, gathers her bits and bobs, her worldly goods, the tale of her days . . . and shuffles along the path, dragging her left leg slightly . . . and round, and up, and out through the Ethelbert Gate . . .

Hundred yards . . .

Took her the best part of another ten minutes . . .
And then the cathedral bells chimed for five o'clock.
Soon be time for Choral Evensong.

George Target, 1977

*The Poor Law of 1834 set up workhouses for the destitute, whose conditions were
extremely harsh: the sexes were divided, so that husbands and wives only saw
each other in the chapel on Sundays. Here is the chapel of the 'house' at Sudbury,
in an anti-Poor-Law poem by a one-time mayor of the town.*

The noble-minded poor, whose lives had past   236
Unstained by parish alms, reduced at last
For some relief, reluctant to apply,
Received permission in 'The House' to die.

The ruined trader, left without a friend,
Or aught which he could borrow, pawn, or spend,
Who in his youth, far better days had known,
Now reaped the harvest he himself had sown.
The hopeless deaf, still took their usual place
Close to the fountain of their Saviour's grace,
Raised their imploring eyes and watched with pain
The moving lips that moved for them in vain.

Here the blind mother, guided by the hand
Of her dear girl, took her accustomed stand,
And as she *felt* the presence of her child,
She raised her sightless eyes to heaven and smiled,
With grateful heart, that God *one* comfort gave
To light her darksome passage to the grave,
For in compassion to her want of sight,
Mother and child they part not, day nor night.

The halt and maim'd, whose race was almost run,
Dragged their weak limbs and entered one by one, –
The wreck of toil-worn men whose life of care
No other home could for their age prepare,
At every step a helping hand they crave,
'Poor human ruins tott'ring o'er the grave.'

G. W. Fulcher, 1845

*Gentlemen could make spectacular drop-outs. Here is Cambridge's answer to
Oxford's 'Scholar-Gypsy', haunting the countryside outside the University.*

In those old robustious days – famous once, but now forgot – flourished   237 the Republic of Upware, a somewhat blackguardly society composed chiefly of muscular undergrads. Admission to the ranks of this precious association was denied to none who could hit hard and drink deep. In the riverside field that still keeps its name of 'Upware Bustle', the Republic held many of its drunken, uproarious carouses, presided over by the singular character who called himself, not President, but 'King of Upware'. Richard Ramsay Fielder, this pot-house monarch 'flourished', as histories would say, *circa* 1860. He was an MA of Cambridge, a man of good family and of high abilities, but cursed with a gipsy nature, an incurable laziness, and an unquenchable thirst: the kind of man who is generally, for his sake and their own, packed off by his family to the Colonies. Fielder perhaps could not be induced to cross the seas; at anyrate, he enjoyed an allowance from his family, on the degrading condition that he kept himself at a distance. He earned the allowance loyally, and found the society that pleased him most at Upware and in the inns of the surrounding Fenland villages; so that on leaving the University he continued to cling to the neighbourhood for many years, becoming a hero to all the dissolute youngsters at Cambridge. He it was who originally painted the apt inscription 'Five Miles from Anywhere', on the gable-wall of this waterside inn, his favourite haunt, where he lounged and smoked and tippled with the bargees; himself apeing that class in his dress: coatless, with corduroy breeches and red waistcoat. A contemporary sketch of him tells of his thin flowing hair of inordinate length, of his long dirty finger-nails, and of the far from aromatic odour he gave forth; and describes his boating expeditions. 'He used to take about with him in his boat an enormous brown-ware jug, capable of holding six gallons or more, which he would at times have filled with punch, ladling it out profusely for his aquatic friends. This vast pitcher or "gotch", which was called "His Majesty's pint" ("His Majesty" in allusion to his self-assumed title), had been made to his own order, and decorated before kilning with incised ornaments by his own hand. Amongst these figured prominently his initials "R. R. F." and his crest, actual or assumed, a pheon, or arrow-head.' Alluding to his initials, he would often playfully describe himself as 'more R. than F.', which means (is it necessary to explain?) 'more rogue than fool'. Eccentric in every way, he would change his quarters without notice and without reason, and would remain in bed, smoking and drinking, for weeks together.

This odd character lingered here for some years after the bargees had gone, and into the time when even the most rowdy of Cambridge undergraduates began to find it 'bad form' to booze and be hail-fellow with the village rapscallions of Fenland. Then Fielder himself 'forswore sack and lived cleanly'; or at anyrate deserted his old haunts. Report tells how he died at last at Folkestone, in comfortable circumstances and in a quite respectable and conventional manner.

Charles Harper, 1902

Edward Fitzgerald was also, in a manner of speaking, a drop-out. A quirky literary figure, he lived in a cottage on his family's estate at Boulge, before moving to Woodbridge.

I never look out   238
Nor attend to the blast;
For all to be seen
Is the leaves falling fast:
 Falling, falling!

But close at the hearth,
Like a cricket, sit I,
Reading of summer
And chivalry —
 Gallant chivalry!

Then with an old friend
I talk of our youth —
How 'twas gladsome, but often
Foolish, forsooth:
But gladsome, gladsome!

Or, to get merry,
We sing some old rhyme
That made the wood ring again
In summer time —
 Sweet summer time!

Then go we smoking,
Silent and snug:
Naught passes between us,
Save a brown jug —
 Sometimes!

And sometimes a tear
Will rise in each eye,
Seeing the two old friends
So merrily —
 So merrily!

Edward Fitzgerald, c.1870

Debenham's naughty boy has his moment of glory.

Dick, the village poacher, had been a very naughty boy, lazy, cheeky, and   239
a bully. He had some respect for my father, who one day caught him
throwing stones at the door of the girls' school and gave him a very sound
'hiding', but the good effect of that was only temporary. He grew up to be
a tall, powerful man, and developed a considerable capacity in the
handling of animals, so that he could earn something, when he chose to
do so, as a cattle drover. Also he possessed the gift of making friends with
and training dogs, especially greyhounds, lurchers and cattle dogs. If he

did not have one of his own he could whistle away the dog of some respectable neighbour and take it for a walk prospecting for hares and planning his next expedition. Though the last of the regular game-keepers had left our neighbourhood, there were still in the 'seventies a good number of hares about, for coursing was a favourite sport, and the Duke of Hamilton's harriers hunted the country, so the farmers liked to be able to show plenty of hares. Never was there a meet of the harriers or a coursing party that Dick did not attend, for his impudence was immense. Next day he would be round with a dog, or perhaps two, in search of a tired hare which might fall an easy prey to them. Again and again he was 'up before the Magistrates', fined, and if he could not pay the fine served a term in prison. Good Mrs Moore, of Crows Hall, sent for him one day and pleaded with him to amend, but neither persuasion nor punishment had any effect. If he were in funds he got drunk and quarrelsome and the police had to drag him to 'the Lock-up'. One day his little brother and sister were seen playing at a curious game. The boy had 'collared' the girl and was marching her down the street and they announced that they were playing at 'Mr Page taking brother Dick to prison'.

Yet somehow he was not entirely unpopular in the parish. Many good people tried to befriend him, and the none-too-good relished his lawbreaking. One day he gained a real triumph and great applause. It was at the first of our athletic meetings. The meeting was excellently organized, and in addition to the races confined to local runners there were cups to be competed for of sufficient value to attract entries from Ipswich and other towns. For the bicycle race, ridden over a rough grass track on lofty bicycles, there was a tremendous struggle between Prentice and Popplewell, two of the best cyclists in Suffolk. Later came the two-mile walking race, and a man with quite a high reputation came on to the ground in proper kit, shorts, spiked shoes and corks to carry in his hands. Most of the spectators thought he would have a walk-over, but no; Dick discarded his coat and waistcoat, kicked off his nailed boots, and in his 'stockinged feet' strode up to the starter. Spectators cheered and chaffed him, expecting to see the 'furriner' win easily, but when the men had travelled a quarter of a mile it was plain that the style and dress of the visitor could not make up for the great stride of the local man. Still, could Dick last out for two miles at this pace, for they must have been travelling at fully six miles an hour? The visitor was in good training and walked with the heel-and-toe step, while the judge had to caution Dick to keep his heels down. Knowing his habits, we doubted if he could last out the distance, but we need not have feared, for near the end of the journey he marched clean away and won, derisively slapping his legs. Great and prolonged applause from the crowd.

James George Cornish, 1938

A scene in Ipswich at the beginning of this century; we can picture it in terms of Edward Ardizzone's lively drawings.

We were marching through a poor quarter of the town. Why we were   240 doing so and on what errand I have forgotten. Our Scoutmaster, a young man, was dressed in regulation uniform and so also were the first four files that followed him. Each carried the appropriate staff and each was decorated with many badges. We that came after were a motley crowd. A few had scout hats, but most wore school caps. The rest of our clothing was most unorthodox: a variety of different coloured jerseys, shorts and stockings. Even the scout scarf was often lacking. Those that carried a staff handled it self-consciously and would from time to time trip over it. All of us seemed to be out of step.

Our route lay alongside a spiked iron railing which formed the fourth side of a square of dilapidated houses. On the other side of the railing a terrible fight was taking place. A man had a woman by the throat and was pressing her head backwards over the railings towards us.

He was a fearful looking creature, very tall and dressed only in ragged shirt and trousers. His head was a great, hairless dome with underneath a wild, ravaged face, haggard and unshaven, like some ghastly drunk out of Hogarth's 'Gin Alley'.

The woman was large and stout and very strong. I was fascinated by the arch of her wide body as she was bent backwards over the spikes and by the indentations the spikes made in the broad expanse of flesh. I was fascinated too by the great swelling biceps of her bare arms as she, in her turn, clutched her assailant's throat. They fought almost silently but with concentrated ferocity. The only sound was the sound of heavy breathing and the occasional grunt. A perfect subject for Daumier.

We boys stared goggle-eyed at this scene until our master turned and in a prissy voice said, 'Eyes front, boys. Remember never to interfere between man and wife.' Obediently, eyes 'fronted', we marched on, though I could not resist an occasional backward glance. It looked like murder.

Edward Ardizzone, 1970

Crime, for so long recorded in East Anglia, has always had its insane element.

Andrew Friday of Raveningham was taken with one horse belonging to   241
John of Hales which he stole at Raveningham. He puts himself on the country and the jurors say that Andrew stole the horse worth 20s. on Friday, 2 June 1307 and kept it until Monday when he sold it to Peter Munk in Norwich market for 8s. But the jurors say that at the time he stole the horse and sold it he was insane. They say that he is a lunatic and in the waning of the moon, he becomes insane. He was insane before and after the theft. They say that fifteen days before the theft Andrew cut down all the trees at his home in Raveningham and replanted them in the ground. When he was put in prison after his arrest he tore at his clothes and the clothes of others in the prison with his teeth. Because he was insane at the time of the felony, he is returned to prison to await pardon.

Norfolk Gaol Delivery Record for 1307 (translation, Barbara Hanawalt)

No murder was more dramatically revealed than when Mrs Marten dreamt (or said she dreamt) about what really happened to her daughter at the Red Barn at Polstead; 'Barnard' is a pseudonym for the murderer, William Corder.

Full of what Hannah had said to her concerning the supposed murder of   242
Maria in the Red Barn, Mrs Marten retired to rest, and remained for some hours awake, deeply reflecting on the horrible suspicions excited in her breast. Towards the middle of the night she fell asleep, and dreamed a singular dream; – not singular from its subject, for her waking thoughts had led to it, but from its remarkable accuracy and prophetic character.

    She dreamed that she was looking in through the door of the Red Barn, and that she saw the body of her daughter lying on the floor in the right hand bay, covered with blood: Barnard was close by, without his coat, working alternately with spade and pickaxe, making a grave. She saw him complete his work, and, when he had finished, deposit the body in the earth, cover it over, and then spread the ground with straw. She then fancied that she entered the Barn – stood upon the grave – removed the straw and the earth with her hands from the body – and plainly saw the features of her daughter; at which a scream burst from her, and she awoke trembling with horror. She told her husband this remarkable dream; and added her full conviction that Maria had been murdered by Barnard, and buried in the Red Barn.

    William Maginn, 1831

The gibbet provided a ghoulish nemesis for another murderer.

'I mind too,' said the old man, 'the last gibbet as ever stood in   243
Huntingdonshire. It was put up on the other side of Alconbury on the Buckden road. Matchan was the man's name. He was a soldier, and had been quartered at Alconbury; and he murdered his companion, who was a drummer boy, for the sake of his money. Matchan's body was hung in chains, close by the road side, and the chains clipped the body and went tight round the neck, and the skull remained a long time after the rest of the body had got decayed. There was a swivel on the top of the head, and the body used to turn about with the wind. It often used to frit me as a lad, and I have seen horses frit with it. The coach and carriage people were always on the look out for it, but it was never to my taste. Oh, yes! I can mind it rotting away, bit by bit, and the red rags flapping from it. After a while they took it down, and very pleased I were to see the last of it.'

    W. H. B. Saunders, 1888

Capital punishment was also the penalty for horse-stealing. Margaret Catchpole risked that punishment when she stole John Cobbold's horse to help her lover, Will Laud.

'Margaret, you must take this lantern, and just move the dark part round,   244 and it will shew you where the old boy's stable-dress is; go up the stairs carefully, and bring it down with you.'

Margaret did so. She went with breathless step to the bedside of the coachman. His stable-dress was upon the floor; she took it up gently, and as cautiously receded with it down to the stable again, closing the door without noise.

'So far so good, Margaret. Now, do you dress yourself there in the empty stall, while I saddle and bridle the further horse.'

This, however, was more than John Cook could do, for Rochford was of such a spirit, and sent out at him with such vengeance, that he dared not go up to him; nor could he without Margaret's help put the saddle or bridle on to Crop. She dressed herself as quickly as she could in the coachman's stable-dress; he being a little fellow, and Margaret rather tall, they only hung about her a little loosely, but were not too long for her. When she came from the stall, after rolling her own things in a bundle, and putting them into the very bottom of the seed-box, under the manger, and covering them with hay, she looked exactly like a young groom. She went up to the Crop horse and patted him on the neck, whilst her companion saddled and bridled him; she then tied some straw round his feet, so that no noise should be made in the stable-yard, and out the gallant fellow was led, ready for such a journey and for such a rider as never before had mounted his back.

'Now my girl,' exclaimed Cook, 'screw up your courage to the start. Come into the meadow. I can let you out on to the Woodbridge road, and then off with you.'

'But where am I to find you? you have not told me that,' exclaimed Margaret.

'Mount! and I will tell you.'

Margaret, with his aid, was soon in the saddle, and once there, she felt her own command over her steed.

'Now, Margaret,' he replied, 'mind what I say: you must sell that horse if you can, at Chelmsford market tomorrow morning; if not, you must ride on to the Bull, in Aldgate, London; but if you regard your own and your lover's safety, you will sell the horse first, and then find your way to the Dog and Bone public-house, at Lambeth: there you will find Will Laud, expecting you. Sell the horse for all you can get; say he is worth a hundred guineas, and that your master, squire John Cook, sent you up to sell him.'

The horse was a strawberry roan colour, remarkable for his action and the spirit with which he went through a journey. His ears were short enough, for, in accordance with a barbarous practice of that day, they were cropped; few that ever knew the horse could forget him; in harness, he carried himself as proudly as if he had been trained to exhibit his beauty, but this was his constant habit; his spirit was such, that he was never touched with a whip, and never exhibited the least disposition to restiveness; free, easy, gentle, noble, swift, untiring, graceful, and grand, he was admired wherever he went; and the short coachman, who occasionally used to ride him, made him, a sixteen-hand horse, look at least a hand higher. What an object was Margaret Catchpole upon him! Her spirit was up as well as Crop's; her resolution to go through all she had undertaken was fixed, and in reply to John Cook's question, when they came to the paddock-gate, 'Are you ready, Margaret?' she replied 'Quite ready!'

'And now, off with you,' said the fellow, as he opened the gate. 'Remember the "Dog and Bone". A hundred guineas for the horse, and you will be a happy woman;' and off started poor Margaret at a sweeping pace for the London road.

Richard Cobbold, 1846

Here is another spirited young woman, one who knew how to manipulate men and other animals. Polly was one of those eccentric characters who seemed to thrive within the confines of the old class system: a sort of Valkyrie to the Wotan of Thomas Coke in the Valhalla of Holkham.

One of Joe's colleagues, but of a different sex, was Polly Fishbourne,   245
keeper of the Church Lodge, who, when I last heard of her, was still alive. She must be about my own age. She had large, black eyes, red cheeks, and white teeth; her hair was cropped like a man's, and she wore a man's hat. The rest of her attire was feminine. She was irreproachable in character, and, indeed, somewhat of a prude. Polly was the terror of poachers, with whom she had frequent encounters, and would give and take hard knocks; but generally succeeded in capturing her opponents and making them answer for their misdeeds at Petty Sessions.

A Norfolk game preserver once offered Polly a shilling a piece for a hundred pheasant's eggs. She nodded her head. Soon after she brought Mr Coke a five-pound note. 'There, Squire,' said she, 'is the price of one hundred of your guinea fowl eggs.' Of course the Squire made Polly keep the five-pound note.

One time that I was staying at Holkham, a bull killed a labouring man in the salt marshes. The savage brute was standing over his victim, and a crowd was assembled at the gate, when Polly appeared at the opposite side. There was a cry, 'Get out of the way, Polly, or the bull will kill you.' 'Not he,' was the reply; 'he knows better.' She was right. The moment he saw her he backed astern to the remotest corner of the inclosure. It turned out that the animal had once attempted to run at her, but she lodged a charge of small shot in his muzzle.

Two young gentlemen once paid a visit to Holkham in the summer time. The dinner hour was half-past three, but the guests were not forthcoming. It was eight in the evening before they put in an appearance, and then looked uncommonly sheepish. At day-break they decamped without beat of drum. It transpired that they had expressed a wish to see the Church, and applied to Polly, the keeper of the Church Lodge. On their way thither one of them attempted to rob the said keeper of a kiss. Luckily for them they were guests at the hall, or she would have treated them as she used to treat the poachers. She resorted to a milder punishment; while they were in the belfry admiring the surrounding scenery, Polly turned the Church key upon them.

George Thomas Keppel, Earl of Albemarle, 1876

Less determined girls, such as these at Helpston, indulged in superstitious fancy.

246

The young girls whisper things of love
And from the old dames hearing move
Oft making 'love knotts' in the shade
Of blue green oat or wheaten blade
And trying simple charms and spells
That rural superstition tells
They pull the little blossom threads
From out the knapweeds button heads
And put the husk wi many a smile
In their white bosoms for awhile
Who if they guess aright the swain
That loves sweet fancys trys to gain
Tis said that ere its lain an hour
Twill blossom wi a second flower
And from her white breasts hankerchief
Bloom as they ne'er had lost a leaf
When signs appear that token wet
As they are neath the bushes met
The girls are glad wi hopes of play
And harping of the holiday
A hugh blue bird will often swim
Along the wheat when skys grow dim
Wi clouds – slow as the gales of spring
In motion wi dark shadowd wing
Beneath the coming storm it sails
And lonly chirps the wheat hid quails
That came to live wi spring again
And start when summer browns the grain
They start the young girls joys afloat
Wi 'wet my foot' its yearly note
So fancy doth the sound explain
And proves it oft a sign of rain

John Clare, 1820

Others were merely simple-minded and accepted marriage proposals un-questioningly, as in this story by an author who lived at Shropham. ('Horus' – Horace – had a house and a job outside East Anglia in one of the shires – 'shares'.)

It was the wife who had desired the red-cheeked Marthy for her son's 247 helpmate.

'Horus ain't strong – a corfin' and a spittin' half 's time t'rough,' she said to her husband. 'He'll, maybe, want some'un to narse 'm t'rough another illness sune, and I don't fancy his a pickin' up none o' them theer hussies from the shares. Marthy, she's a good liver, and she ha' got religion.'

And so it was with his mother's entire approval – at her suggestion, indeed – that Bob, the prayers being over, invited the visitor to take a walk with him.

'I reckon I'll be a-walkin' home to Gran'mawther's,' Marthy said. 'Th' road's free; I s'pose yew can come along wi' me, ef so be's yew wush tew.'

So she put on her sensible straw hat and tied her scarf beneath her chin, pulled on her fresh-washed gloves, and sallied forth into the sweet summer evening with Horus Nobbs. Along the white road, lying between the trim thorn fences, they went; through the narrow green lane, with its straggling hedges of sweet-briar, honeysuckle, and blackberry nearly meeting above their heads; across the broad fields where the barley and wheat, fast whitening to harvest, waved breast-high as they passed.

And during that walk, the short cut to Marthy's home, the amorous Horus, as Mrs Harper was afterwards proud and pleased to record, 'oped all 's mind'.

Marthy could not be said to possess that intimate knowledge of him which young women are advised to acquire of the men they promise to marry. She had walked home with him once from chapel; she had seen him twice pass her window; she had looked down on the top of his head through the 'discourse'; she had sat in his embrace through tea. Yet Marthy was by no means afraid; and it is probable that she was not running more than the average risks. It is said that the women who pride themselves on knowing the men they marry sometimes find themselves mistaken.

No doubts and trepidations on the subject came to agitate the simple mind of Marthy Milch. That a man could be other than he seemed was a proposition too complex for her intellect to grasp. He belonged to chapel-folk, he had got religion, his father held forth beautiful, he had good clothes to his back, and a house over his head 'i' th' shares'. What could maiden desire more?

'Gran'mawther, th' young chap ha' axed me to walk along on 'im, and I ha' said 'm yes,' she said when she had bidden good-night to Horus at the house door.

Mary Mann, 1902

But the nicest girls are those who are the most natural, and indulge in mild flirtation. Robert Arbib was a sergeant in the US Army Engineers, stationed at Debach during the War.

I do not know who mentioned it first. Perhaps it was Earl, who always   248 had a weather-eye cocked for a pretty girl, or I – never far behind in the critical appreciation of beauty. But one day early that autumn one of us said, 'You know, this little village of Sudbury has more pretty girls per square foot than any town I've ever seen!' And the other agreed.

Our errands around Sudbury each morning introduced us to many of them, and the rest turned our heads as we walked through the Market Hill or down North Street on our business. We could never solve the enigma of where the pretty girls came from, or why on this island of attractive girls Suffolk seemed to stand out, and, in Suffolk, Sudbury above the rest. But we were sure we had found a secret and unexplored paradise. 'Perhaps they take all the ugly girls out in the woods when they are three years old, and exterminate them,' I once said. The suggestion was heatedly denied by several natives.

Often on our way to town, Earl and I argued the matter. Perhaps it was some peculiar combination of racial heritage. Perhaps it was a rare and salubrious climate known only in this part of the world. Perhaps it was just a felicitous accident. We never did reach a plausible solution, but there it was – which nobody could deny.

When we stopped in for our morning coffee at Mrs Searle's bakery and tea shop, there was Peggy, a pert, blue-eyed blonde of eighteen, and Millie, a quaint, shy, dark-haired, large-eyed girl with a soft low voice. There, too, was Thelma, a tall, willowy, pale-skinned, chestnut-haired, blue-eyed girl, and Fay, red-haired, sparkling with laughter.

It was like a gallery! Peggy always had smart talk with the customers, and twitched her skirt between the tables in the back room – and Fay had a captivating twinkle – but little Millie just smiled shyly – and one day, when she had asked me what had become of an American sergeant of whom she had become fond, and I answered he had been transferred, she looked at me wistfully with her large black eyes, and said pensively, in her musical voice, 'Just when you get to know someone . . . they always go away. . . .'

At the Post Office we were waited on by Olive, of the heart-shaped face and the cascade of black hair – Daisy, snub-nosed, red-haired, pixie-eyed, and saucy, and Joan, graceful, slender, blue-eyed, and the darling of the town.

At the Board of Inland Revenue – there we found tiny Pat with a head of beautiful curls, and Kay, tall, blonde, grey-eyed and graceful. At Boot's the chemist we were served by Molly, who would be judged a blonde beauty in any town around the world. At Cundy's the florist we would admire Audrey – tall, raven-haired, and darkly beautiful. At the Gainsborough House, though still a child, there was beautiful Marie. At the milliners there was another pretty one, whose name we never learned, for, alas, our errands never took us to the milliner.

And then, too, there was Daphne.

Robert Arbib, 1947

East Anglians were traditionally stolid and robust.

The Inhabitants of this County are strong and robust, sharp and cunning. The Food of the Commonalty is much upon Puddings and Dumplings, which has produced the Proverb of *Norfolk Dumplings*, as the Eating Beans so much in *Leicestershire* has proverbially nick-named the People *Leicestershire Bean-Bellies*. Nor may the People be ashamed of their Food, it being certainly the wholsomest and nourishing to the human Body, not breeding such ill Juices as Flesh doth. It is true, the People are said to be   249 litigious and much given to Law-Suits, on which Account it is, that this County is said to be more full of Lawyers, especially Attorneys, than other Counties are. . . .

Thomas Cox, 1724

A dry humour lurked just below the surface. This author's father lived at Monk Soham in his capacity as Archdeacon of Suffolk.

Among the other Guildhall people were old Mrs 'Ratty' Kemp, widow of 250 the Rat-catcher; old one-eyed Mrs Bond, and her deaf son John; old Mrs Wright, a great smoker; and Mrs Burrows, a soldier's widow, our only Irishwoman, from whom Monk Soham conceived no favourable opinion of the Sister Isle. Of people outside the Guildhall I will mention but one, James Wilding, a splendid type of the Suffolk labourer. He was a big strong man, whose strength served him one very ill turn. He was out one day after a hare, and a farm-bailiff, meeting him, tried to take his gun; James resisted, and snapped the man's arm. For this he got a year in Ipswich jail, where, however, he learnt to read, and formed a strong attachment for the chaplain, Mr Daniel. Afterwards, whenever any of us were driving over to Ipswich, and James met us, he would always say, 'if yeou see Mr Daniel, dew yeou give him my love.' Finally, an emigration agent got hold of James, and induced him to emigrate, with his wife, his large family, and his old one-legged mother, to somewhere near New Orleans. 'How are you going, Wilding?' asked my father a few days before they started. 'I don't fare to know rightly,' was the answer; 'but we're goin' to sleep the fust night at Debenham' (a village four miles off), 'and that'll kinder break the jarney.' They went, but the Southern States and the negroes were not at all to their liking, and the last thing heard of them was they had moved to Canada.

So James Wilding is gone, and the others are all of them dead; but some stories still remain to be cleared off. There was the old farmer at the tithe dinner, who, on having some bread-sauce handed to him, extracted a great 'dollop' on the top of his knife, tasted it, and said, 'Don't chüse none.' There was the other who remarked of a particular pudding, that he 'could rise in the night-time and eat it'; and there was the third, who, supposing he should get but one plate, shovelled his fish-bones under the table. There was the boy in Monk Soham school who, asked to define an earthquake, said, 'It is when the 'arth shug itself, and swallow up the 'arth'; and there was his schoolmate, who said that 'America was discovered by British Columbia.' There was old Mullinger of Earl Soham, who thought it 'wrong of fŏoks to go up in a ballune, as that fare so bumptious to the Almighty'. There was the actual balloon, which had gone up somewhere in the West of England, and which came down in (I think) the neighbouring parish of Bedfield. As it floated over Monk Soham, the aeronaut shouted, 'Where am I?' to some harvesters, who, standing in a row, their forefingers pointed at him, shouted back, 'Yeou're in a ballune, bor.' There was old X, who, whenever my father visited him, would grumble, talk scandal, and abuse all his neighbours, always, however, winding up piously with 'But 'tis well.' There was the boy whom my father put in the stocks, but who escaped by unlacing his 'high-lows', and so withdrawing his feet. There was the clergyman, preaching in a strange church, who asked to have a glass of water in the pulpit, and who, after the sermon, remarked to the clerk in the vestry, 'That might have been gin-and-water, John, for all the people could tell.' And, taking the duty again there next Sunday, he found to his horror it *was* gin-and-water: 'I took the hint, sir – I took the hint,' quoth John, from the clerk's desk below.

Francis Hindes Groome, 1895

Low life naturally spoke in the vernacular. This was full of complicated vowel sounds which Robert Forby, an early etymologist, disparaged.

Ou and Ow.   251

In these last of our diphthong sounds we have the greatest difficulty to encounter, whether in vindicating our practice, or in conveying an idea of it to those who never heard it. In truth, we make very strange havoc with them. They have, with us, three different sounds, all equally departing in different ways from euphony, and from approved usage; sounds which cannot be represented, and to which it is not to be conceived that any natural organs can give easy and habitual utterance, if any utterance at all, but those of a native East-Angle, or of an old he-cat.

1. The first is a broad twanging sound somewhat, but not exactly, as if it were written *au-w*. These three letters are not to be considered as a triphthong; the *w* standing independent, and ready, either to apply its force to an initial vowel following, or to rest in itself, if nothing follows, as in observation *aw* 1.

Ex. Ought – low – owe – moult.
        Dough – mow – glow – soul, &c.

2. The second is considerably narrower, and may be attempted by endeavouring to sound the *open a* with *w* after it, as above described.

Ex. Power – sour – devour.
        Shower – scour – our.

3. The third is narrower still; and may be described as about midway between the legitimate sound of *ou* and that of long *u*. Or it may be easier to attempt the pronunciation (should any one think of attempting it at all) by lengthening out *long u*, instead of *open u*, as in the former case.

Ex. Cow – sow – plow.
        Now – crowd – proud.

Robert Forby, 1830

Forby's excellent definition of the most common form of address in East Anglia.

BORH, BOR, *s.* a term of very familiar address, generally understood to   252 be a coarse pronunciation of the word *boy*. A different account of it is proposed with some confidence. If boy is actually sometimes pronounced as if it were spelled *baw*, it is the sole instance of our so perverting the power of the diphthong *oy*; we either pronounce it as others do, or we narrow it to long *i*; we never call joy *jaw*, nor a toy a *taw*; we do not talk of *emplaw*ing or *destraw*ing, but of *emply*ing or *destry*ing. This one seeming instance of such perversion is therefore likely to have arisen from our not understanding the term we use; besides, it may be remarked, that this word is applied indiscriminately to persons of both sexes and of all ages; and though it may be common for elderly people to address as *boys* those who are much their juniors, or if they have been long intimate, to call each other in jocular familiarity old boys; or if old men, affecting juvenile airs, be so called, yet it would surely be too absurd for old women to give to each other the appellation of *boy*. Now among so many traces as we have of Saxon antiquity, so many instances of Saxon words traditionally retained in their original form and use, it cannot be extravagant to conjecture that the word is, in fact, *bor*, and directly refers to the well-known frame of Saxon society, in which those who constituted every little community, or township (*borg*), were mutually and formally bound by law to and for each other, under a petty local magistrate, or conservator of the peace, called the *borsholder*, *i.e.* the *bor's older*, or *elder*. This official title still exists in some districts. The word under our consideration would thus signify townsman, neighbour, sworn friend, &c., much in the same way as our seamen call each other messmate, and our soldiers comrade. It is to be observed that it is actually a part of the word neighbour (A.S. *neah*, prope, and *borh*); and why may it not exist in the simple as well as in a compound form? If this explanation be admitted, one old woman may, without absurdity, say to another (as often happens), 'Co' *bor*, let's go a sticking in the 'Squire's plantations.' And the other may answer, 'Aye, *bor*, so we will.'

Robert Forby, 1830

Outsiders were not encouraged to attempt the vernacular.

A pert little octogenarian, clad in homely attire, and with straps below his 253
knees, as land-workers wear them, like Horatio, held the bridge. A felt hat topped his wise small grey head, and a fringe of fox-tinted beard half-mooned his aged chin. 'Billy', as his co-workers called him, acted as ferryman, levering off and chain-manipulating the heavy pontoon in and out the gap – out as impatient yachts-folk needed, and closed when hay-wagons at spells demanded.

Billy had a lively tongue, soft at will as a cat's paw, when her claws lie *perdu*; and also voiced frank, even tart, opinions upon men and things which, spoken in the dear old Norfolk brogue, warmed my heart towards this rustic riverside philosopher. A wagon had just rumbled over, and Old Man started to shift fallen hay. Looking up, he spake:

'Now, then, togither, du yow want ter go trew?'

'Bor,' said I, 'we dew; *I'm* comin' trew, as sune as yow shift yer owd pontune!'

'Yow're werry clever, yung man!' he rebukefully remarked, but by no means offensively. I thought of the forty-two children of Beth-el, who mocked Elisha, and I relented. I know how sanguinary can be two she bears!

'But I'm broad Norfik myself,' I said, 'and I'm proud on it.'

'Well, then, I arn't,' he snapped; 'an' if I'd hed yar chances of bein' edjicated, *I'd* speak plain English!'

Bravo! I thought; but I saw I had ruffled the dear old boy's feelings.

Arthur Patterson, 1923

In fact outsiders, especially those who brought innovation, were deeply resented.

I am bound to express my belief that Maychester will never help to   254 return a Liberal to the House of Commons for the Market Waldron Division of Landshire, but hope springs eternal in the breast of Parliamentary candidates, and I was not surprised to learn from the doctor a month or more ago that the young gentleman who seeks to capture the district for Liberalism was summering the country.

But I thought no more about the matter until last week, when I sat in the porch surveying my garden and the lane beyond that passes Father William's cottage. The veteran was tending some tomato-plants.

Down the road I saw a cloud of dust heralding a fast-flying motor-car. In less time than it takes me to set the words down the Liberal candidate has reached the old man's cottage, and, with brakes hard set, was trying to steer clear of the garden. The wheels must have skidded, I think; certainly the appearance of the trim-cut hedge was not improved, and the candidate, who seems to know even less about motor-cars than politics, looked quite flushed as he backed out on to the road.

For a moment Father William stared aghast to see his hedge assaulted. Then he gave tongue.

'Do ye come a-breakin' down an ole man's garden?' he screamed. 'I'll pay ye, ye varmint!' So saying he shuffled hurriedly within, to reappear in a moment, crook-stick in hand. Without another word he aimed a deadly blow at the car. 'Do ye take that!' he cried, his eyes ablaze, his red shawl flying in the breeze. I think that in the moment of his wrath and excitement machine and driver were one – a twentieth-century centaur.

'I say, my friend, you mustn't hurt the car,' said the perturbed candidate. 'It's quite an accident; I'm very sorry, but the hedge isn't hurt. And what a nice garden you've got!'

'An' ye wanted to break into it, I doubt, ye waster!' screamed Father William, feeling that he realized the facts of the case at last. 'Do ye come nigh agin wi' that gre't ugly ole machine o' yourn, an' I'll gi'e it a strook that'll break it an' you too.'

'Now, my good friend,' began the candidate, plainly discomfited.

'That's a lie,' broke in the veteran. 'I ain't no fr'en' o' yourn, an' never weren't; an' if th' p'liceman were passin' along, I'd gi'e ye to 'im, an' 'e'd take ye, an' no mistake! Arter me wegebles, I shouldn't wonder, an' put 'em in y'r cart an' ride off. Worse nor a poacher ye are, an' so I'll tell ye!'

'Now, please don't be so impatient,' pleaded the candidate soothingly. 'I've driven down here on purpose to have a chat with you. People say you're the oldest inhabitant – '

'An' no doubt you've come to deny ut,' interrupted Father William, with fine sarcasm. 'Ye're down 'ere wi' no good purpose, I'll be bound. Why don't ye keep that gre't beast o' yourn quiet, 'stead o' lettin' it stand shiverin' an' shakin' like it's got ague? Do ye think I raise me wegebles f'r fools like that to come a-tramplin' on?'

S. L. Bensusan, 1907

Old men recollected the exploits of their youth.

After the tea had 'tricolated' down their throats, and other things also, extra fuel was put on the fire, long clay pipes were lit, and then tongues began, very slowly at first, to wag, not to me, but to each other. Old Jimmy, who had been fifty years team-man on one farm, and old Tom, who had been sailor, labourer, and poacher in turns, talked thus to each other, as nearly as the vernacular can be given in print: – 255

'Tom, bor, de yow mind the time when we used to ha' to go down to Blakeney arter a cargo o' rum?'

'Oh! ah! bor! thar a' du, an' orl.'

I interpolate a question, like putting a bit of coal on the fire, 'Well, what did you do?'

'Well! 'twas like this here. Whensumever a ship was expected to come in from Holland, we used to drive down, each one in a hoss and cart, every night, for which we'd get half a crown if she worn't there, and five shillun if she wor. Then, if you will me believe, we'd have the cargo out o' the ship and into the carts and away we'd go, all in a quarter of an hour. As soon as uvver we were gone yow could hear the guns of the preventive men a-blazing away arter us. Du they never catched us; 'cause why, they knew where to find a keg for themselves. They just blazed away to let folks know they'd *werry near* catched us.' At this not a muscle of their phlegmatic faces moved.

To my question as to what became of the 'stuff', I had for answer: 'There was allust [always] folks to take it; sometimes we hid it away in Edgefield Great Wood, sometimes in the chambers upstairs. I have seen this here house where we are now a-settin' so crammed wi' casks in the room upstairs that we had to prompt the ceiling up wi' larch poles to keep the floor from coming through. Listen here!' (and he tapped the floor with his heel) 'de you hear how holl' that sounds? Well, there's a cellar there and that used to be full an' all. Then we allust left a keg just inside the parson's gate.' (Alas for the good old times of fifty years ago!)

'What for?'

'Why! just to keep his mouth shut, by opening it.'

Morley Adams, 1913

And death collected old men. It caught up with Hobson when safe in bed – he who had led a charmed life driving coaches between Cambridge and London. Hobson also hired out horses, but you always had to take the one nearest the stable door ('Hobson's choice').

Here lies old Hobson. Death hath broke his girt,   256
And here, alas! hath laid him in the dirt;
Or else, the ways being foul, twenty to one
He's here stuck in a slough, and overthrown.
'Twas such a shifter that, if truth were known,
Death was half glad when he had got him down;
For he had any time this ten years full
Dodged with him betwixt Cambridge and *The Bull*.
And surely Death could never have prevailed,
Had not his weekly course of carriage failed;
But lately, finding him so long at home,
And thinking now his journey's end was come,
And that he had ta'en up his latest inn,
In the kind office of a chamberlin
Showed him his room where he must lodge that night,
Pulled off his boots, and took away the light.
If any ask for him, it shall be said,
'Hobson has supped, and's newly gone to bed.'

John Milton, 1631

But death could also catch up with men still actually in the driving seat.

'The post,' he said, 'was brought out from Braintree by cart in them days;   257
and at the time I'm tellin' you of, the job was contracted out to a man that
lived over at Benfield. He drove a little closed-in box of a cart, on high
wheels, with painted spokes nigh as thin as matches. A mule drew the
cart and sometimes you'd meet it fair flyin' along the roads. On the way
back to Braintree each night, the postman – he wore a little ol' pill-box
hat, I remember – used to call at Larkfield, Shepfield, and Stalling to pick
up the mail-bags. There he sat, perched up on top of his little red cart, in a
sort of fenced-in seat. The mail-box was padlocked at the back; and each
post-master – or whatever you like to call 'em, for mostly they did a
dozen other jobs besides – had his own key. He'd hurry out with the
mail-bag, unlock the box, fling the bag in, and then lock it up again.
"Night, Joe!" he'd say; and without so much as a word from the driver,
or a flick o' the whip, away that ol' mule 'ld goo like a streak of lightnin'.
He knew the roads just as well as Joe himself did.

'Well, we used to have rare hard winter weather then – sometimes
it 'ld be below zero. More'n once I've played games on the pond when I
was a kid: bowlin' for oranges instead of coconuts, you know. Why, the
water would be frozen so thick that even the ground underneath was
frozen too. But as I was sayin', there'd be ol' Joe, sittin' up there on his
high seat, all muffled up to the ears so's you couldn't tell whether he

answered you or not. And one mighty cold night, he came rattlin' along the road same as usual, and called at all the post offices like he did every blessed night of the year. It was so cold that whenever he stopped, the post-master just flung the mail-bag into the back of the cart, locked up the box as quick as ever he could, and scuttled off indoors again out of the weather. "Night, Joe!" he called, and away went the mule. When they got to Braintree, they pulled into the post office yard, and somebody came out to collect the bags. "You've had a cold ride to-night, Joe, and no mistake," he said. But Joe never answered a word. He just sat up there on his perch, without so much as movin' a hand – for he was frozen dead in his seat. And nobody ever knowed whereabouts on the road it happened.'

C. Henry Warren, 1939

High Life

The rich man in his castle, the poor man at his gate. Laurence Jones' father was the owner of Cranmer Hall, near Fakenham.

That this was a world of pre-ordained classes, we never doubted. We felt no sense of patronage when, on Christmas Eve, the cottagers on the estate crowded into the decorated Servants' Hall, each man bringing with him a capacious red-and-white spotted handkerchief. This he unrolled upon a long trestle table, and we children set upon each handkerchief, with our bare hands, a chunk of raw and bleeding beef, and a packet of raisins done up in thick purple paper with a piece of holly stuck into it. My father came in and wished them all a Merry Christmas, and they wished him the same, not forgetting the young ladies and gentlemen. We were not class-conscious, because class was something that was there, like the rest of the phenomenal world; moreover, they were all our respected friends, who simply happened to be 'the poor', and consequently could not expect to dine, like ourselves, off turkey and plum-pudding. When we visited them in their homes, we were prone to envy them for their warmth and cosiness, the shell-boxes, the grandfather clocks, the china dogs upon the mantelpiece, rather than to compare their cramped dwellings unfavourably with our own. Nobody told us that the widow Grimmer was bringing up two boys on five shillings a week from the parish, and lighting in her grate, from time to time, a piece of brown paper, in order that she and the children might warm their hands, for three or four fleeting seconds, when the paper flamed and roared in the draught of the crooked chimney. Did my father, the kindest of men, know this? He was paying his farm-labourers, married men with families, fourteen shillings a week. But they were lucky, for they got free milk and butter from Mrs Olley's dairy. Did my father know that young Willy Woodhouse, aged seventeen, who worked

in the carpenters' shop, walked seven miles in the morning, with his
tool-bag on his back, to repair the barn at Kettlestone, and seven miles
home again at night? Old John Basham, the head-carpenter, drove there
in his cart, to keep an eye on the work. My father swore by old John
Basham, and selected, for old John's tombstone, after much thought, the
text: 'The path of the just is as a shining light, that shineth more and more
unto the perfect day'. But if John Basham was about to return from
Kettlestone half an hour before knocking-off time, not once did it occur
to his just mind to wait and give his workmen, or at worst their heavy
tools, a lift home in his pony-cart. He rode the path of the just behind his
pony, and Sam and young Willy trudged again the seven miles of dusty
lanes. Estate carpenters, in those days, received class as something
'given', as we did, together with most of the men on the place. Hard
work, thoroughness, and pride in the job were the marks of those men;
their endurance, patience, and asceticism were taken for granted by
themselves as much as by their employer.

Laurence Jones, 1955

Grandees could still be put in their place by direct talk from accepted 'characters'.

When I became big enough to manage a team, I had the honour of   259
driving the London and Norwich Royal Mail. I generally selected the
stage from Bury to Thetford, the last of my journey homewards. At the
'Bell Inn' of the latter town I used to sit down to a most sumptuous
breakfast of eggs, buttered toast, fried ham, &c. &c., and all for love and
not money. I was a prime favourite with the landlady, Betty Radcliffe, so
much so that for the many years that as man and boy I frequented her
hostelry, she would never accept a sixpence from me. Betty wore a high
cap, like that in which Mrs Gamp is seen in Dickens's novel; a flaxen wig,
which she appeared to have outgrown, for it ill concealed her grey hairs.
Being the sole proprietress of post-horses into Norfolk, she assumed an
independent demeanour and language, to which every one was
compelled to submit.

When the Duke of York changed horses at the 'Bell', on his way to Mr
Tom Thornhill's of Riddlesworth, he always had a talk with Betty. As he was
paying her one morning for the horses, she jingled the money in her hand,
and said to his Royal Highness, 'I may as well take a little of your money, for
I have been paying your father's taxes for many a long day.'

Prior to one of those ruinous election contests in which Messrs Coke
and Wodehouse (afterwards Lords Leicester and Wodehouse) engaged, the
former said to Betty, 'I want all your post-horses for the next fortnight.'
Betty gave Mr Coke a knowing wink, and said, 'I dare saa you do, but cub
baw, [come, boy] along w' me. What do you see painted on that board?'
'The "Bell" of course.' 'And what on the other side?' 'The "Bell" too!' 'Just
so,' said Betty. 'Don't you see that my sign is painted o' both sides? You shall
have half my horses, but Wuddus [Wodehouse] the other half.'

George Thomas Keppel, Earl of Albemarle, 1876

This fictional prelate of the established church seemed not to realize that 'silly Suffolk' is a corruption of 'selig [holy] Suffolk' – the Suffolk of the fifteenth-century churches.

'Yes, indeed,' said the bishop, 'I think Suffolk is a very nice county; and as   260
we are only a mile or two from Norfolk, I'll say as much for Norfolk too.
"It's an ill bird that fouls its own nest." '
    'I like a county in which there is something left of county feeling,'
said Lady Carbury. 'Staffordshire and Warwickshire, Cheshire and
Lancashire have become great towns, and have lost all local distinctions.'
    'We still keep our name and reputation,' said the bishop: 'silly
Suffolk!'
    'But that was never deserved.'
    'As much, perhaps, as other general epithets. I think we are a
sleepy people. We've got no coal, you see, and no iron. We have no
beautiful scenery, like the lake country – no rivers great for fishing, like
Scotland – no hunting-grounds, like the shires.'
    'Partridges!' pleaded Lady Carbury, with pretty energy.
    'Yes; we have partridges, fine churches, and the herring fishery.
We shall do very well if too much is not expected of us. We can't increase
and multiply as they do in the great cities.'
    'I like this part of England so much the best for that very reason.
What is the use of a crowded population?'
    'The earth has to be peopled, Lady Carbury.'
    'Oh yes,' said her ladyship, with some little reverence added to her
voice, feeling that the bishop was probably adverting to a divine
arrangement. 'The world must be peopled; but for myself I like the
country better than the town.'
    'So do I,' said Roger; 'and I like Suffolk. The people are hearty, and
radicalism is not quite so rampant as it is elsewhere. The poor people
touch their hats, and the rich people think of the poor. There is
something left among us of old English habits.'
    'That is so nice,' said Lady Carbury.
    'Something left of old English ignorance,' said the bishop. 'All the
same I dare say we're improving, like the rest of the world. What
beautiful flowers you have here, Mr Carbury! At any rate, we can grow
flowers in Suffolk.'

Anthony Trollope, 1875

The class system extended also into the towns, such as Lynn, with the pernicious distinction between 'gentlemen' and 'tradesmen'.

Except those of the learned professions, and *very few* besides, all the   261
principal families of this town are in fact *tradesmen*; yet even these are here
very capriciously and superciliously distinguished into *gentlemen* and *trades-men*; though the former retail their goods, or sell their commodities in
small quantities, as well as the latter: and surely a man who buys corn by
the bushel, the coomb, or the quarter, and sells coals by the chalder and
half chalder, and his deals in any small quantity the buyer may wish, and

his bottled wine by single dozens, is to all intents and purposes as much a tradesman as a grocer, a linen-draper, an ironmonger, or a druggist. What is then the ground of this distinction? Is it education? No: our tradesmen in general have been brought up at the grammar-school, and the others can seldom or ever pretend to any higher advantage. Nor do they possess minds more cultivated by reading and knowledge of the world; for there is every reason to believe that the tradesmen are at least their equals in those respects, and some of them perhaps very much their superiors. But is not fortune or *wealth* the ground of this distinction? No: many of those denominated tradesmen are known to be much more wealthy, as well as much more intelligent and respectable, than some of those who have arrogated to themselves the dignified name of gentlemen. On what then can this curious distinction be founded? It may very truly be answered, On pride, arrogance, ignorance, impertinence, and vulgar servility.

William Richards, 1812

Millers, too, had their pride; in this anecdote it came before a fall.

At Trumpington, not far from Cambridge town,   262
A bridge goes over where the brook runs down
And by that brook there stands a mill as well.
And it's God's truth that I am going to tell.
  There was a miller lived there many a day
As proud as any peacock and as gay;
He could play bag-pipes too, fish, mend his gear,
And turn a lathe, and wrestle, and poach deer.
And at his belt he carried a long blade,
Trenchant it was as any sword that's made,
And in his pouch a jolly little knife.
No one dared touch him, peril of his life.
He had a Sheffield dagger in his hose.
Round was his face and puggish was his nose;
His head on top was bald, just like an ape.
He was a market bully in such shape
None dared lay hand on him or come too near
Without him swearing that they'd buy it dear.
  He was a thief as well of corn and meal,
And sly at that; his habit was to steal.
Simpkin the Swagger he was called all round.
He had a wife whose breeding was renowned.
Town-clergyman, no less, her father was;
Gave her fine brass for dowery, because
He wanted to have Simpkin his relation.
The nuns had given her an education.
Simpkin would take no woman, so he said,
Unless she were a virgin and well-bred,
To save the honour of his yeoman stock;
And she was proud, pert as a magpie cock.

It was a proper sight to see the pair
On holidays, what with him strutting there
In front of her, his hood about his head,
And she behind him all decked out in red,
Like Simpkin's hose, for scarlet-red, he had 'em.
No one dared call her anything but 'Madam',
And there was no one bold enough to try
A bit of fun with her or wink an eye.
It would have been as much as ask old Swagger
To murder you with cutlass, knife or dagger,
For jealous folk are dangerous, you know,
At least they want their wives to think them so.
And then her birth was smirched to say the least;
Being the daughter of a celibate priest
She must maintain her dignity, of which
She had as much as water in a ditch.
She was a sneering woman and she thought
That ladies should respect her, so they ought,
What with her well-connected family,
And education in a nunnery.

Geoffrey Chaucer, fourteenth century (translation, Nevill Coghill)

*High life has always been closely concerned with dowries and marriage
settlements. Elizabeth Paston of Oxnead was determined to marry the widower
Scroope, whatever her mother, brother John or cousin Elizabeth Clere might
say. Here is Elizabeth Clere's urgent report to John Paston.*

Trusty and well-beloved cousin, I commend me to you, desiring to hear   263
of your welfare and good speed in your matters, the which I pray God
send you to his plesaunce and to your heart's ease.

Cousin, I let you weet that Scroope hath been in this country to see
my cousin your sister, and he hath spoken with my cousin your mother,
and she desireth of him that he should show you the indentures made
between the knight that hath his daughter and him, whether that
Scroope, if he were married and fortuned to have children, if those
children should inherit his land, or his daughter, the which is married.

Cousin, for this cause take good heed to his indentures, for he is
glad to show you them, or whom ye will assign with you; and he saith to
me he is the last in the tayle of his livelihood the which is three hundred
and fifty marks (233*l*. 6*s*. 8*d*.) and better, as Watkin Shipdam saith, for he
hath taken a compt of his livelihood divers times; and Scroope saith to
me if he be married and have a son and heir, his daughter that is married
shall have of his livelihood fifty marks (33*l*. 6*s*. 8*d*.) and no more; and
therefore, cousin, meseemeth he were good for my cousin your sister
with that ye might get her a better; and if ye can get a better I would
advise you to labour it in as short time as ye may goodly, for she was
never in so great sorrow as she is now-a-days, for she may not speak with
no man, whosoever come, ne not may see nor speak with my man, nor
with servants of her mother's, but that she beareth her an hand

otherwise than she meaneth; and she hath since Easter the most part been beaten once in the week or twice, and sometimes twice on a day, and her head broken in two or three places. Wherefore, cousin, she hath sent to me by Fryar Newton in great counsel, and prayeth me that I would send to you a letter of her heaviness, and pray you to be her good brother, as her trust is in you; and she saith if ye may see by his evidences that his children and hers may inherit, and she to have reasonable jointure, she hath heard so much of his birth and his conditions, that and ye will she will have him, whether that her mother will or will not, notwithstanding it is told her his person is simple, for she saith men shall have the more dainty [*deyute*] of her, if she rule her to him as she ought to do.

Cousin, it is told me there is a goodly man in your inn, of the which the father died lately, and if ye think that he were better for her than Scroope, it would be laboured, and give Scroope a goodly answer, that he be not put off till ye be sure of a better; for he said when he was with me but if he have some comfortable answer of you he will no more labour in this matter, because he might not see my cousin your sister, and he saith he might have seen her and she had been better than she is; and that causeth him to deem that her mother was not well willing; and so have I sent my cousin your mother word; wherefore, cousin, think on this matter, for sorrow oftentime causeth women to beset them otherwise than they should do, and if she were in that case, I wot well ye would be sorry: cousin, I pray you burn this letter, that your men nor none other men see it; for and my cousin your mother knew that I had sent you this letter, she should never love me. No more I write to you at this time, but Holy Ghost have you in keeping. Written in haste, on Saint Peter's day, by candle light.

Elizabeth Clere, 1454

Margaret (Peggy), the heroine of a short play, was equally determined to refuse Lambert and Serlsby, despite their landholdings at Fressingfield and Laxfield, for she had a better catch in Lacy, Earl of Lincoln.

Lambert	Peggy, the lovely flower of all towns,	264
	Suffolk's fair Helen, and rich England's star,	
	Whose beauty, temper'd with her huswifery,	
	Makes England talk of merry Fressingfield!	
Serlsby	I cannot trick it up with poesies,	
	Nor paint my passions with comparisons,	
	Nor tell a tale of Phoebus and his loves:	
	But this believe me, – Laxfield here is mine,	
	Of ancient rent seven hundred pounds a-year,	
	And if thou canst but love a country squire,	
	I will enfeoff thee, Margaret, in all:	
	I cannot flatter; try me, if thou please.	
Margaret	Brave neighbouring squires, the stay of Suffolk's clime,	
	A keeper's daughter is too base in gree	
	To match with men accounted of such worth:	
	But might I not displease, I would reply.	

L.   Say, Peggy; naught shall make us discontent.
M.   Then, gentles, note that love hath little stay,
            Nor can the flames that Venus sets on fire
            Be kindled but by fancy's motion:
            Then pardon, gentles, if a maid's reply
            Be doubtful, while I have debated with myself,
            Who, or of whom, love shall constrain me like.
S.   Let it be me; and trust me, Margaret,
            The meads environ'd with the silver streams,
            Whose battling pastures fatten all my flocks,
            Yielding forth fleeces stapled with such wool
            As Lemnster cannot yield more finer stuff,
            And forty kine with fair and burnish'd heads,
            With strouting dugs that paggle to the ground,
            Shall serve thy dairy, if thou wed with me.
L.   Let pass the country wealth, as flocks and kine,
            And lands that wave with Ceres' golden sheaves,
            Filling my barns with plenty of the fields;
            But, Peggy, if thou wed thyself to me,
            Thou shalt have garments of embroider'd silk,
            Lawns, and rich net-works for thy head-attire:
            Costly shall be thy fair habiliments,
            If thou wilt be but Lambert's loving wife.
M.   Content you, gentles, you have proffer'd fair,
            And more than fits a country maid's degree:
            But give me leave to counsel me a time,
            For fancy blooms not at the first assault;
            Give me but ten days' respite, and I will reply,
            Which or to whom myself affectionates.

Robert Greene, 1594

*François René de Chateaubriand, then a young man of twenty-five, fled France
in 1793 and lodged with a clergyman at Bungay. The clergyman's wife made a
tactical error when she suggested the lodger should marry her daughter, but for
Chateaubriand it was merely another romantic episode for his brilliant
autobiography.*

'Sir,' she said in English, 'you have noticed my confusion: I do not know   265
if Charlotte pleases you, but it is impossible to deceive a mother's eyes:
my daughter has undoubtedly conceived an attachment for you. Mr Ives
and I have discussed the matter together: you suit us in every respect; we
believe that you will make our daughter happy. You no longer have a
country of your own; you have lost your relatives; your property has
been sold; who then could call you back to France? Until you inherit our
possessions, you will live with us.'
     Of all the sorrows I had endured, this was the greatest and most
painful. I threw myself at Mrs Ives's feet; I covered her hands with my
kisses and my tears. She thought I was weeping with happiness, and she

began to sob for joy. She stretched out her arm to pull the bell-rope; she called her husband and daughter.

'Stop!' I cried. 'I am a married man!'

She fell back in a faint.

I went out and, without going back to my room, left the house on foot. On arriving at Beccles I took the mail-coach for London, after writing a letter to Mrs Ives of which I regret that I did not keep a copy.

François René de Chateaubriand, 1850 (translation, Robert Baldick)

Conjugal fidelity was rewarded in a curious manner at Dunmow, with a flitch of bacon.

You shall swear by the custom of your confession,   266
That you never made any nuptial transgression
Since you were married man and wife,
By household brawls, or contentious strife;
Or otherwise in bed or at board,
Offended each other in deed or word;
Or since the parish clerk said amen,
Wished yourself unmarried again;
Or in a twelvemonth and a day
Repented not in thought any way.
But continued true, and in desire,
As when you joined hands in holy choir.
If to these conditions, without all fear,
Of your own accord you will freely swear,
A whole gammon of bacon you shall receive,
And bear it hence with love and good leave;
For this our custom at Dunmow well known,
Though the pleasure be ours, the bacon's your own.

Anon., eighteenth century

Some were able to flout convention and live in unconjugal fidelity, as did George Walpole of Houghton Hall, the profligate third Earl of Orford, with his mistress, Patty Turk.

At the head of Lord Orford's table was placed, for the reception of his 267 visitors, a person whom he denominated simply 'Patty'; and that so unceremoniously, that all the most intimate of his associates addressed her by the same free appellation.

Those, however, if such there were, who might conclude from this degrading familiarity, that the Patty of Lord Orford was 'every body's Patty', must soon have been undeceived, if tempted to make any experiment upon such a belief. The peer knew whom he trusted, though he rewarded not the fidelity in which he confided; but the fond, faulty Patty loved him with a blindness of passion, that hid alike from her weak perceptions, her own frailties, and his seductions.

In all, save that blot, which, on earth, must to a female be ever indelible, Patty was good, faithful, kind, friendly, and praise-worthy.

Fanny Burney, 1832

The grave is no barrier for true love, as attested by this inscription on the memorial to Sarah Cargill at Mulbarton.

Dear Love, one Feather'd minute and I come   268
To lye down in they darke Retireing Roome
And mingle Dust with thine, that wee may have,
As when alive one Bed, so dead one Grave;
And may my Soul teare through the vaulted Sky
To be with thine to all Eternitie.
O how our Bloudless Formes will that Day greet
With Love Divine when we again shall meet
Devest of all Contagion of the Flesh
Full filled with everlasting joys and Fresh
In Heaven above (and 't may be) cast an eye
How far Elizium doth beneath us lye.
                    Deare, I disbody and away
                    More Swift than Wind
                    Or Flying Hind
                    I come I come away.

Eighteenth century

But, equally, the grave brings no rest for family feuds, as witness these inscriptions at Bramfield. The Nelson family seem to have had a free hand in composing Arthur Applewhaite's epitaph, as well as really letting go in the account of his widow's death.

Here lies the body of ARTHUR APPLEWHAITE   269
Second Son of HENRY APPLEWHAITE
of Huntingfield in this County Gent
(Who was Favourite and Bayliff to
HENRY HEVENINGHAM, HENRY HERON
and JOHN BENCE Deceased, and remains
so to ALEXANDER BENCE and GEORGE
DASHWOOD. All Esquires, and Successively
Owners of the Heveningham-Hall Estate,)
Who died on the ninth day of September
A:D 1733. And in the 39th Year of his Age.
He Married BRIDGETT the Eldest Daughter,
and at length, Sole Heiress of LAMBERT
NELSON late of this Parish Gent, By whom
he had no issue. And to whom (Having by
his Father's Instigation made no will)

He left no Legacy, But a Chancery-
Suit with his Eldest Brother For her
own Paternal Estates In this Town,
and Blyford.

Between the Remains of her Brother EDWARD,
And of her Husband ARTHUR
Here lies the Body of BRIDGETT APPLEWHAITE
Once BRIDGETT NELSON.
After the Fatigues of a Married Life,
Born by her with Incredible Patience,
For four Years and three Quarters, bating three weeks;
And after the Enjoiment of the Glorious Freedom
Of an Easy and Unblemisht Widowhood,
For four Years and Upwards,
She Resolved to run the Risk of a Second Marriage Bed
But DEATH forbad the Banns –
And having with an Apoplectick Dart,
(The same Instrument, with which he had Formerly
Dispatch't her Mother,)
Touch't the most Vital part of her Brain;
She must have fallen Directly to the Ground,
(as one Thunder strook,)
If she had not been Catch't and Supported
by her Intended Husband.
Of which Invisible Bruise
After a Struggle for above Sixty Hours,
With that Grand Enemy to Life,
(But the certain and Merciful Friend to Helpless Old Age,)
In Terrible Convulsions Plaintive Groans, or Stupefying Sleep
without Recovery of her Speech, or Senses,
She Dyed, on the 12th day of Sept in ye Year of our Lord 1737
and of her own Age 44

Sarah Hare's will is extraordinary, both in its stipulations about simple funeral arrangements and in its provision for a wax effigy, which can still be seen in Stow Bardolph Church.

I SARAH HARE youngest daughter of Sir Thomas Hare Bart and Dame   270
Eliz. his wife, and youngest to the present Sir Thomas Hare Bart of Stow
Hall in the County of Norfolk do here with my own hand write this my
last Will and Testament in the manner following. *First* I resign my soul to
Almighty God with great willingness trusting in his mercy. *Secondly* my
body to be Interred as soon as conveniency will permit that I may not be
any way offensive to the living, in the method I here direct, which is to
have my body wrap'd in one of my own blanketts in place of a Burial
Dress which I forbid my coffin to be made of the best Elm lin'd with a
thinn lead with a flap of lead sawder'd down over me, not to have a nail or
any ornament that is not absolutely necessary, Except a plate with my

coat of arms and with this inscription. they that humble themselves shall be Exalted. I desire I may be convey'd to the burial place of our family in Stow Church in the cheapest method possible either cart wagon or any (way but water) not expensive with my own servant to attend me if I have none at the time of my Death any poor body having their thargoo bord and two guineas for their trouble. I desire Six of the poor men in the parish of Stow or Wimbotsham may put me in to the ground they having five shillings a piece for the same. I desire all the poor in the Alms Row may have two shillings and sixpence each person at the Grave before I am put in. This I hope my Executor will see firstly performed before Sunset. After my just debts which now do not amount to five pounds and funeral charges are paid I give to my Brother George Hare all I am possest off at my death. Except what I shall the after dispose of and appoint him my executor to this my will if he be living, if he be not then my nephew Thomas Leigh and if he is not living then to my two nieces Eliz. and Mary Hare jointly or to the survivors of them. I give to my mother anything she pleeses to take. I give Rosanna Lady Hare Sir Ralph Hares picture I wear at my watch and to my niece Mary Hare my cozens Earls picture with a pebble at the back which I generally wear at my arm. I give to my servant that is with me at the time of my Death all my linen that she has in her keeping except my two best suits of lace and all my Cloates except my two best gowns which with the two suits of lace I desire may be given to any unfortunate person(?) not too proud to wear them or too mean. I desire to have my face and hands made in wax with a piece of crimson satin thrown like a garment in a picture hair upon my head and put in a case of Mahogany with a glass before and fix'd up so near the place were my corps lyes as it can be with my name and time of Death put upon the case in any manner most desirable if I do not execute this in my life I desire it may be done after my Death. If my nephew Thomas Leigh is not my executor than I give to him my Repeating Watch with the Chain and Seals to it except my Coat of Arms and Twenty Pounds in money to be paid him then.

Sarah Hare, 1743

Family inheritance is always a subject of immediate concern. Samuel Pepys, an influential Whitehall official, suffered some rude shocks when penetrating into deepest fenland in pursuit of his interest in his uncle's will.

17th [September]. Up, and my father being gone to bed ill last night and   271 continuing so this morning, I was forced to come to a new consideration, whether it was fit for to let my uncle and his son go to Wisbeach about my uncle Day's estate alone or no, and concluded it unfit; and so resolved to go with them myself, leaving my wife there, I begun a journey with them, and with much ado, through the fens, along dikes, where sometimes we were ready to have our horses sink to the belly, we got by night, with great deal of stir and hard riding, to Parson's Drove, a heathen place, where I found my uncle and aunt Perkins, and their daughters, poor wretches! in a sad, poor thatched cottage, like a poor barn, or stable, peeling of hemp, in which I did give myself good content to see their manner of preparing of hemp; and in a poor condition of habitt took them to our miserable inn, and there, after long stay, and hearing of Frank, their son, the miller, play upon his treble, as he calls it, with which he earns part of his living, and singing of a country bawdy song, we sat down to supper; the whole crew, and Frank's wife and child, a sad company, of which I was ashamed, supped with us. And after supper I, talking with my aunt about her report concerning my uncle Day's will and surrender, I found her in such different reports from what she writes and says to the people, and short of what I expected, that I fear little will be done of good in it. By and by newes is brought to us that one of our horses is stole out of the stable, which proves my uncle's, at which I am inwardly glad – I mean, that it was not mine; and at this we were at a great loss; and they doubting a person that lay at next door, a Londoner, some lawyer's clerk, we caused him to be secured in his bed, and other care to be taken to seize the horse; and so about twelve at night or more, to bed in a sad, cold, nasty chamber, only the mayde was indifferent handsome, and so I had a kiss or two of her, and I to bed, and a little after I was asleep they waked me to tell me that the horse was found, which was good newes, and so to sleep till the morning, but was bit cruelly, and nobody else of our company, which I wonder at, by the gnatts.

18th. Up, and got our people together as soon as we could; and after eating a dish of cold cream, which was my supper last night too, we took leave of our beggarly company, though they seem good people, too; and over most sad Fenns, all the way observing the sad life which the people of the place (which if they be born there, they do call the Breedlings of the place) do live, sometimes rowing from one spot to another, and then wadeing, to Wisbeach, a pretty town, and a fine church and library, where sundry very old abbey manuscripts; and a fine house, built on the church ground by Secretary Thurlow, and a fine gallery built for him in the church, but now all in the Bishop of Ely's hands. After visiting the church, &c., we went out of the towne, by the help of a stranger, to find out one Blinkhorne, a miller, of whom we might inquire something of old Day's disposal of his estate, and in whose hands it now is; and by great chance we met him, and brought him to our inn to dinner; and instead of being informed in his estate by this fellow, we find that he is the next heir to the estate, which was matter of great sport to my cozen Thomas and me, to see such a fellow prevent us in our hopes, he being Day's brother's daughter's son, whereas we are but his sister's sons and grandsons; so that, after all, we were fain to propose our matter to him, and to get him to give us leave to look after the business, and so he to have one-third part, and we two to have the other two-third parts, of what should be recovered of the estate, which he consented to; and after some discourse and paying the reckoning, we mounted again, and rode, being very merry at our defeat, to Chatteris, my uncle very weary, and after supper, and my telling of three stories, to their good liking, of spirits, we all three in a chamber went to bed.

19th. Up pretty betimes, and after eating something, we set out and I (being willing thereto) went by a mistake with them to St Ives, and there, it being known that it was their nearer way to London, I took leave

of them there, they going straight to London and I to Brampton, where I
find my father ill in bed still, and Madam Norbery (whom and her fair
daughter and sister I was ashamed to kiss, but did, my lip being sore with
riding in the wind and bit with the gnatts), lately come to town, come to
see my father and mother, and they after a little stay being gone, I told my
father my success. And after dinner my wife and I took horse, and rode
with marvellous, and the first and only hour of, pleasure, that ever I had
in this estate since I had to do with it, to Brampton woods; and through
the wood rode, and gathered nuts in my way, and then at Graffam to an
old woman's house to drink, where my wife used to go; and being in all
circumstances highly pleased, and in my wife's riding and good company
at this time, I rode, and she showed me the river behind my father's
house, which is very pleasant, and so saw her home, and I straight to
Huntingdon, and there met Mr Shepley and to the Crown (having sent
home my horse by Stankes), and there a barber came and trimmed me,
and thence walked to Hinchingbroke, where my Lord and ladies all are
just alighted.

   Samuel Pepys, 1663

*For sheer highmindedness, no one could compete with the Gurneys of Earlham,
whose Quaker principles made for exacting standards. This diarist was only
twelve years old. (Keswick was her uncle's house nearby; and John Pitchford was
a young neighbour, and a Roman Catholic.)*

I always get up at five or six, which I call late. I read till breakfast, which I   272
enjoy amazingly; the breakfast is a little after eight. I am most busy all the
morning at lessons. I have about an hour for play. We dine at three. In
the afternoon I write my French exercise and journal, and study botany,
which I think is a most charming employment; to study nature in any
way is delightful. We drink tea about six, and have the most pleasant
evenings. We all sit and work while Kitty reads to us. We have been
reading Hayley's 'Triumph of Temper', which I only like tolerably. I went
to Keswick yesterday. Elizabeth and I had a large syllabub, and sucked it
through straws. I think my mind has been in a very good state. I am
improving. It is very pleasant to think so sometimes. One of my chief
faults is speaking unkindly to Betsy: she does so provoke me. She
behaves in some things so aristocratically because she is the eldest, and
nothing makes me so angry as that. How very pleasant is Pitchford's
company! We had a charming walk, and then we came in and sat round
the fire with Pitchford. He talked most interestingly, principally about
religion. I can't say how much I admire what he said – the happiness he
had in prayer, and he showed what a *most* delightful thing real devotion
is, and what a comfort and support religion is to the mind. He spoke so
charmingly and became so animated about it, it was enough to make one
religious. I am determined I will be religious – *really* so, I mean. When
Pitchford was gone, I went to bed, and lay awake till Kitty came. What
Pitchford had said had got so completely into my mind, that I thought
about it the whole time, and somehow Kitty and I fell into talk about it.

She said that it was only very lately that she had felt *real* devotion, and that it had made her far happier. I now intend to make it my aim to follow Pitchford and Kitty: I never saw such perfect characters as they. The last time I was at Keswick, Elizabeth told me she wondered we were not all more charming than we are, living with Kitty. It rather hurt me: I don't know why, but it did. I believe it was because I felt it was true. I am determined I will try to make myself worthy of the pains that such a person as Kitty takes with me.

I really see and know my own faults. I know that I have a great many, and that it will require time and patience to cure them. I do not think I have a bad temper, but, on the contrary, very good. I am very affectionate, and my heart is open to warm impressions. I can't bear restraint, and it is difficult to govern me by strictness, though very possible to do it by kindness and persuasion. I think I am not selfish, but the contrary. I have a bold forwardness, which is disgusting. I oppose all restraint with too much vigour. I always tell my opinions and think them better than those of other people who are wiser than I am. I think I am self-conceited. I have no mildness in my character, for I only see the virtues of a few, and look down with contempt upon the general run. I am wanting in real fortitude, though nothing is so useful.

Louisa Gurney, 1797

The Gurney family in action at Cromer. Elizabeth Fry became a prominent prison reformer.

We very much enjoyed our stay at Cromer, especially the daily intercourse which it afforded with our precious sister, Elizabeth Fry, who was our near neighbour. She, as you know, is always engaged in endeavouring in some way or other to benefit her fellow-creatures, and very sweet it is to be able to be co-workers with her for a season in her labours of love. There are a great many sailors at Cromer, and we had some extremely interesting meetings with them (not exactly religious meetings), which commenced in a very simple way. At certain seasons of the year, not having anything to do, they are often lounging about the cliff for hours together; and one day, looking over a tract which seemed peculiarly applicable to them, I proposed to dear Joseph that we should ask them to come into our large dining-room in the evening, and read it to them. He, being always ready to uphold me in every good word and work, immediately agreed, and so we strolled about the cliff and invited them in as we happened to meet with them scattered about in little companies. Quite a large number came, and I read to them the tract called 'The Two Seamen', to which they listened with the most profound attention, and afterwards Joseph addressed them very suitably, when they departed apparently well satisfied with the opportunity. On mentioning it to our sister Fry, and also that we intended having them in very soon again, she seemed much pleased with the plan, and said she would like to be with us when we met next time. Accordingly a few evenings afterwards we had the room nearly full, and it was an occasion certainly not to be forgotten. The most profound silence reigned while I read to them a very impressive tract entitled 'The Roll-Call, or How will you answer it?' Then Joseph spoke to them, and dear Elizabeth addressed them very sweetly, and then appeared in solemn and most striking application. It was a time of unusual interest, and one which I cannot at all do justice to by my imperfect mode of description, the sailors were so deeply impressed by the whole thing. We had one or two very interesting meetings afterwards, but I think this was the most striking, there was such great solemnity from the first, and the tract, which perhaps you have read, seemed so completely to rivet their attention. Then, when Joseph in a solemn manner exhorted them to be prepared for that great day wherein ten thousand times ten thousand would be summoned to appear before the judgment-seat of Christ to hear the last roll called, the most profound solemnity prevailed, and I could almost fancy that I heard the general response, 'How shall I answer it?' But I must not fill my sheet about Cromer, or I could tell you many interesting anecdotes – our visits to the cottages of the coast-guardsmen, establishing a library for sailors, &c.

Eliza Gurney, 1842

Life at the rectory, as here portrayed, could be excessively formal.

The period succeeding breakfast at the Rectory on Sunday mornings was, 274 in theory, devoted to meditation suitable to prepare the mind for the religious exercises of the day. In reality, the Rector disappeared into his study, Mrs Burgess scanned a volume of sermons, Marina, of a younger and more rebellious generation, fidgeted, sewed, or leaned upon the casement, gazing out upon the prospect, if possible more blankly peaceful on that day than upon any other. Theodore wandered in the bereaved and empty garden, on damp paths between bare, well-manured beds, all asleep in expectation of the season to come. He caught sight of a face and figure at the upper windows once and again, but made no sign, so strong upon him was the habit of the place and hour. Then the first bell began, regular and monotonous, insistent and compelling. He ran in, changed his coat, secured his books, and, as the party assembled, joined them, at the Rector's word, 'It is time to go!'

The Rector walked with his sister-in-law, Theodore had the felicity of offering his arm to Marina. She took it with a glance up at him, no word. So along the quiet street to the lych-gate, from whence the path under the limes, between the gravestones, was lined with bare-headed labourers, their bonneted wives and bobbing children, all waiting for the Rectory party to go in, and following upon its heels as soon as it did so.

R. H. Mottram, 1929

Life at college (in this case Trinity, Cambridge) could be excessively hedonistic; not surprisingly, Thackeray failed to get a degree.

Sunday. I have missed a day! but I trust you will forgive me the offence   275
when I relate the circumstances which led to the omission. I had taken a
desperate ride with Carne (after lectures) to Lord Herveys place at
Wimpole about 9 miles from here, in Wimpole Park we gallopped for
about half an hour and finally lost our way, that is to say found that we
had fifteen miles to ride home instead of nine, at a quarter to three we
were seven miles from Cambridge, and at ten minutes past three we were
trotting very quietly down Trumpington Street! – All wh. things made
me very tired, however I worked resolutely with my private tutor, and
after returning from him read resolutely on by myself till about nine
o'clock when unluckily I fell asleep till ten, & then woke with such a
splitting headache that I retired to bed, directly I was comfortably settled
in baide the headache left me, it was all owing to this cruelly unpleasant
position of my head over the back of the sofa – This morning I felt vastly
better for my ride, & went to Chapel in a most perfect state of bodily
contentment only my joints were rather stiff with my yesterday's
exertion – Poor Carne is quite done up with his exertion, & looks most
miserably 'seedy'. We saw an ugly house, a delightful park, and some
good pictures, & besides this I have had enough exercise to keep me going
for a week – My Wine arrived yesterday – The Sauterne is pekooliarly
good, the men come and drink it and then caution me not to [serve] it at
wine parties – The wine parties are miser[ably] stupid things in my
opinion. I was at one on Thursday and at another to day – I shall keep
clear of them. Tomorrow I intend to commence a steady, and systematic
course of reading. I shall always 'sport my oak' while I am engaged in my
studies – I fear I shall find it difficult to send a Journal a week, I ought to
send two, I have taken these two pages already so I must say no more till
tomorrow and see how my reading agrees with me. Good night dear
Mother.

   William Makepeace Thackeray, 1829

This Cambridge lounger, one hopes, was likewise flunked.

>   I rise about nine, get to breakfast at ten,   276
>   Blow a tune on my flute, or perhaps make a pen;
>   Read a play till eleven, or cock my lac'd hat;
>   Then step to my neighbour's, till dinner, to chat.
>   Dinner over to *Tom's*, or to *Clapham's* I go,
>   The news of the town so impatient to know;
>   While LAW, LOCKE, and NEWTON, and all the rum race,
>   That talk of their modes, their ellipses, and space,
>   The seat of the soul, and new systems on high,
>   In holes, as abstruse as their mysteries, lie.
>   From the Coffee-House then I to Tennis away,
>   And at six I post back to my college, to pray:
>   I sup before eight, and secure from all duns,
>   Undauntedly march to the *Mitre* or *Tuns*:
>   Where in punch or good claret my sorrows I drown,

And toss off a bowl, to the best in the town:
At one in the morning, I call what's to pay,
Then home to my chambers I stagger away,
Thus I tope all the night, as I trifle all day.

Anon., 1750

High life most obviously hit East Anglia when the Court was at Newmarket.

On the seventeenth of October [1695] William went to Newmarket, now   277
a place rather of business than of pleasure, but, in the autumns of the
seventeenth century, the gayest and most luxurious spot in the island. It
was not unusual for the whole Court and Cabinet to go down to the
meetings. Jewellers and milliners, players and fiddlers, venal wits and
venal beauties followed in crowds. The streets were made impassable by
coaches and six. In the places of public resort peers flirted with maids of
honour; and officers of the Life Guards, all plumes and gold lace, jostled
professors in trencher caps and black gowns. For the neighbouring
University of Cambridge always sent her highest functionaries with loyal
addresses, and selected her ablest theologians to preach before the
Sovereign and his splendid retinue. In the wild days of the Restoration,
indeed, the most learned and eloquent divine might fail to draw a
fashionable audience, particularly if Buckingham announced his intention of holding forth; for sometimes His Grace would enliven the dulness
of a Sunday morning by addressing to the bevy of fine gentlemen and
fine ladies a ribald exhortation which he called a sermon. But the Court
of William was more decent; and the academic dignitaries were treated
with marked respect. With lords and ladies from St James's and Soho,
and with doctors from Trinity College and King's College, were mingled
the provincial aristocracy, fox-hunting squires and their rosy cheeked
daughters, who had come in queer-looking family coaches drawn by
carthorses from the remotest parishes of three or four counties to see
their Sovereign. The heath was fringed by a wild gipsy-like camp of vast
extent. For the hope of being able to feed on the leavings of many
sumptuous tables, and to pick up some of the guineas and crowns which
the spendthrifts of London were throwing about, attracted thousands of
peasants from a circle of many miles.

Thomas Babington Macaulay, 1855

*Most especially when Charles II was engaged upon another seduction. The
anonymous lady was Louise de Kérouaille (alias 'Quierovil' or 'Carwell'), Louis
XIV's very successful spy at Charles' Court.*

This over, I went that night with Mr *Tressurer* to *Euston*, a palace of my   278
L:[*Arlingtons*] where we found Monsieur *Colbert* (the *French Ambassador*)
& the famous new *french* maid of honor, *Mademoisell Quierovil* now
comeing to be in great favour with the K — : here was also the *Countesse*
of *Sunderland*, & severall Lords & Ladies more who lodged in the house:

during my stay here with my Lord *Arlington* neere a fortnight; Came his Majestie almost every second day with the Duke, who commonly returnd againe to New-market; but the King lay often here, during which time I had twice the honor to sit at Dinner with him, with all freedome: It was universaly reported that the faire Lady — was bedded one of these nights, and the stocking flung, after the manner of a married Bride: I acknowledge she was for the most part in her undresse all day, and that there was fondnesse, & toying, with that young wanton; nay 'twas said, I was at the former ceremonie, but tis utterly false, I neither saw, nor heard of any such thing whilst I was there, though I had ben in her Chamber & all over that appartment late enough; & was my selfe observing all passages with curiosity enough: however twas with confidence believed that she was first made a *Misse* as they cald these unhappy creatures, with solemnity, at this time &c.

John Evelyn, 1671

His neglected queen, Catherine, had to content herself with more innocent frolics. The grand ladies went to the fair riding side-saddle on horses ridden by their escorts.

The Court returns not till Saturday, so there is little news. Last week   279
there being a Faire near Audley End, the Queen, the Dutchess of Richmond, and the Dutchess of Buckingham, had a frolick to disguise themselves like country lasses, in red petticoats, wastcoats, &c. and so goe see the Faire. Sir Bernard Gascoign, on a cart-jade, rode before the Queen, and another stranger before the Dutchess of Buckingham, and Mr Roper before Richmond. They had all so overdone it in their disguise, and look'd so much more like Antiques than Country volk, that as soon as they came to the Faire the people began to goe after them; but the Queen going to a booth to buy a pair of yellow stockins for her sweet hart, and Sir Bernard asking for a pair of gloves, stitched with blue, for his sweet hart, they were soon, by their gebrish, found to be strangers, which drew a bigger flock around them. One amongst them had seen the Queen at dinner, knew her, and was proud of her knowledge: this soon brought all the Faire into a crowd to stare at the Queen. Being thus discovered, they, as soon as they could, got to their horses; but as many of the Faire as had horses got up with their wives, children, sweet-harts, or neighbours behind them, to get as much gape as they could till they brought them to the court gate. Thus, by ill conduct, was a merry frolick turned to a pennance.

M. Henshaw, 1670

Royal visits in later years became highly respectable affairs, as when Queen Victoria and Prince Albert stayed at Wimpole after a visit to Cambridge.

27 October: 280
Attended Prayers in an old Chapel in the house, & then breakfasted, after

which we walked out. It was very cold, but fine. The pleasure grounds &
gardens are very nice, & all in excellent order. The house built of red
brick, is large, & has 2 wings & 2 flights of steps outside. Albert went out
shooting. We lunched downstairs with the Company, in the Library, a
fine large room, with a bow window. The 7 Children were there – nice
children. Victor, a year & ½ old, is my godson, a fine boy, & the youngest
of all is a fine baby boy, 3 months old. At 3 I drove out with Ldy
Hardwicke, Ldy Normanby, & Ldy Mt Edgecumbe, Albert riding with Ld
Hardwicke, & the other Gentlemen. We drove over Bourne, Ld de la
Warr's place.

   We dined at ½ p. 7. The Duke of Rutland & Ld Exeter gone but
otherwise, the same Party, with the addition of the High Sheriff & the 2
County Members. After dinner, we went into the Gallery, which was full
of guests, & there was a very pretty little Ball. The room was charmingly
decorated with flowers. All the Masters of Colleges from Cambridge,
with their families, & several of the young Nobility, & a number of the
neighbours, the ladies being wonderfully well dressed, were there. The 4
eldest children appeared, very nicely dressed, & little Agneta looked so
pretty. I danced 3 quadrilles, with Ld Hardwicke, Ld Canning & Ld
Caledon. We went to supper at 11, & after that, retired.

28 October:
After our breakfast we walked to the Farm which is beautiful, & we were
shown a heifer being fattened for the Show at Smithfield, a great beauty,
also the young calves, pigs, & fowls. Albert was interested in examining
the various ploughs. We also visited the Dairy, which is very pretty.

   At ¼ p. 11, we left Wimpole, after I had given Ldy Hardwicke a
bracelet, & my godson a small present. Ld Hardwicke & his brothers
accompanied us to Ragston, 6 miles, where we 1st changed horses.

   Queen Victoria, 1843

*To conclude, here is their son, the Prince of Wales, leading high life and low life
together in a communal romp at the servants' ball at Sandringham.*

One year the Marlborough House servants came down by special train,   281
and the rival establishments were in great force, the decided belle of the
evening being Madame Francatelli, who did not belong to the household
but was invited out of compliment to the distinguished *chef*, and was
most becomingly dressed and not at all forward or flirtacious. The ball
opened with a country dance, the Prince and Princess leading off with the
heads of the respective departments, and the Duchess of Teck, whose
good-nature and frank enjoyment made her a great acquisition, with
another of the upper servants. One year the Princess's coachman, the
most diminutive man in the room, was her partner, and the contrast was
rather striking. The house-party, equerries, ladies-in-waiting, and all
invited from the neighbourhood, were ordered to join in, no shirking or
sitting out allowed, and when the sides had been made up, the Prince and
Princess set off with their partners, round and round, down the middle

and up again, and so on to the end, the Prince the jolliest of the jolly and the life of the party, as he is wherever he goes. I never saw such amazing vitality. His own Master of the Ceremonies, signalling and sending messages to the band, arranging every dance, and when to begin and when to leave off, noticing the smallest mistake in the figures, and putting people in their places. In the 'Triumph', which is such an exhausting dance, he looked as if he could have gone on all night and into the middle of next week without stopping, and I really believe he could. He is an antidote to every text and sermon that ever was preached upon the pleasures of the world palling upon the wearied spirit. They never pall upon his, and year after year he comes up 'to time' with renewed capacity for revelry and junketings. It was a mercy to have a Quadrille now and then for a little rest. The Marlborough housekeeper, who was attired in a pea-green silk, danced it in the old polite style, holding up her gown in points, and dropping a little curtsey to her partner each time she came forward, like Mrs Fazziwig of immortal memory. Then a jig was started, and it was so pretty to see the way the Princess danced it, while the state liveries of the footmen and green velvet of the game-keepers and Highland costumes, mixed up with the scarlet coats of the country gentlemen, and the lovely toilettes and the merry tune, made a sight to be seen or heard. Almost before one dance was ended the Prince started another, and suddenly the Scotch pipers would screech out and the Prince would fold his arms and fling himself into a Highland fling, and so on fast and furious until far into the small hours of the morning, with supper intervening, when our former partners, the footmen, waited upon everyone as demurely as if they had not at all been careering about together just before.

Louisa Cresswell, 1887

List of Sources

Textual sources are listed by passage number. In the List of Sources, the publication date given for a work is that of the edition consulted, which is not necessarily the first edition of that work. In the main text, however, the date given at the end of a quoted extract is that of the year in which the work was first printed – or, in some cases, assumed to have been written.

1   A. E. Fletcher, *Thomas Gainsborough*: New York, 1904 (pp. 1–2)
2   Jack Burton, from *The City of Churches*: Norwich, 1987
3   John Norden, 'Essex'; in *Camden Society*: London, 1840 (p. 7)
4   Arthur Young, *General View of the Agriculture of the County of Suffolk*: 1794 (pp. 11–12)
5   William Cobbett, *Rural Rides*: London, 1886 (Vol. 1, pp. 57–8)
6   Thomas Tusser, from 'A Comparison between Champion Country and Severall'; in *The Five Hundred Points of Good Husbandry*: London, 1812 (pp. 203–6)
7   Robert Reyce, 'The Breviary of Suffolk'; in *Suffolk in the XVIIth Century*: London, 1962 (pp. 13–14)
8   Reginald Beckett, *Romantic Essex*: London, 1907 (pp. 119–20)
9   Elihu Burritt, *A Walk from London to John O'Groats*: New York, 1864, (pp. 63–4)
10 George Crabbe (the younger), *The Life of George Crabbe*: Oxford, 1932 (pp. 150–2)
11 Celia Fiennes, *Journeys*, edited by Christopher Morris: London, 1947 (pp. 144–6)
12 Sir Alfred Munnings, *An Artist's Life*: London, 1950 (pp. 29–30)
13 Charles Dickens, *Pickwick Papers*: London, 1910 (p. 213)
14 Simon Dewes, *A Suffolk Childhood*: London, 1959 (pp. 207–8)
15 John Skelton, from 'Philip Sparrow'; in *Complete Poems*, edited by Philip Henderson: London, 1948 (pp. 71–2)

16   William Hurn, 'Heath-Hill': 1777
17   Michael Hamburger, from 'In Suffolk'; in *Collected Poems*: Manchester, 1984 (pp. 337–8)
18   William Broome, from 'The Oak and the Dunghill'; in J. Gathorne-Hardy (Earl of Cranbrook), *Parnassian Molehill*: Ipswich, 1953 (pp. 43–4)
19   William Cobbett, *Rural Rides*: London, 1886 (Vol. 2, pp. 298–9)
20   John Clare, from 'The Mores'; in *Selected Poems and Prose*, edited by Eric Robinson and Geoffrey Summerfield: Oxford, 1967 (pp. 169–70)
21   Ronald Blythe, 'Our Villages'; in Celia Jennings, *Suffolk for Ever*: Bury St Edmunds, 1989 (p. 174)
22   John Constable, 'Discourses'; in *Suffolk Records Society*: Woodbridge, 1970 (Vol. 14, p. 67)
23   John Constable, 'Discourses'; in *Suffolk Records Society*: Woodbridge, 1970 (Vol. 14, pp. 14–15)
24   C. R. Leslie, *Memoirs of the Life of John Constable*: London, 1845 (pp. 313–14)
25   W. A. Dutt, *Highways and Byways in East Anglia*: London, 1901 (p. 403)
26   Laurens van der Post, 'Edward Seago: the Land and the Painter'; in *Writers of East Anglia*, edited by Angus Wilson: London, 1977 (p. 103)
27   Michael Drayton, 'Poly-Olbion'; in *Works*: London, 1876 (Vol. 3, p. 16)
28   George Gissing, *The Private Papers of Henry Ryecroft*: London, 1903 (p. 267)
29   Jean Ingelow, from 'The Waveney'; in J. Gathorne-Hardy (Earl of Cranbrook), *Parnassian Molehill*: Ipswich, 1953 (pp. 129–30)
30   Edmund Spenser, from 'The Faerie Queene'; in *Poetical Works*: Oxford, 1929 (p. 269)
31   John Milton, from 'Lycidas'; in *English Poems*: Oxford, 1951 (p. 37)
32   C. Henry Warren, *Content with what I have*: London, 1967 (p. 171)
33   Sir Thomas Browne, 'The Natural History of Norfolk'; in *Works*, edited by Geoffrey Keynes: London, 1931 (Vol. 5, p. 404)
34   W. A. Dutt, *A Guide to the Norfolk Broads*: London, 1923 (p. 33)
35   Edward Seago, *A Canvas to Cover*: London, 1947 (pp. 90–1)
36   Ralph Knevet, from 'Funeral Elegies': 1637
37   Ernest R. Suffling, *The Land of the Broads*: London, 1895 (pp. 247–9)
38   Richard Lubbock, *Observations on the Fauna of Norfolk*: 1849 (pp. 247–9)
39   Arthur Ransome, *The Big Six*: London, 1940 (pp. 51–3)
40   From 'The Yarmouth Water Frolic', in the *Norfolk Chronicle*, 1777; in J. Goodwyn, *East Anglian Verse*: Ipswich, 1974 (p. 25)
41   John Knowlittle (Arthur H. Patterson), *Through Breckland in a Breydon Punt*: Norwich, 1920 (pp. 32–3)
42   Percy Lubbock, *Earlham*: London, 1922 (pp. 180–2)
43   H. M. Doughty, *Summer in Broadland*: London, 1899 (pp. 45–9)
44   Ernest R. Suffling, *How to Organise a Cruise on the Broads*: London, 1899 (pp. 78–80)
45   Christopher Davies, *The Swan and her Crew*: London, 1876 (pp. 38–40)
46   Arthur Ransome, *Coot Club*: London, 1934 (pp. 46–8)
47   Alan Savory, *Norfolk Fowler*: London, 1953 (p. 98)
48   Charles Kingsley, *Hereward the Wake*: London, 1877 (pp. 11–13)
49   William Dugdale, *The History of Imbanking and Draining*: London, 1772 (pp. 171–2)
50   Joseph Needham, *History is on our side*: London, 1946 (p. 63)
51   'Entomology on Wicken Fen'; in *The Cambridge Graphic*, 11 May 1901 (p. 20)

52 Felix' 'Life of St Guthlac'; in Charles W. Jones, *Saints' Lives and Chronicles in Early England*: New York, 1947 (p. 135)

53 'Liber Eliensis' (translation); in Sydney Waterlow, *In Praise of Cambridge*: London, 1912 (p. 83)

54 Michael Drayton, from 'Poly-Olbion'; in *Works*: London, 1876 (Vol. 3, pp. 32–3)

55 Thomas Fuller, *The History of the Worthies of England*: London, 1840 (Vol. 1, p. 221)

56 'Fen Bill Hall's Chain of Incidents'; in W. A. Dutt, *The Norfolk and Suffolk Coast*: London, 1909 (p. 391)

57 'Powtes Complaint'; in William Dugdale, *The History of Imbanking and Draining*: London, 1772 (p. 391)

58 Annie Berlyn, *Sunrise-Land*: London, 1894 (p. 262)

59 William Cobbett, *Rural Rides*: London, 1886 (Vol. 2, p. 313)

60 Charles Kingsley, *Alton Locke*: London, 1877 (p. 122)

61 Christopher Morley, *The Fen Country*: London, 1925 (pp. 220–1)

62 Dorothy L. Sayers, *The Nine Tailors*: London, 1936 (pp. 60–1)

63 John Cowper Powys, *Autobiography*: London, 1934 (p. 183)

64 Rupert Brooke, from 'Grantchester'; in *Collected Poems*: London, 1918 (pp. 55–7)

65 A. C. Benson, *From a College Window*: London, 1906 (pp. 273–5)

66 Frances Cornford, 'Cambridgeshire'; in *Collected Poems*: London, 1954 (p. 49)

67 Daniel Defoe, *A Tour through the Whole Island of Great Britain*: London, 1927 (Vol. 1, pp. 80–1)

68 William Gilpin, *Observations on Several Parts of the Counties of Cambridge, Norfolk, Suffolk and Essex*: London, 1809 (pp. 28–9)

69 James John Hissey, *A Tour in a Phaeton*: London, 1889 (pp. 274–6)

70 Edward Thomas, *The Icknield Way*: London, 1913 (pp. 94–5)

71 W. G. Clarke, *In Breckland Wilds*: Cambridge, 1925 (p. 10)

72 Michael Home, *Spring Sowing*: London, 1946 (pp. 13–14)

73 Charles J. Cornish, *Nights with an Old Gunner*: London, 1897 (pp. 28–30)

74 Jane Hales, *The East Wind*: Hunstanton, 1969 (pp. 10–11)

75 Theodore Watts-Dunton, *Aylwin*: London, 1900 (p. 3)

76 Agnes Strickland, from 'Seaside Flowers'; in *Historic Scenes and Poetic Fancies*: London, 1850 (pp. 322–3)

77 W. A. Dutt, *The Norfolk and Suffolk Coast*: London, 1909 (pp. 190–1)

78 Frances Cornford, 'The Coast, Norfolk'; in *Collected Poems*: London, 1954 (p. 82)

79 Annie Berlyn, *Sunrise-Land*: London, 1894 (pp. 39–40)

80 George Crabbe, from 'The Village'; in *Tales, 1812 and other Selected Poems*: Cambridge, 1967 (pp. 2–3)

81 Clement Scott, 'The Garden of Sleep: A Summer Song'; in *Poppy-Land*: London, 1897 (pp. 1–2)

82 Charles J. Cornish, *Nights with an Old Gunner*: London, 1897 (pp. 24–6)

83 S. Baring-Gould, *Mehalah*: London, 1884 (pp. 1–3)

84 Francis Engleheart, from 'Pin Mill'; in *A Selection of Poetry*: Ipswich, 1965 (p. 18)

85 S. L. Bensusan, *A Countryside Chronicle*: London, 1907 (pp. 17–18)

86 J. Wentworth Day, *Harvest Adventure*: London, 1946 (pp. 97–8)

87 Richard Cobbold, *The History of Margaret Catchpole*: London, 1946 (pp. 233–4)

88   George Crabbe, from 'The Borough'; in *Tales, 1812 and other Selected Poems*: Cambridge, 1967 (pp. 110–11)

89   Thomas Nash, *Works*, edited by Ronald McKerrow: London, 1905 (Vol. 3, pp. 179–80)

90   James Ford, *Aldeburgh Described*: 1815 (pp. 24–5)

91   Arthur Ransome, *We Didn't Mean to Go to Sea*: London, 1937 (pp. 62–3)

92   George Crabbe, from 'The Borough'; in *Tales, 1812 and other Selected Poems*: Cambridge, 1967 (pp. 57–8)

93   Robert Reeve, article in *The Ipswich Journal*, 1770; in Alfred Suckling, *Histories and Antiquities of the County of Suffolk*: 1848 (Vol. 2, pp. 63–4)

94   Edward Fitzgerald, *Letters*, edited by A. M. Terhune: Princeton, 1980 (Vol. 2, pp. 400–1)

95   John Betjeman, 'East Anglian Bathe'; in *Collected Poems*: London, 1958 (pp. 128–9)

96   Imogen Holst, *Britten*: London, 1966 (p. 15)

97   Anne Nichols, from 'A Journal of a very young Lady's Tour'; in James Ford, *The Suffolk Garland*: 1818 (pp. 84–5)

98   A. J. Swinbourne, *Memories of a School Inspector*: 1912 (p. 44)

99   Jonathan Mardle (Eric Fowler), *As I was a-sayin'*: Norwich, 1950 (p. 96)

100   R. S. Joby, *Forgotten Railways*: Newton Abbot, 1977 (Vol. 7, pp. 79–80)

101   Tacitus, 'Works'; in *Bohn Classical Library*: London, 1854 (p. 375)

102   G. A. Henty, *Beric the Briton*: London, 1893 (pp. 72–4)

103   Roger of Wendover, 'Flowers of History', translated by J. A. Giles; in *Bohn Classical Library*: London, 1849 (p. 198)

104   Julian Tennyson, *Suffolk Scene*: London, 1940 (pp. 145–6)

105   *Anglo-Saxon Chronicle*, edited by Dorothy Whitelock: London, 1961 (p. 87)

106   From 'The Ballad of the Bigod of Bungay'; in Alfred Suckling, *History and Antiquities of the County of Suffolk*: 1846 (Vol. 1, p. 135)

107   Augustus Jessopp, article in *The Nineteenth Century*, Feb. 1884; in John James Raven, *The History of Suffolk*: London, 1895 (pp. 104–5)

108   Edgar Powell, *The Rising in East Anglia*: Cambridge, 1896 (pp. 13–14)

109   John Capgrave, *The Book of the Illustrious Henries*, translated by Francis Hingeston: London, 1858 (pp. 200–1)

110   Alexander Neville, 'The Norfolk Furies', translated by Richard Woods; in James Halliwell-Phillipps, *The Norfolk Anthology*: London, 1852 (pp. 59–60)

111   Agnes Strickland, *Lives of the Queens of England*: London, 1842 (pp. 284–6)

112   John Foxe, *The Acts and Monuments*, edited by J. Pratt: London, 1877 (Vol. 8, pp. 425–6)

113   William Dowsing, *Journal*: 1643 (pamphlet entry 124)

114   Joseph Hall, 'Hard Measure'; in John Jones, *Bishop Hall, His Life and Times*: London, 1826 (pp. 406–7)

115   Earl of Clarendon (Edward Hyde), *The History of the Rebellion*: London, 1826 (Vol. 4, pp. 98–100)

116   John Campbell, *The Naval History of Great Britain*: London, 1818 (Vol. 2, pp. 190–2)

117   Earl of Albemarle (George Thomas Keppel), *Fifty Years of my Life*: London, 1876 (Vol. 2, pp. 107–8)

118   S. Baring-Gould, *Cheap Jack Zita*: London, 1893 (pp. 123–7)

119   Jane White, *Norfolk Child*: London, 1973 (p. 171)

120   Bernard Goldringham; in John Nichols, *The Progresses and Public Processions of Queen Elizabeth*: London, 1823 (Vol. 2, pp. 137–8)

121   James Woodforde, *The Diary of a Country Parson*, edited by John Beresford: Oxford, 1949 (pp. 198–200)

122   James Wentworth Day, in *The East Anglian Magazine*: Ipswich, November 1970

123   William of Newburgh, 'Of the Green Children'; in Joseph Stevenson, *The Church Historians of England*: London, 1856 (Vol. 4, part 2, pp. 436–7)

124   Ralph of Coggeshall; in Mike Reynolds, *About Suffolk*: Woodbridge, 1978 (p. 155)

125   Jocelin of Brakelond, *Chronicle*, edited and translated by L. C. Jane: London, 1907 (pp. 166–70)

126   Margery Kempe, *The Book of Margery Kempe*, modern version by W. Butler-Bowdon: London, 1936 (pp. 237–8)

127   J. Glyde, *The Norfolk Garland*: Norwich, 1872 (p. 237)

128   Desiderius Erasmus, 'Peregrinatio Religionis Ergo'; in *Colloquies*, translated by N. Bailey: New York, 1878 (pp. 8–9)

129   'The Report of a Strange and Wonderful Spectacle'; in Alfred Suckling, *History and Antiquities of the County of Suffolk*: 1846 (Vol. 1, pp. 125–6)

130   Matthew Hopkins, *The Discovery of Witches*, edited by Montague Summers: London, 1928 (pp. 50–1)

131   *East Anglian Notes and Queries* for January 1967; edited by S. Tymms: Lowestoft, 1869 (Vol. 3, p. 57)

132   John Glyde, *The Norfolk Garland*: London, 1872 (pp. 31–2)

133   M. R. James, 'Oh Whistle and I'll come to you, my lad'; from *Ghost Stories of an Antiquary*: London, 1905 (pp. 203–5)

134   Margaret Wilson's account in Harry Price, *The Most Haunted House in England*: London, 1940 (p. 134)

135   O. G. S. Crawford, in *Antiquity*, March 1940

136   Angus Wilson, *Anglo-Saxon Attitudes*: London, 1956 (pp. 179–80)

137   George Borrow, *Lavengro*: London, 1901 (Vol. 1, pp. 131–2)

138   Sir Thomas Browne, 'Repertorium'; in *Works*, edited by Geoffrey Keynes: London, 1931 (Vol. 5, pp. 168–9)

139   Henry James, *Portraits of Places*: London, 1883 (pp. 301–4)

140   William Wordsworth, 'Sonnet on King's College Chapel'; in *Complete Poetical Works*: London, 1888 (p. 639)

141   Thomas Gray, from 'Ode for Music'; in *Gray's Poems, Letters and Essays*: London, 1966 (p. 16)

142   John Kirby, *The Suffolk Traveller*: 1764 (pp. 14–15)

143   Daniel Defoe, *A Tour through the Whole Island of Great Britain*: London, 1927 (Vol. 1, p. 49)

144   John Evelyn, *Diary*, edited by E. S. de Beer: Oxford, 1959 (p. 371)

145   Hilaire Belloc, *The Hills and the Sea*: London, 1906 (pp. 141–2)

146   George Bloomfield, 'Thetford Chalybeate Spa': 1821

147   Daniel Defoe, *A Tour through the Whole Island of Great Britain*: London, 1927 (Vol. 1, pp. 54–5)

148   R. W. Ketton-Cremer, *Norfolk Assembly*: London, 1957 (pp. 224–5)

149   Percy Lubbock, *Earlham*: London, 1922 (pp. 134–5)

150   C. H. Spurgeon, *Memories of Stambourne*: 1892 (pp. 3–4)

151   Anon. (William Maginn), *The Red Barn, A Tale, Founded on Fact*: London, 1831 (pp. 3–5)

152   Frederic J. Gardiner, *Village Life in the Fens*: Wisbech, 1908 (pp. 27–8)

153   Adrian Bell, *A Street in Suffolk*: London, 1964 (pp. 97–8)

154   Sir Alfred Munnings, *An Artist's Life*: London, 1950 (pp. 78–9)

155   Eileen Power, *Medieval People*: London, 1925 (pp. 147–8)

156   Robert Reyce, 'The Breviary of Suffolk'; in *Suffolk in the XVIIth Century*: London, 1962 (pp. 21–2)

157   Rowland Parker, *The Common Stream*: London, 1976 (p. 260)

158   John Betjeman, in *Norfolk Country Churches and the Future*: Woodbridge, 1972

159   John Kirby, *The Suffolk Traveller*: 1764 (pp. 116–17)

160   L. P. Hartley, *The Shrimp and the Anemone*: London, 1951 (pp. 169–72)

161   Dorothy L. Sayers, *The Nine Tailors*: London, 1936 (pp. 35–6)

162   Shane Leslie, *The Cantab*: London, 1926 (pp. 1–3)

163   James Withers, from 'My Native Village'; in *Poems*: 1856 (pp. 2–3)

164   Francis Blomefield, *Topographical History of the County of Norfolk*: 1805 (Vol. 1, pp. 130–1)

165   Charles Dickens, *Pickwick Papers*: London, 1910 (p. 313)

166   Agnes Strickland, *Lives of the Queens of England*: London, 1842 (pp. 291–2)

167   A. C. Benson, *The Upton Letters*: London, 1905 (pp. 283–5)

168   Charles Harper, *The Newmarket, Bury, Thetford and Cromer Road*: London, 1904 (pp. 317–18)

169   Lady Beauchamp-Proctor, 'Journals': 1772

170   James Grigor, *The Eastern Arboretum*: London, 1841 (pp. 98–9)

171   Horace Walpole, *Correspondence*, edited by W. S. Lewis: London, 1965 (Vol. 32, pp. 140–3)

172   Frederick Augustus Hervey; in Vere Foster, *The Two Duchesses*: London, 1898 (pp. 116–17)

173   Arthur Young, *Autobiography*, edited by M. Betham-Edwards: London, 1898 (p. 105)

174   François La Rochefoucauld, *A Frenchman's Year in Suffolk*, translated and edited by Norman Scarfe; in *Suffolk Records Society*: Woodbridge, 1988 (Vol. XXX, p. 33)

175   François La Rochefoucauld, *A Frenchman's Year in Suffolk*, translated and edited by Norman Scarfe; in *Suffolk Records Society*: Woodbridge, 1988 (Vol. XXX, pp. 138–40)

176   Dr Edward Rigby, 'Holkham, Its Agriculture'; in *The Pamphleteer*: London, 1819 (Vol. 13, No. 26, p. 472)

177   Lady Beauchamp-Proctor, 'Journals': 1772

178   James Grigor, *The Eastern Arboretum*: London, 1841 (p. 126)

179   James Howell; in Allan Jobson, *Portrait of Suffolk*: London, 1973 (p. 173)

180   Percy Lubbock, *Earlham*: London, 1922 (pp. 163–6)

181   Lady Bedingfeld, *Jerningham Letters*, edited by Egerton Castle: 1896 (Vol. 2, pp. 164–6)

182   John Hadfield, *Love on a Branch Line*: London, 1959 (pp. 51–3)

183   Eileen Power, *Medieval People*: London, 1925 (pp. 153–4)

184   James Woodforde, *The Diary of a Country Parson*, edited by John Beresford: Oxford, 1949 (p. 539)

185   James Ewing Ritchie, *Christopher Crayon's Recollections*: London, 1898 (pp. 78–80)

186   Augustus Jessopp, *The Coming of the Friars*: London, 1866 (pp. 88–9)

187   Camilla Gurdon, *Suffolk Tales and other Stories*: London, 1897 (pp. 8–9)

188   George Goldsmith Carter, *Looming Lights*: London, 1945 (pp. 1–2)

189   Charles Dickens, *David Copperfield*: London, 1910 (pp. 29–31)

190   Thomas Tusser, 'A Description of Time and the Year'; in *The Five Hundred Points of Good Husbandry*: London, 1812 (p. 66)

191   François La Rochefoucauld, *A Frenchman's Year in Suffolk*, translated and edited by Norman Scarfe; in *Suffolk Records Society*: Woodbridge, 1988 (Vol. XXX, pp. 125–6)

192   H. Rider Haggard, *A Farmer's Year*: London, 1899 (pp. 53–5)

193   A. M. W. Stirling, *Coke of Norfolk and his Friends*: London, 1912 (p. 447)

194   From 'There's Olluz Summat'; in Charles E. Benham, *Essex Ballads*: 1897

195   H. W. Freeman, *Joseph and his Brethren*: London, 1928 (pp. 18–21)

196   Admiral Lord Nelson, *Dispatches and Letters*, edited by Nicholas Young: London, 1844 (Vol. 1, p. 295)

197   Leonard Thompson; in Ronald Blythe, *Akenfield*: London, 1969 (p. 37)

198   Robert Bloomfield, from *The Farmer's Boy*: London, 1845 (p. 67)

199   Nathaniel Kent, *General View of the Agriculture of the County of Norfolk*: 1796 (pp. 39–40)

200   Adrian Bell, *Corduroy*: London, 1930 (pp. 35–8)

201   Edwin Hewitt, from "Liza Green's 'Lotment'; in C. A. F. Mason, *Contemporary East Anglian Poetry*: Bury St Edmunds, 1928 (pp. 64–5)

202   James George Cornish, *Reminiscences of Country Life*, edited by Vaughan Cornish: London, 1939 (pp. 5–6)

203   Robert Bloomfield, from *The Farmer's Boy*: London, 1845 (pp. 15–16)

204   Thomas Cox, *Magna Britannia*: 1724 (Vol. 5, p. 276)

205   Nathaniel Kent, *General View of the Agriculture of the County of Norfolk*: 1796 (pp. 102–3)

206   Agnes Strickland, from 'The Harvest'; in *Historic Scenes and Poetic Fancies*: London, 1850 (p. 321)

207   Sir John Cullum, *The History and Antiquities of Hawstead*: London, 1784 (p. 191)

208   Michael Home, *Autumn Fields*: London, 1944 (pp. 84–5)

209   'Quill' (John Lushington), 'Harvest Cart in Suffolk'; in John Glyde, *The New Suffolk Garland*: Ipswich, 1866 (pp. 407–8)

210   'Quill' (John Lushington), 'Gleaning Time in Suffolk'; in John Glyde, *The New Suffolk Garland*: Ipswich, 1866 (p. 408)

211   George Ewart Evans, *Ask the Fellows who Cut the Hay*: London, 1956 (pp. 64–5)

212   Robert Hughman, from 'Suffolk'; in J. Gathorne-Hardy (Earl of Cranbrook), *Parnassian Molehill*: Ipswich, 1953 (pp. 140–1)

213   Sir John Cullum, *The History and Antiquities of Hawstead*: London, 1784 (pp. 222–3)

214   M. Biddell; in Herman Biddell, *The Suffolk Stud Book*: 1880 (p. 648)

215   W. G. Clarke, *Norfolk and Suffolk*: London, 1921 (pp. 251–3)

216   Arthur Young, *General View of the Agriculture of the County of Norfolk*: London, 1804 (p. 73)

217   Mrs Gerard Cresswell, *Eighteen Years on the Sandringham Estate*: London, 1887 (pp. 68–72)

218   T. W. Turner, *Memoirs of a Gamekeeper*: London, 1954 (pp. 51–3)

219   Kenneth Clark, *Another Part of the Wood*: London, 1974 (pp. 16–17)

220   L. Banville, *Journals of a Norfolk Gamekeeper*, edited by Norma Virgoe and Susan Yaxley: London, 1986 (p. 100)

221   Henry James, *Portraits of Places*: London, 1883 (p. 304)

222   Thomas Holcroft, *Memoirs*: 1816 (Vol. 1, pp. 44–6)

223   Mervyn Coke, 'Waterbeach Riding'; in *Writers of East Anglia*, edited by Angus Wilson: London, 1977 (p. 9)

224   Edmund Blunden, 'Winter: East Anglia'; in *Poems*: London, 1930 (pp. 101–2)

225   William Kemp, 'Kemps Nine Daies Wonder'; in *Camden Society*: London, 1840 (Vol. 11, p. 9)

226   W. H. Barrett; in Alan Bloom, *The Skaters of the Fens*: Cambridge, 1958 (pp. 60–1)

227   Shane Leslie, *The Cantab*: London, 1926 (pp. 87–8)

228   Edward Fitzgerald, 'Euphranor'; in *Selected Works*, edited by Joanna Richardson: London, 1962 (pp. 93–4)

229   *Norfolk Chronicle*, 16 Jan. 1869; in *Norfolk Annals*, compiled by Charles Mackie: Norwich, 1901 (Vol. 2, pp. 186–7)

230   Edward Moor, *Suffolk Words and Phrases*: London, 1823 (pp. 63–5)

231   Ken Rice, Neal Manning and Eric Johnstone, *Blue and White Crusade*: Ipswich, 1978 (p. 78)

232   George Borrow, *Lavengro*: London, 1901 (Vol. 1, pp. 45–7)

233   Augustus Jessopp, *Arcady for better or worse*: London, 1882 (pp. 180–3)

234   Wonba Smythe, *The Waterman of the River Cam*: 1825 (pp. 8–9)

235   George Target, 'Welcome to Norwich a Fine City'; in *Writers of East Anglia*, edited by Angus Wilson: London, 1977 (pp. 30–1)

236   G. W. Fulcher, from 'The Village Paupers', edited by E. A. Goodwyn: Beccles, 1981 (pp. 22–3)

237   Charles Harper, *The Cambridge, Ely and King's Lynn Road*: London, 1902 (pp. 237–9)

238   Edward Fitzgerald, from 'Old Song'; in Victor Allan, *East Anglian Enchantment*: Ipswich, 1947 (p. 40)

239   James George Cornish, *Reminiscences of Country Life*, edited by Vaughan Cornish: London, 1939 (pp. 42–4)

240   Edward Ardizzone, *The Young Ardizzone*: London, 1970 (pp. 63–4)

241   Norfolk Gaol Delivery Records, 1307–16, translated by Barbara Hanawalt; in *Norfolk Records Society*: Norwich, 1976 (Vol. 44, p. 30)

242   Anon. (William Maginn), *The Red Barn, A Tale, Founded on Fact*: London, 1831 (pp. 587–8)

243   W. H. B. Saunders, *Legends and Traditions of Huntingdonshire*: London, 1888 (pp. 103–4)

244   Richard Cobbold, *The History of Margaret Catchpole*: London, 1846 (pp. 250–2)

245   Earl of Albemarle (George Thomas Keppel), *Fifty Years of my Life*: London, 1876 (Vol. 2, pp. 232–4)

246   John Clare, *The Shepherd's Calendar*, edited by Eric Robinson and Geoffrey Summerfield: Oxford, 1967 (pp. 169–70)

247   Mary E. Mann, 'A Dulditch Courting'; in *The Fields of Dulditch*: London, 1902 (pp. 106–8)

248   Robert S. Arbib, *Here We Are Together*: London, 1947 (pp. 65–6)

249   Thomas Cox, *Magna Britannia*: 1724 (Vol. 3, p. 364)

250   Francis Hindes Groome, *Two Suffolk Friends*: London, 1895 (pp. 31–3)

251   Robert Forby, *The Vocabulary of East Anglia*: Newton Abbot, 1970 (Vol. 1, p. 99)

252   Robert Forby, *The Vocabulary of East Anglia*: Newton Abbot, 1970 (Vol. 1, p. 33 of dictionary)

253   John Knowlittle (Arthur H. Patterson), *The Cruise of the Walrus*: Norwich, 1923 (pp. 72–3)

254   S. L. Bensusan, *A Countryside Chronicle*: London, 1907 (pp. 175–7)

255   Morley Adams, *In the Footsteps of Borrow and Fitzgerald*: Norwich, 1913 (pp. 171–2)

256   John Milton, 'On the University Carrier, Who sickened in the time of his vacancy, being forbid to go to London, by reason of the Plague'; in *English Poems*: Oxford, 1951 (p. 19)

257   C. Henry Warren, *Happy Countryman*: London, 1946 (p. 26)

258   L. E. Jones, *A Victorian Boyhood*: London, 1955 (pp. 69–71)

259   Earl of Albemarle (George Thomas Keppel), *Fifty Years of my Life*: London, 1876 (Vol. 1, pp. 312–14)

260   Anthony Trollope, *The Way We Live Now*: London, 1875 (pp. 74–5)

261   William Richards, *The History of Lynn*: 1812

262   Geoffrey Chaucer, from 'The Reeve's Tale'; in *The Canterbury Tales*, translated by Nevill Coghill: London, 1956 (pp. 135–6)

263   *Paston Letters*, edited by John Fenn: London, 1924 (Vol. 1, pp. 70–1)

264   Robert Greene, 'Friar Bacon and Friar Bungay'; in A. H. Thorndike, *Minor Elizabethan Drama*: London, 1910 (Vol. 2, pp. 202–3)

265   François René de Chateaubriand, *Memoirs*, translated by Robert Baldick: London, 1961 (p. 189)

266   A. D. Bayne, *Royal Illustrated History of Eastern England*: Yarmouth, undated (Vol. 1, pp. 49–50)

267   Mme d'Arblay (Fanny Burney), *Memoirs of Doctor Burney*: London, 1832 (pp. 101–2)

268   Nikolaus Pevsner, *North-West and South Norfolk*: London, 1962 (p. 262)

269   Inscriptions at St Andrew's Church, Bramfield

270   Sarah Hare's will

271   Samuel Pepys, *Diary*, edited by H. B. Wheatley: London, 1893 (Vol. 3, pp. 281–4)

272   Louisa Gurney's Journal; in Augustus Hare, *The Gurneys of Earlham*: London, 1895 (Vol. 1, pp. 64–5)

273   Eliza Gurney, letter to Mary Anna Longstreth; in Augustus Hare, *The Gurneys of Earlham*: London, 1895 (Vol. 2, pp. 166–8)

274   R. H. Mottram, *The Boroughmonger*: London, 1929 (pp. 191–2)

275   William Makepeace Thackeray, *Letters*, edited by Gordon Ray: Oxford, 1945 (Vol. 1, pp. 36–7)

276   'The Lounger', in *The Student, or the Oxford and Cambridge Monthly Miscellany*: Oxford, 1750

277   Thomas Babington Macaulay, *History of England*: London, 1879 (Vol. 4, pp. 176–7)

278   John Evelyn, *Diary*, edited by E. S. de Beer: Oxford, 1959 (pp. 559–60)

279   M. Henshaw, letter to Sir R. Paston; in Lord Braybrooke (Richard Neville), *The History of Audley End*: 1836 (pp. 90–1)

280   Queen Victoria, *Journal*: Royal Archives

281   Mrs Gerard Cresswell, *Eighteen Years on the Sandringham Estate*: London, 1887 (pp. 177–8)

Index

References are to page numbers

East Anglia

The National Trust
East Anglia Region

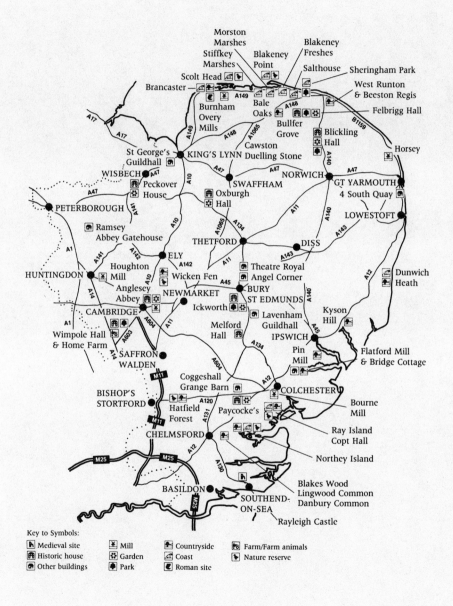

Morston
Marshes
Stiffkey
Marshes
Blakeney
Point
Blakeney
Freshes
Scolt Head
Salthouse
Sheringham Park
Brancaster
A149
West Runton
& Beeston Regis
Burnham
Overy
Mills
Bale
Oaks
A148
Felbrigg Hall
A17
A149
A148
A1065
Bullfer
Grove
Blickling
Hall
A17
St George's
Guildhall
KING'S LYNN
Cawston
Duelling Stone
Horsey
WISBECH
A47
A10
A140
A47
Peckover
House
SWAFFHAM
A47
NORWICH
GT YARMOUTH
PETERBOROUGH
A47
Oxburgh
Hall
4 South Quay
A141
A10
LOWESTOFT
Ramsey
Abbey Gatehouse
A1065
A134
A11
A140
A143
A1
A141
A142
THETFORD
DISS
A142
ELY
A11
A143
HUNTINGDON
A10
Houghton
Mill
A142
Wicken Fen
Theatre Royal
Angel Corner
A12
Dunwich
Heath
A14
Anglesey
Abbey
NEWMARKET
A45
BURY
ST EDMUNDS
A140
CAMBRIDGE
A604
Ickworth
Lavenham
Guildhall
Kyson
Hill
A1
A604
A11
Melford
Hall
A45
IPSWICH
Wimpole Hall
& Home Farm
A14
A603
Pin
Mill
Flatford Mill
& Bridge Cottage
SAFFRON
WALDEN
A604
A12
M11
Coggeshall
Grange Barn
COLCHESTER
BISHOP'S
STORTFORD
A120
Bourne
Mill
M11
Hatfield
Forest
A131
Paycocke's
Ray Island
Copt Hall
CHELMSFORD
A12
Northey Island
M25
M25
A130
Blakes Wood
Lingwood Common
Danbury Common
BASILDON
M25
SOUTHEND-
ON-SEA
Rayleigh Castle

Key to Symbols:
Medieval site
Mill
Countryside
Farm/Farm animals
Historic house
Garden
Coast
Nature reserve
Other buildings
Park
Roman site